THE LAST GREAT ERA OF OPERA: THE 1940s THROUGH THE 1970s

RECOLLECTIONS AND HISTORY

Copyright © 2010 by Robert F. Feist
All rights reserved. No part of this publication may be reproduced without permission from the publisher, except by reviewers to quote brief passages.

Published in the United States by
Integral Design
17116 NE 83rd Court
Redmond, Washington 98052

Library of Congress Cataloging-in-Publication Data

Feist, Robert F., 1928-
    The Last Great Era of Opera; The 1940s through the 1970s
    Recollections and History

    ISBN 978-0-578-04684-6
    Music, General

THE LAST GREAT ERA OF OPERA:
THE 1940s THROUGH THE 1970s

RECOLLECTIONS AND HISTORY

ROBERT F. FEIST

This book is dedicated with love to my parents Robert and Mary Feist.

CONTENTS

Foreword v

Preface vi

CHAPTER ONE—The First Year in Italy as a Fulbright Fellow 1

CHAPTER TWO—The Years of Great Singers in Italy 14

CHAPTER THREE—Operas in Other Cities and My Debut as a Conductor 20

CHAPTER FOUR—Some of the Fulbright Fellows Become Famous 30

CHAPTER FIVE—My Youth and Introduction to Opera in Cincinnati, Ohio 34

CHAPTER SIX—My Second Year as a Fulbright and Superb Opera 50

CHAPTER SEVEN—The Baths of Caracalla and Visiting Germany 67

CHAPTER EIGHT—More Opera in Italy and a Trip to Ireland 80

CHAPTER NINE—Two Seasons at the Red Gate in Augsburg, Germany
and then an Unusual Summer 86

CHAPTER TEN—The Rockefeller Foundation Grant, Eastern Europe
and Moscow and Introduction to the Letters from Russia 117

CHAPTER ELEVEN—Back to Rome and I Begin Teaching 149

CHAPTER TWELVE—Trips to New Zealand and Australia
Conducting Many Operas 151

CHAPTER THIRTEEN—Teaching in Rome and an Invitation to Perform in
the Mid-East and North Africa, Introductions to Letters from
Maestro Gavazzeni and Letters from Maestro Gui 175

CHAPTER FOURTEEN—The Glory Years of the Past Are Gone 253

Acknowledgments 266

Frank Guarerra, well-known opera star of the Metropolitan Opera. He died in November, 2007.

FOREWORD

I first met Robert Feist at the Cincinnati Zoo Opera before he went off to Europe to seek his fame as a musical coach and conductor.

I continued in my career as a baritone at the Metropolitan, San Francisco and other major opera companies.

It was not until many years later that we met up in Seattle where we both had been engaged on the faculty of the School of Music at the University of Washington. There we enjoyed opportunities to collaborate on productions of many operas—all skillfully and extremely well rehearsed—providing the students with a glimpse into the way operas are prepared for the stage and the way the opera world functions. These preparations resulted in extraordinarily fine performances of very enjoyable and educational value for grateful students as well as for the public. It was wonderful and I am proud of the outstanding work we did together.

Maestro Feist has conducted a large number of the great singers and majority of operas in the repertory encompassed in the era of this book. His impressive knowledge of the opera idiom, his years of study, his experiences, his exceptional expertise as conductor, first-rate pianist and exceptional coach, and—last but not least—his life-long love of opera, are apparent in the way he chronicles and presents the information in this volume.

The Last Great Era of Opera provides a special opportunity for opera afficionados, students and opera historians alike—indeed for all those who have been enchanted by and cast under the spell of the opera muse as we have been.

Here the reader can indulge himself with a joyful trip through the annals of one of the "greatest eras" in opera history. This is an experience you will enjoy and I am grateful and excited that, at last, this volume is in print.

—Frank Guarerra
February 25, 2007

PREFACE

Although the title of this book implies many decades of opera, from my youth into the 1970s when I left Italy, it will continue more or less in that fashion with, however, the following interjection that has only been spurred on by recent events here and internationally; the death of Luciano Pavarotti. This has affected everyone in the opera world and even the non-operatic world—that this great tenor made such an impression on everyone that he touched. I'm not going to dwell on it, because everyone has read the newspapers and seen the news on TV, but of course, I knew him. I heard him in many performances in Italy and therefore was well impressed with his style, his voice and everything about him, far superior in my opinion, to his companions, Domingo and Carerras.

But, the death itself suddenly struck me as being one of so many in the past years—I'm going to say the past seven years. I've gone through all my clippings and accounts of things that have happened and I think most opera buffs would be interested in these.

For example, in July 2001 came the death of Gina Cigna, the greatest dramatic soprano of that era who sang and I think recorded, the first *Turandot* on RPM Records. She was already over 100. She was 101 in 2001. And in December of the same year came the death of Edward Downes, the very well-known intermission host of the quiz on the Metropolitan Opera broadcast, whom I also knew because he came here to the University of Washington to lead a mini quiz at one of my performances. He was my guest. In the same year came the death of one of my dear friends who was a fellow Fulbright (along with Anna Moffo), Bill Harper, who died around age 70.

Then in 2002 came the death of the great dramatic soprano Eileen Farrell, who was 82. She died in March, 2002 and we all knew her from opera, concerts and recitals. Hers was a remarkable voice that would be hard to equal today. Then shortly after that in March of 2002 came the death of the great Russian, Yevgeni Svetlanov, the Russian conductor whom I thought was the best of all and whom I worked with in both Milano and at the Bolshoi in Russia.

Soon after in 2003 came the death of Jerome Hines; this bass who was so famous in America, died at age 81. Prior to that in 2000, his wife, the soprano Lucia Evangelista passed away.

Then in March of 2003 came the death of the wonderful lyric soprano, Nadine Conner at the age of 96. We had all grown up hearing her from the Met and everywhere even in Cincinnati, I also heard her in New York, a remarkable lyric soprano who did everything well. Then also in the year 2003 came the death of the tenor Barry Morrell at age 75 who had sung *Tosca* with me much earlier, around 1976 in New Orleans, and I'll never forget that.

In October of 2004 came the surprising death of Robert Merrill at age 87, one of our greatest baritones. Two months later in 2004 came the death of the great Spanish coloratura or lyric coloratura, Victoria de los Angeles at age 81, whom I heard countless times, and unforgettable in *Manon* in Rome. The biggest shock of all was the death in 2004 of Renata Tebaldi, a name as famous as Pavarotti, who sang with him and with every other major tenor. She was 82 when she passed away and I heard her innumerable times in Italy and in New York.

In 1999 had occurred the death of Ruby Mercer, a name maybe not familiar to all of you. She was the editor and founder of the *Opera Canada* magazine, covering all events of opera in Canada. I will get to her later in my book because she became a very dear friend and she was present at my own debut with the Fulbright singers in Spoleto in 1955 of the Rome Opera.

In 2005 the founding director of the Seattle Opera, Glynn Ross passed away at age 90. He was no longer here (in Seattle) and had been the General Director of the Arizona Opera, after he had resigned from the Seattle Opera. And then in the year 2005 came the death of the famous conductor, Maestro Serge Comissiona who was Romanian and whom I had seen many times, even in London. He died at age 76.

Shortly after that in December came the death of George Jellinek with whom I had a correspondence about publishers and the subject of certain sopranos who had lost touch with me, and George with all of his 25 years of broadcasts and intermission features will be well-remembered by all who read *Opera News*. In June of 2005 came the really great surprise of the death of the incredible dramatic soprano, Ghena Dimitrova. She was 64, which is quite young to pass away. She had been the living symbol of roles such as *Turandot* and Abigaille in *Nabucco* which I don't think anyone has ever equaled. Luckily I saw her do these roles and I have them on video. In 2005 also came the death of Maestro Hermann Michael, a German who suddenly made a debut here, maybe five or six years before that conducting a *Tannhäuser* we will always remember. He suddenly appeared from Germany and made an impression, came back for years conducting concerts and operas, until he returned or he moved to Arizona as the conductor of the Arizona Symphony. He was 68. Shortly after that, in the year 2005 came the death of the famous Australian coloratura called June Bronhill, who was 71. She had had a very big career in London at Covent Garden and Sadlers Wells in more light repertoire until she returned to Australia and where I encountered her and she sang many performances with me.

The big blow was in March of 2006 when my beloved friend, Anna Moffo, passed away at the age of 73, which we did not expect nor anticipate at all. There will be much more about her in the course of my book. In March of that year also came the death of the famous, perhaps the most famous Marschallin in *Rosenkavalier*, Elizabeth Schwarzkopf, who died at the age of 90 after an extensive, world-wide career. Shortly after that came the death of Birgit Nilsson, perhaps the greatest Wagnerian soprano, at the age of 87. And that was another blow having heard her countless times in Europe and in America.

Lo and behold, shortly after September of 2006, came the death of the great Astrid Varnay, who ranks almost with Birgit Nilsson in Wagner repertoire. She started out at the Met at the age of 18 or 20, and then went to Europe and had her huge career there, where I heard her always, even in Bayreuth, and she was 88. In September of 2006 came the death of the world-famous composer, Menotti, whom everyone knows from his operas and for his "Festival of Two Worlds," where I conducted for two years. He was 95.

Who can one add? Well, the latest shock was the death of Beverly Sills, which covered all the newspapers probably in the world. She died in July of 2007 at the age of 78 and one needs not add any more comment of her immense career as a singer and administrator and lover of opera.

Now that is an extensive list only bringing to mind, somewhat, the subject of this book of what we have lost, and it is these singers that we have lost that remind us that their substitutes are not with us—a few perhaps. But, when I get around to discussing the gala for Joseph Volpe, I will then quote from the *New York Times*, where, in a very important article they discuss the fact that we are in a "lost generation of singers," meaning the loss of all those singers that I mentioned and many, many others that go back to the 40s, 50s and 60s, who are no longer with us and whom I experienced in person or as friends through my years. You will encounter long sections about these singers or conductors that I worked with in the course of my career. A few may have been missed, despite my editing of the text. An example would be some close friends maybe in Germany and Australia whose changes of address have made our contacts diminish and fail. But the ongoing remembrance of these singers is what makes everything vital. That is why, in the course of this book, you are going to encounter all of these singers whom I have mentioned, who have passed away, and many, many more preceding them, who lived and worked and sang in the 40s, 50s and 60s and into the 70s, starting, at least in my case, in Cincinnati, at the famous Summer Opera, and then into New York and then in Europe, where everything continued, more or less as I thought it had been, for a century. We then realized that the continuation of great singing had started way back, went back through the first great era (the era of Caruso) and continued into the so called "last great era" that I am discussing. It was on the verge of falling in the 1970s and now many, many critics world-wide have made comments on this fact and they ask: "Where are we now?"

This was very apparent when I returned to the United States in 1975. There are a vast amount of operas contained herein and a list of singers that would amaze anyone if they encountered them today. But we must remember that we have had behind us an incredible amount of superb opera world-wide until the 1960s diminished and the 1970s came along when the decline was quite apparent.

So my book will start where I think it should with my first year in Rome at the Rome Opera House as a Fulbright. The three years that I spent there, hearing every great singer in the world, and after that my move to Germany and also, in between, I am going back to my youth as a teenager in Cincinnati and explain in some detail how I encountered these great singers for the first time, in Cincinnati. It was then the second great opera company in the United States, before Chicago and San Francisco, which many people do not know.

So, we begin with Rome, then comes a break and I return to Cincinnati and then I return to Europe to Rome and then I move to Germany an on up until the present. And then we end with the question mark, the big question mark of" where do we go from here.?" So, I hope the rest of this is not only informative and entertaining but of vital importance to anyone who loves opera. I trust it will serve that purpose.

Robert Feist standing next to the poster for the Bicentennial Concert in Rome which he conducted in 1976.

CHAPTER ONE
The first Year in Italy as a Fulbright Fellow

It began, of course, on the boat from New York where all of the Fulbright Fellows set sail from New York to Naples. On this long voyage of nine days or so, we all got to know each other quite well. They were not all musicians. Many were there on their way to study other things. Because the Fulbright Fellowship involves many areas of concentration and study, it could be in the fine arts or history or many aspects of music. So, upon landing in Naples we went by bus along the coast to Rome. We spend one night in Rome and many of us took a long walk down the Via Nazionale, a big, long street that ends at the Piazza Venezia, famous because that is where Mussolini gave his addresses to the nation from the top of the balcony of the famous building overlooking the square. And, on his side was the equally famous monument to Victor Emmanuel which was often called the "wedding cake" because of its many steps, statues and so forth.

After this we returned to the hotel and then we were taken to Perugia. Perugia is a wonderful old historic city between Rome and Florence. We spent several weeks there to become acquainted with Italian history and language. We were in the Università per Stranieri, the university for foreigners. We were all lodged in various homes. Many of us shared rooms or a dwelling with an Italian family whom we got to know. I shared a room and my roommate was a tenor whom I met on the boat, Bill Harper. Also in this building were two composers and as the weeks went on we got to know the others and where they lived. We were constantly in class taking Italian lessons and learning basic facts about the history of the country. Evenings after dinner, at the house where we stayed, we would wander up to the main square and sit there at an outdoor cafe drinking wine or coffee and sharing our views on this new country. This was the best way to get acquainted with each other as we did for those three or four weeks.

As for performances, the only thing we saw was the opera *Parsifal*, of all things, the *last* one we would have expected in Italy! It was a guest performance in the main opera house in Perugia done by an imported cast of Germans as was then the case in Italy, and conducted by Tullio Serafin, perhaps considered the greatest maestro of that period. We enjoyed it although we were looking for something Italian at the same time. A few weeks later we attended a performance of Beethoven's *"Missa Solemnis"* in a famous cathedral in the city. It was conducted by Fernando Previtali and sung by, of all people, Lina Pagliughi. She was a soprano we knew from recordings as *Gilda* and *Lucia* and I didn't know if she was still alive. But she sang very well as did the others and the performance was stimulating.

Besides this, our singers arranged to have a recital done by us to introduce us to the Perugia populace. So we all decided on what arias or songs to sing and we did it in a room, not a castle, just a very nice spacious aula (hall) and I accompanied them in arias and duets from Puccini, Verdi and others, and I still have a program, as a matter of fact. It was very successful and we enjoyed it very much. It was our first performance in Italy.

After this event and a few days later, we were carried off on a trip. This was a sight-seeing trip with a touring bus which took us to see little neighboring hillside cities that later we got to know better. We got to see Assisi and the famous cathedral, actually two—one on top of the hill and one at the bottom. Besides this city of Assisi, with its wonderful cathedrals, we saw Todi, an interesting city, Orvieto and a few others. Then we returned to Perugia for the night. A few days later we were taken by bus again to Rome. It had already been arranged or was soon arranged, where we would stay.

We had the option of either getting together with friends and sharing an apartment or living in a very big apartment in a hotel. Everyone chose their own means and their own friends. Now I had come over on the boat with three other Fulbright Fellows, becoming "buddies," let us say, and we got to know each other quite well and not all were musicians. One was the tenor, Bill Harper. There was also a sociologist, Jim Taccini, and an arts or history major, Pete Chiacchieri. We four decided we could live well together.

So, with an agent in Rome, we found an excellent apartment, more or less in a new section of Rome. It was an apartment that I would have considered new even in America. So, we settled into this apartment which was totally furnished. We had a cleaning woman who came weekly, whom we sometimes saw and sometimes did not, and we ate all of our meals out, which was customary. I don't think we ever cooked or had any meals done in the apartment. Now as for the center, it was very interesting because it was varied. It had nothing to do with the other Fulbrights who were there for art, history, sociology or other matters such as that. Since we were all connected with opera, these six or seven of us were deposited more or less at the Rome Opera house called the Teatro dell' Opera, the main theater in the city. The singers had their own schedules to learn roles and coach. They coached with various conductors whom we called the *maestri sostitutti*, assistant conductors, at the Rome Opera, such as the famous Luigi Ricci, who wrote a book on Puccini, and Giuseppe Bertelli. They were very well-known in the theater because they were there daily. The singers coached with them and then would get together several times a week with their stage director who was a more or less retired stage director, Riccardo Picozzi, a wonderful old gentleman who was in his 70s and was agile as someone in his 50s.

And we worked in a building almost next door to the Rome Opera on the top floor where we ran through various scenes from operas that he chose. I was always then chosen to play for all of these rehearsals, which I did very gladly. I got to know Maestro Picozzi and his wife because they would invite me to their home which was nearby. I would occasionally go there maybe for dinner and conversation and I even coached other singers, meaning singers not from our group. Later you will read a letter from Elsa Picozzi to my parents.

But, back to the Fulbrights. Now as they were doing their work within, I myself was immediately deposited inside the Rome Opera house. This was a surprise that would have been the envy of any other American student or student conductor, because I had discussed with them where I was going and they thought initially they would send me to the conservatory, which is the Conservatorio di Santa Cecilia. The Santa Cecilia Conservatory is where most up-and-coming singers and conductors study. But, I had done all that.

I had two degrees, Bachelor and Masters in America and so I would be repeating myself. So, therefore, people who managed the Fulbright Commission realized that. The Fulbright Commission in Rome was headed by a woman and her staff. But the man in charge of us was Signor Pallotelli, a wonderful old gentleman we got to know very well. He organized everything we did. In my case he arranged for me to go to the Rome Opera house. So, from the very beginning I was every day inside the opera house working backstage with all the other assistant conductors. Fortunately I had a good grasp of Italian. I had no problem with that. What I did was what the other conductors did. I would indicate entrances and exits to the singers during rehearsals with orchestra or piano, even where they come in and go off the stage. So it turned out that what I found myself in the middle of was an incredible production with a cast hard to be equaled today. The opening opera of the season was *La Forza del Destino*. The cast was Renata Tebaldi; also Aldo Protti, the baritone; Gino Penno, the tenor and Giulietta Simionato as Preziosilla. The bass was Giulio Neri . The other bass was Renato Capecchi, who was really a baritone and was doing a rather buffo bass role. Well, this cast was amazing. I had never heard anything like it of this caliber in America and it turned out that Penno, the tenor, only lasted a few years and then he more or less disappeared. I suppose he retired because his voice was rather tight and pushed, though he sang all the notes well. The others were all superb.

The conductor was Gabriele Santini, who became one of my two or three favorite conductors of my career in Europe. A very disciplined man who put up with no nonsense and often had a rather vicious tongue at the orchestra, which made for a lot of comment and even jokes. He was certainly a firm taskmaster and their performances were without doubt superb. I was course able, because of my capacity, to wander around sometimes. I would go into the auditorium and sit in the orchestra level which we call the "platea," the main floor of the auditorium and watch the conductor. Sometimes when it was necessary, I would be back stage working with the singers on their entrances and this went on for all of the performances, perhaps five or six of that series.

It turned out that our Fulbright singers had a box seat. They had subscribed to a box which would take them to all of the operas of the season which were remarkable. So, on those nights when they appeared, obviously we would get together. They would come downstairs at intermission, and I would run out from backstage and meet them and we would discuss it and hash over how wonderful the performance was and we all agreed we had never heard anything of this caliber. So, that went and the whole year progressed in this fashion; they learning their repertoire with Picozzi and me learning all the other operas with the conductors, assistant conductors backstage while I was working there at the Rome Opera house.

So, that was the schedule, more or less, for the year. The second opera of that particular season of 1954-1955 was a German opera. It was *Rosenkavalier* by Strauss and by that time as I have said, the Italians had already picked up the habit or practice of importing German casts for German operas. Prior to this, it had been the case that most of the foreign operas were sung in Italian though they be German, French or whatever. So, here we had a *Rosenkavalier* with a superb cast that frankly, again, amazed me. It was headed by the soprano, Maria Reining of Vienna who was long a star there as the Marschallin even though she probably was overshadowed by Elizabeth Schwarzkopf, who did not come while I was there. The Octavian was the incredible soprano Sena Jurinac who became a friend and remains so until this day. Jurinac was the star of the Vienna Opera too, doing almost every sort of role with Von Karajan. She was chosen by Von Karajan to sing many roles, not only *Rosenkavalier*, but other Strauss roles, a lot of Mozart and Verdi such as *Otello* and *Don Carlo*.

Other cast members were Deszö Ernster as Baron Ochs and Gustav Neidlinger who sang Faninal. He returned actually a year later to sing *Die Meistersinger,* and Sophie, the daughter of Faninal, was sung by Rita Streich, a very well-known coloratura soprano of that year. Hilde Rössel Maydn, a famous secondary singer who got to know me as I was always backstage telling them where to go on and when to get off and conducting something offstage. She had me coach her in some other roles, just whenever she had time or I had time between performances.

The same occurred with the American baritone, Norman Foster, who was learning a role in Mozart for a performance in Italian. So I coached him on that too. We got along very well and a very, very long cast composed of some Italians and some Germans. This was conducted by another guest, of course, from Germany, Rudolph Moralt, who came several times to Rome and I saw him there and also later in Munich. The performances were excellent.

As it turned out I was able to leave in the middle of this series of performances, maybe after the fourth or third because we had planned a trip, several of us Fulbright students, a Christmas trip to take us up to Germany where we had never been. So Harper, the tenor, Irene Callaway, the soprano and I set out by train and went to Munich. At Munich we stayed at a hotel and were shown by the hotel manager, just by looking out at the streets, the devastation still left from the bombing of World War II. Churches and other things too were still in ruins.

It was quite a shock. We didn't stay very long. We went on to Salzburg which we saw briefly and then to Vienna. There we stayed a few days and of course wanted to go to the opera. Well, the Vienna Staatsoper, the state opera house, was in ruins. It had been bombed and not yet rebuilt which happened a few years later.

So, the Vienna state opera was performing in a smaller, very well-known theater called the Theater an der Wien. The theater, in which, by the way, Mozart's *Magic Flute* had its Viennese premiere. So, we went to this little theater and stood, (I *think* we stood) and saw a wonderful performance of Mozart's *Magic Flute*, right where it had been born. That was a very wonderful historic occasion. Following Vienna, having seen the whole city and everything in it, we returned to Munich where we split up. We stayed in a pension. We split because I had an important date with a soprano from Italy, who was going to sing in Germany a recital under the auspices of some group. I had to rehearse with her for her recital, not in Munich, but in a nearby little town. So the others went on. I don't know where they went, but eventually to Rome.

A few days later I myself got on a train, and went to Switzerland and got off the train at Interlaken where I had met, by arrangement, two other Fulbright friends of mine. One was a soprano who was a friend from the Perugia weeks, Audrey Nossaman, and she had studied at Milan that whole fall. She had chosen Milan instead of Rome to make her studies with a maestro there and she occasionally came to Rome to visit us. The other person we met was a good friend of ours, again from the boat. His name was Lennie Mastrogiacomo. He was studying in Rome as a piano major and they both came to Interlaken to see Switzerland. So, we got on a train, as all tourists do, and went up this incredible mountain to see Gründewald, the small town on the way up and then finally taking the chair lift up to the top. It was spectacular introduction for us to the mountains of the Swiss Alps which none of us had seen. So that was our New Year's Eve, to spend New Year's Eve in Interlaken celebrating the Swiss Alps and after that we returned to Rome.

As it turned out, in late December and into January, the Rome Opera had scheduled a double bill. One was an opera, the very famous *Amahl and the Night Visitors* by Gian Carlo Menotti which actually had never been seen in Rome. The other was a staged performance of Carl Orff's' "Carmina Burana" with much more ballet and the singing was done from the side or from the pit. Well, of course, I had no work to do on it as I had missed rehearsals, but I saw it and all of the performances. One could say that Pederzini, a well-known mezzo did the mother in *Amahl* and though shaky on top was still quite good and one of the three kings was Renato Capecchi, also very well-known. The conductor of both works was Oliviero de Fabritiis, known to many Americans for his many visits to America including stints at the San Francisco Opera above all. I saw him frequently over the years in many operas and I will comment more on him at a later time when we get to an opera of some substance.

Well, after that came a performance, a production, let us say, of Puccini's *Butterfly*. Now that was nothing of a revelation to me. I knew it, of course, having seen many, many performances in America, so I thought I knew it more or less, by memory.

The cast was somewhat different, somewhat unusual. The soprano who did *Butterfly* was Onelia Fineschi although I saw her some years later in Vienna. Pinkerton, the tenor, was Alvinio Misciano, totally unknown to us and even now unknown. He was a very, very light-voiced Pinkerton. The main figure to us was Sharpless, sung by Afro Poli, a very well-known baritone who was, more or less, ending his career, but he sang very well. The staging was totally conservative and the conductor Alberto Paoletti was an associate conductor at the theater who only did repeats of various works, nothing extraordinary, and I was never very much a fan of his. So, the *Butterfly* did not leave exactly a lasting impression.

The work that followed that left quite an impression because it was my first encounter anywhere except by recordings, with Maria Callas. She sang Cherubini's *Medea*, one of her fundamental great roles. In this *Medea* the conductor was again the one I admired so much, Santini. He did a superb job. Assisting Callas was the great bass Boris Christoff, the first time I heard him in the theater. He was excellent, as was the secondary lyric soprano, and that was Gabriella Tucci, whom I got to know very well and she sang all over Italy and even at the New York Met. The tenor was Francesco Albanese, no relation whatsoever to Licia, but a very fine tenor in this role and the maid of *Medea* was sung by the great Fedora Barbieri. How to try today to equal a cast such as that? I was quite"bowled over," you would say. The staging was traditional as was typical in Italy in those days. The Director was Margherita Wallman, who did much of the staging for operas in Rome and I did my usual backstage work which gave me a chance to meet Callas. I can still remember very much between acts, standing on the stage—an empty stage. She was looking at the scenery to decide where her entrance was and where it was not and we had a conversation. She realized I was an American. We spoke some Italian and we spoke some English and, of course, her English was perfect. So that was a fine chance to meet Callas and later to hear her. Well, her vocal condition was still good but with the usual problems that constantly reasserted themselves, meaning pitches anywhere above her B flats were difficult. She had more or less backed out of the high Cs and it was particularly noticeable if it occurred at the end of a trio or duet or at the end of an act. And that was the Callas that I first encountered. I saw her many times thereafter. And we all very much enjoyed the chance to see her.

On the heels of the above double bill came another double bill and it was an unusual combination. The first was an opera/ballet in one act by a contemporary Italian called Antonio Veretti called *Burlesca* or *Burlesque*. I do not recall anything about it except that I did not care for it. The cast included, of all people, the famous mezzo Cloe Elmo who debuted with the Met years later and it had Rizzieri who sang very often in Rome. *Burlesca*, the opera, did not enthuse me but the conductor certainly did. He was the other great conductor that I knew, became friends with, and ended up having correspondence with him until he died, Maestro Gavazzeni of La Scala, who came to Rome almost every year for one or two operas. He was very flamboyant although clear in his direction and a lot of people criticized him for being too "plateale" meaning "for the public" to you, but I didn't find that to be the case and I got to know him very well.

He conducted very well and not only that, the other opera was another what we call, a "knockout." It was my first experience in person with Puccini's one-act *Il Tabarro* which is one of three one-act operas, that he wrote that premiered in New York. This *Tabarro* is at times my favorite Puccini. This time it had a superb cast which I don't think I'll ever see again. Headed by Tito Gobbi, as Michele, the first time I had ever seen Gobbi, Lo Forese, the tenor, who was superb, but had a short career, and the soprano was Clara Petrella.

Writing of Clara Petrella and her immense impact forces me to make this interjection. I first heard her on several LP records, while still at the Cincinnati College of Music. One was

Tabarro, recorded by the RAI in Rome to mark the 25th anniversary of the death of Puccini in 1949, and this LP was easily available anywhere in the USA on the label CETRA-SORIA.

Like many others of that era, she was superb but with singers not her equal and unknown to me when I was in Rome; Reali, baritone, Glauco Scarlini, tenor under Giuseppe Baroni, conductor, also new to me. The other set of LPs was Montemezzi's masterpiece *L'Amore Dei Tre Re*, rarely done in the USA, and which I never ran into in Italy in 20 years. We were lucky to learn that this great post-verismo composer had been living and teaching in California until his death. They brought him to the Cincinnati Zoo Opera to conduct this opera, which played to about half the theater only, but was raved about by the press and public. It came back the next year under Cleva with some other singers.

I was captivated, had the score, went to orchestra rehearsals with Montemezzi, and cannot imagine better casts. On the discs it had oddly cast a famous baritone, Bruscantini, in the heavy leading bass role of Archibaldo, and another lyric baritone, Capecchi, as Manfredo, both known to me in Rome Opera performances of other works. The LP tenor was Amadeo Berdini, not at all up to his role, even a crack!. The conductor was Arturo Basile, known to LP record fans and to me in Italy, and the RAI Orchestra.

However Petrella dominated the entire opera for all my friends who heard it, but in Cincinnati we had two casts, all excellent. The French mezzo, Lily Djanel, known at the Met for *Carmen* mostly, my favorite Puccini tenor at the time in Cincinnati, Armand Tokatyan, baritone George Czaplicki as Manfredo, and the aging great basso, Virgilio Lazzari, from the Met and always at the Cincinnati Opera each summer as Archibaldo--superb. The next year we had Norina Greco as Fiora, always fine in all her roles, but not a Petrella! Charles Kullman as the tenor, Avito and Robert Weede, the baritone. So I was well versed in the opera through these live shows and my LPs and regret that I never saw Petrella as Fiora in Italy at all.

It remains a mystery why the Met had not done the opera since February 10, 1941. I still have an *Opera News* issue of that week when it was broadcast and cover shows Montemezzi rehearsing the singers Grace Moore and Charles Kullman with the great Ezio Pinza as the Archibaldo and Richard Bonelli as Manfredo. I did not hear it, not yet having been caught up in Opera until my first *Barber* that summer at the Zoo with Bidu Sayao. So, as all wonder, if and when, these masterpieces will return to an American opera house? For those wishing to see Petrella in a performance, they can look for the excellent video filmed by the RAI in Italy of her *Tabarro* with Picchi, the old but excellent Tagliabue, and great camera work. To bad she never sang in the USA as Bing felt she was "not suitable" to the American taste.

Now the Petrella story could go on and on which I will comment on as I go through this book. She was a lyric spinto soprano with warm, dark and with extremely pungent qualities which some would complain about because the pitch was not always stable and with so much passion. Her voice and this dark color way down into the low voice and into the chest voice made her the very fixture of attention. Well, that was it for me. I fell for Clara Petrella and stayed hooked with her performances for years and years and luckily have several of her operas on recordings. So, this *Tabarro* was a wonderful production in all ways and due mainly to Petrella and Gavazzeni. The other singers were equally good.

So, that was probably the second big highlight of that year. But they didn't stop. This was Rome. This was like the Met in a very unusually good season. This opera now in a theater that observed what we call the Stagione System meaning one opera and then another opera done in a row with three or five performances as opposed to the repertoire type which alternates every night, such as the Met. We now had *Werther* of Massenet in that year which the Italians were still singing in Italian instead of French and the conductor was again Gavazzeni, who galvanized us all and not only that, here I was introduced in person to Giuseppe di Stefano. Well, he has remained my favorite tenor and his style was so superb. I used to come out of backstage and stand down more or less in the front line row next to the orchestra to watch him sing his arias and the sensation was more than enough to make your hair stand on end.

In addition to him was of all people, Clara Petrella, again singing the role of Charlotte, which can be sung by a soprano or a mezzo and in this case a soprano. She was again completely devastating as was di Stefano. Their singing together, I guess we would say was "mind-blowing." The role of Sophie, her sister, was sung by, again an introduction to me, Renata Scotto. This was the young Scotto, a coloratura because she never undertook anything heavier. When she was going to Edinburgh, jumping in and taking a role of Callas in *Sonnambula*; well she was charming, sweet and sang wonderfully with her tiny lyric voice. So, the entire experience was a thrill.

As we approached the end of the season we had another double bill to follow that. This was a double bill by the famous contemporary Italian, Pizzetti. In this we had a double bill consisting of the ballet, *La Pisanella*, a sort of a ballet which I frankly did not care for and I don't think I saw it much and the other opera was *La Straniero, The Stranger*. It had a cast that was rather good. Mirto Picchi was was known for many dramatic roles in Puccini and Verdi. His soprano was Gabriella Tucci whom I got to know very well later and she even came to the Met and sang for years here and in Europe. The bass was Mario Petri, excellent and the bass was a friend of mine who made his debut with me in Spoleto, Mazzola. This was conducted by Angelo Questa, another new conductor to me but very well-known in Italy and on recordings. This opera I've seen several times because they brought it up again in Naples and I saw it there with Maestro Gavazzeni, but here it was conducted by Angelo Questa. He was a good, no-nonsense conductor and not particularly a friendly man though I did visit him once at his home to ask for advice about my career. But I have very little more to say about Questa because I had not become a fan of his works in general.

But that, however is not the case for the next opera. Because then we suddenly received the great *Un Ballo in Maschera* of Verdi. We former Fulbrights that are still in touch still recall this and how we were absolutely "bowled over" when we heard di Stefano, Gobbi and Antonietta Stella on the stage in this opera and the Oscar was the American coloratura Gianna d' Angelo, who had made quite a career in Italy. The conductor again was the great Santini. Well you could not top this. The sounds of these three principal singers, in their prime, in great roles was hard to believe. And I think the one that "knocked us out," if you want to put it that way, was Antonietta Stella. I had never heard her before and she has remained to this day my favorite dramatic or spinto soprano in any roles and her Amelia was the beginning of this long friendship until I saw her a few years ago in Rome. Di Stefano too was in his prime as was Gobbi and the conductor was Santini. So, another memorable session in which I was backstage all the time telling Stella and Gobbi when to go on and to go off.

And following this we had another double bill conducted by de Fabritiis, whom I mentioned earlier. One was a one-act opera by Mascagni which I had never heard of called *Zanetto*, an opera that is seldom done and very, very rarely performed anywhere and I must say

I conducted the American premiere of it in Cincinnati which was broadcast on NPR (National Public Radio), but that is another story. Here we had the two people in the cast, Simionato and Rosanna Carteri doing this simple one-hour opera that was very beautiful and sung so gorgeously. The other companion opera to this was a well-known work by Mascagni called *L'amico Fritz* which I had never seen. And it is short enough to be billed with another opera. The staging was excellent, the cast terrific. Rosanna Carteri was the soprano and my first encounter there on the stage in Rome was Tagliavini in very good estate. The other roles and conducting by Fabritiis were memorable. The cast and the singing, everything about it was quite moving and I will never forget that because I don't think I've seen *L'amico Fritz* since.

Three leading singers in the cast of Prokoviev's *Angelo di Fuoco* at the 1959 Spoleto Festival at lunch in a nearby restaurant. Left to Right—Rolando Panerai, Florindo Andreolli, and Leyla Gencer, singers.

CHAPTER TWO
The Years of Great Singers in Italy

Now I go to the great, great Rossini under my other favorite conductor. At this point we reach an opera that was a new one to me and that had started a very strong interest on my part in Rossini. Because the opera was *Cenerentola* and we had never heard it in America, at least I had never heard it, and this was the achievement of the conductor, Vittorio Gui. He became one of my idols and one of my friends. He was very famous and an old man; he was responsible, let's say, for the enormous revival of Rossini in the world. It started in Italy around 1925, I think, when he did a production of a rare Rossini opera *L'Italiana in Algeri* in Torino, and then he continued to do them. But all of us had forgotten Rossini over the years in Italy and also in the USA except at Glyndebourne, where Gui was a very famous resident conductor, almost every season for years and years and years.

Well, *Cenerentola* appeared in Rome and I was there backstage doing everything, and the cast was incredible. We had, of all things, Giulietta Simionato, whom I grew to love and it was the first time I heard a mezzo singing the roles that Rossini had written for a mezzo. In America we were used to coloratura sopranos singing Rossini and things of that nature. But, they were really written for a mezzo, a lyric mezzo, with coloratura ability and Simionato was the chief among all of them. And we were just dazzled. I could not believe what she accomplished in this role. And with her was Sesto Bruscantini and Ian Wallace, an Englishman, as Don Magnifico, who probably belonged to the Glyndebourne cast whom Gui always had in England. The tenor was Juan Oncina, a Spaniard. He was very good in this high leggiero tenor repertoire and the others were the two girls, Clorinda and Tisbe, well-known, but not stars.

Well, the opera was amazingly successful and for me it was the opening of an entire new era. As I then heard over the years, many more Rossinis. And through these performances, I got to know Simionato. I would see her backstage and the others too, but especially Gui, and I will dwell on him later when I get to another chapter and when I used to visit him at his home in Florence as I did with aged Tullio Serafin at his home and who met me on the road later.

After this came *La Traviata,* which, of course, I had seen countless times in America and

The first inside page from a program of the debut concert of the Fulbright singers with Conductor Robert Feist.

especially in Cincinnati. The thing about this opera is that it was scheduled to be sung by Tebaldi who cancelled, not suddenly, but with quite a bit of notice. I couldn't figure it out.

Talking to all the other conductors, we got the feeling that she was realizing that Violetta was a little bit too hard for her in the first act, even if she had sung it many times. So, suddenly we had Elena Rizzieri, who was a well-known lyric coloratura, who did a good job. We had the tenor Prandelli, whom I had mentioned earlier and he was the Alfredo. Gino Bechi we knew from recordings and I was surprised to find him still living. But there he was and he did a very good Germont, a bit frazzled on top.

The rest of the cast were the normal secondary people that you found in Rome at the time. The conductor was Vincenzo Bellezza, whom I didn't get to know. I spoke to him occasionally, but he had had an extensive career all over, including some nine or ten years at the Metropolitan Opera, as well as La Scala. But, Bellezza, by this time, was being a little careless or old, or not very dominating and his rehearsals were somewhat chaotic. He was always talking on his stand to make the orchestra shut up because they were always yapping and gossiping and making noise. So, it was very distracting to find this in the Rome Opera House. But, that was typical of Bellezza at that era, and so therefore I never really pursued a contact with him. And so the *Traviata* was what we call a sort of normal repertoire piece with nothing outstanding.

However, the next two operas were what we call not *blockbusters*, but were certainly extreme rarities that I had never seen. The first was *Cyrano de Bergerac* by Alfano. As readers will know, Franco Alfano was the man who was chosen by Ricordi to complete Puccini's *Turandot,* which he had left unfinished at his death. But, people did not know that Alfano wrote many operas himself, maybe ten or more, which were very rarely heard if at all. And now, as I write this, we know that the Metropolitan Opera finally produced it in New York, this past year, with Domingo, the first time it was ever heard in the United States which actually puzzles all of us. You can't imagine why it took that long. It is a marvelous opera and it has been recorded. I have a recording from the Italian radio, the RAI with American singers, Olivia Stapp and William Johns.

This performance was a "knockout," my favorite term, because it starred Ramon Vinay who was celebrated in Italy, as he was all over the world for his *Otello* and for other works that

I heard him sing. I heard him sing *Samson and Delilah* in Naples and other operas. But here he was doing *Cyrano* and marvelously. Roxanne was Anna de Cavalieri, a name that Italians knew by *that* name, but Americans would know her as Ann McKnight. She was discovered by Toscanini and sang Musetta in his famous *La Boheme* in New York on NBC Radio with Albanese. At any rate de Cavalieri had been in Italy for some time, not as a pupil, but as a protégé of Tullio Serafin, as was Callas, and turned into a lyric-spinto and beautiful voice that carried all over the theater and she was a marvelous Roxanne.

So those two made up the chief roles in this cast, but also they had such people as Mario Borriello, who was very well-known and Christiano, the main tenor role, was sung by Gustavo Gallo who did a very excellent job. The staging was excellent in all ways, very normal. And the conductor was Franco Ghione, another very well-known name, one that I knew even before coming to Europe from various old recordings on the normal 78rpm label. He was quite old but did a very excellent job with this opera. I, of course, saw all performance and I was thrilled to do it. To be able to see it and to work backstage with these people and all of the Fulbright singers who congratulated everybody. They also met with me at the intermission to rave about the fact they had been able to see this rare, rare opera which finally, now this year (2006) has had its American premiere and will be actually broadcast by the Met this coming season.

Having finished that rarity, we had one more. This was an opera that is considered really not an opera, but an oratorio. This is how you hear it most often, "The Damnation of Faust" by Berlioz. Well, here was a staging, and it is often staged, but not as frequently done as it is as a concert piece. It is one of Berlioz's best scores, and it was staged by Herbert Graf. Graf was well-known to all in America for his years and years at the Metropolitan Opera, one of the main stage directors there. There the staging was excellent and the singers were very good. The Faust was Mirto Picchi again, this dramatic tenor who was heard in many dramatic roles throughout Italy. Margarita was Miriam Pirazzini, an excellent mezzo, whom I later met in Germany when she worked with me. The bass baritone as Mephistofeles was Mario Petri, and another fine bass, Plinio Clabassi also sang a leading bass. So this was a superb performance and was conducted by Franco Capuana, a very excellent conductor, known through recordings and for his work all over Italy and outside of Italy.

There, that first season turned out to be, really, an introduction to all of us of the great music and of the great singers in Italy, but that is the subject of the next chapter. For now, I want to digress to say that in the middle of this opera and my work backstage, we had free time, of course.

Backstage at my conducting debut in Spoleto with the Rome Opera Orchestra. Congratulating us is the famous Ruby Mercer, former Met star and then the founder of *Opera Canada* magazine. From left to right—Signor Pallotelli, Maurine Norton, Peter Binder, Irene Callaway, Robert Feist, Ruby Mercer, Bill Harper, Gimi Beni and Anna Moffo.

CHAPTER THREE
Operas in Other Cities and My Debut as a Conductor

We generally arranged that we would meet for lunch. It happened to be a nice, small trattoria on a street near the opera across from the Ministry of Finance. So we had a small table and we would congregate there sometimes three of us, sometimes five and we would meet other friends who were not in the music world, all Italians. We would have a light lunch with the usual pasta, meat, salad and wine at a ridiculously inexpensive price and then go back to our own task. For me, it meant that I had several hours off because nothing resumed at the Rome Opera until maybe 5:00 p.m. for the evening performance at nine. And we, of course, had much time to see the city.

We saw everything in Rome over the course of a year. So it wasn't like tourists who arrive and then have three days or one week to try to see Rome and then another week for Florence. We had a year. So we took our time and saw everything and there is no use listing them all because they are what everybody knows; the Roman Forum, Piazza Venezia and Piazza del Popolo, Fontana di Trevi, all the fountains, St. Peter's Square, St. Peters and all the other major basilicas. We all had the time to see them leisurely and to admire this amazing amount of art, history and beauty that is Rome.

Of course there is a lot of commotion. Italians are not quiet. They are noisy and the traffic is confusing, but it is far worse now. Then there were not many cars. I have photos showing just a few cars parked, a few little Fiats, or whatever they are, and yes, the noise was always present. It was hard for everybody to be quiet for any particular reason. Still we enjoyed it. We really put up with it because it was a extremely wonderful place to be at that time. The world was quiet, nothing was happening that was bad and we enjoyed life very much, not only in Rome but we had several visits outside of the city. We often went to Naples It is only two hours by train to see maybe an opera and to visit the whole city of Naples. I saw *Samson and Delilah*, with Vinay and, of all people, the great legendary mezzo, Ebe Stignani, whom I never thought I would see and it was wonderful, even though in Italian which was the custom.

Then we went to Florence on a major trip, somewhere in May, I think. It was during the May Festival with the *Maggio Musicale*, and we went there for one particular reason. We hit a

Right—A view of the beautiful Teatro Nuovo in Spoleto, Italy..

CITTA DI SPOLETO
TEATRO LIRICO SPERIMENTALE
IX STAGIONE

Venerdì 23 Settembre 1955 - Ore 21

CONCERTO
VOCALE E STRUMENTALE

Con la partecipazione dei vincitori del
"PREMIO FULBRIGHT"
assegnati al "Teatro Lirico Sperimentale" dalla "Commissione Americana per gli Scambi Culturali con l'Italia"

DIRETTORE
Maestro ROBERT FEIST

Soprani	IRENE CALLAWAY
	ANNA MOFFO
	MAURINE NORTON
Tenore	WILLIAM HARPER
Baritono	PETER BINDER
Basso	GIMI BENI

Orchestra del Teatro dell' Opera di Roma

ROBERT FEIST
di Cincinnati (HO)

DIRETTORE D'ORCHESTRA

Above—Mr. Feist in his "Direttore d' Orchestra" role at the Concert of Fulbright Scholars featuring Irene Callaway, Anna Moffo, Maurine Norton, William Harper, Peter Binder and Gimi Beni, September 23, 1955.

weekend of two operas that were incredibly cast. We heard *Otello* and *Falstaff* on successive nights. The *Otello* had a cast you could not equal today with Mario del Monaco who was the reigning Otello of the day and with him Tito Gobbi and Renata Tebaldi. This was an amazing cast and it was under Gabriele Santini. It was superb in all ways. I can remember the public bursting into applause after a simple thing such as a high note in the third act where you normally would not have applause, but in Italy you do and that set the place on fire.

The next day we went back to the same theater for *Falstaff,* which had another great cast, headed by Tebaldi again and Pirazzini and a very wonderful Falstaff who was a surprise; it should have been Gobbi, but he couldn't sing two nights in a row of heavy roles, so they brought in the veteran Mariano Stabile, who had been the Falstaff for decades in Italy and I thought he had died. But there was Stabile doing Falstaff, his key role, and we were just in heaven. We couldn't believe we were hearing Stabile in person.

Everybody else was also terrific, the names of which I do not have in front of me. But those two nights were an introduction to opera in Florence and I saw many, many more over the next years. We also saw the whole city, which is the treasure chest of art in Italy. Everything about Florence is art—all the works of Botticelli, Michelangelo, and so forth. We saw them all in all of the museums. We went through the all the streets. We saw the Academia in which the famous statue "David" is found. In short we had a wonderful tour of that city and it grew to be practically our favorite outside of Rome.

Then somewhere in that spring, they took us up to Milan and it was our introduction to Milan. There, in addition to seeing the city, which is simply a big industrial city in the sense that it is all business there, and not that much of scenic art to see. The great Duomo is fantastic and the Piazza del Duomo is another marvel plus the Galleria. This is the gallery that is near La Scala, which is filled with shops, restaurants and bars, and everybody congregates to just chat and gossip about what is happening in Milan especially at the opera. Because the other side of the gallery is La Scala and that is what we really wanted to see plus visit the other historical sites. But, over the course of days, we saw three different works. We saw first of all—Callas in another one of her roles. And this was her leading role in *La Sonnambula* by Bellini, one of her signature roles, extreme coloratura and wonderful acting. I liked her better in this than *Medea* because there were no attempts at straining for extreme high notes and it was quite beautiful. In addition to which it was conducted by, of all people, Leonard Bernstein, who had been brought to La Scala a year or so before making his debut there with another opera. And there, suddenly, here he is doing *La Sonnambula*, which he had probably not even heard before. But he was wonderful and the ovations went on and on and one and they turned on the lights in the whole theater for the curtain calls, which they never do. The rest of the cast I don't recall because I don't have the program here, I but I imagine that the tenor was Cesare Valletti or someone of his stature.

The next night or two nights later, we saw a double bill, and this had the *Cavalleria Rusticana* with, to my joy and amazement, Giulietta Simionato, again doing the soprano role of Santuzza, which is occasionally done, but I never expected to see her in it and it was marvelous. She was partnered by Giuseppe di Stefano. So that was quite a duo for this opera. And, of course, di Stefano by this time was already engaging in the heavier repertoire, which was to doom him later on, because instead of staying with the lyrical roles like *Manon* or *Faust* and *Boheme*, he gradually took on the heavier roles including this one and *Pagliacci* and *Tosca* and on and on and on, which can be mentioned later on. However, it was a stunning performance. On the double bill with that was the one-act opera *Zanetto*, which I have already mentioned having seen it in Rome and it was extremely well done, again with Carteri and Simionato.

Finally we had the debut in Italy of the American conductor, Thomas Schippers. Of course he was brought in by Menotti, his patron, and this was in 1955 and he was not yet known with the Spoleto Festival. But they did the opera *The Saint of Bleeker Street*, a premiere for Italy or for Milano and Menotti was the stage director and it had a very good cast. But, David Poleri had done it in America and the rest of the cast was very similar to that in America. We enjoyed it. The public enjoyed it too, though it is not my favorite Menotti opera. Still, though having been there for the Italian premiere, it was a great joy in addition to seeing the rest of the city.

We returned to Rome and to conclude this chapter, it brings us to the big moment which was our debut in Italy. They knew that they were going to have the American singers take part in the Teatro Lirico Sperimentale, the experimental opera theater in Spoleto, Italy. This small town, about an hour up from Rome, on the way to Florence, had been created as a festival about ten years before by the city itself and by Adriano Belli, who was an administrator or

Robert Feist with his parents, Robert and Mary Feist in New York before his departure to Italy as a Fulbright Scholarship winner.

Mr. Feist on the occasion of his debut conducting the Rome Opera Orchestra in the Teatro Nuovo in Spoteto, Italy, September, 1955.

Left to right—Signora Saragat, Robert Feist, the future Prime Minister of Italy, Giuseppe Saragat, Anna Moffo, Bill Harper and Leonard Mastrogiacomo at a recital given in the villa of the Saragats.

Right—Fulbright vocal winners received awards from Claire Boothe Luce at a reception at the American Embassy in Rome. *Left to right:* Claire Boothe Luce, Mr. Feist, bass Beni, soprano Norton, soprano Moffo and tenor Harper.

a banker, as a means for making a stage for all the young singers in Italy who won national competitions or the competition in honor of Beniamino Gigli. Well, the number of Italian singers who could do this would be endless; there's no place to recount them. But, of all people, Franco Corelli, Antonietta Stella and countless others made their debuts in Spoleto in that little town in years prior to us.

The Americans joined it around 1953 and I knew some of the singers later when they moved elsewhere. Among them was the fine tenor, Jean Cox, who made his debut there in *The Barber of Seville* and later moved on to Mannheim, I believe. To my delight he was engaged in Augsburg as Otello in one of my very own performances. Admittedly too heavy for him, but he did it superbly and later sang Wagner roles in Germany and even the USA including (I think) the Met in New York where he moved into heavy tenor repertoire. Also Edith Lang, a fine spinto soprano, who debuted in *Butterfly* in Spoleto and later became a leading soprano in Hamburg and a friend of mine, singing Tosca and other roles. But for us, what they chose was an opera that they thought they could well undertake at that point in training and that was *Don Pasquale* by Donizetti, a lyric comedy opera. Well they rehearsed in Rome of course, staging and everything and I played for all of the rehearsals, but I was not going to conduct it. It was conducted by Maestro Bertelli, one of the main assistants.

Somewhere in the course of the summer, before this occurred, the administrators came to me, including Maestro Ricci, one of the chief assistants and he said: "Well the singers are making their debut and so are you." Well, I fell over almost. I said: "But I have never conducted." He said: "Well you will now. It would be absurd to have these American singers make their debut with the Rome Opera Orchestra (which always moves up to Spoleto for the debut season in September) and not have you conduct as well." Well, I explained to him that in college as an undergraduate and graduate I had only really studied conducting as a college course, but had never conducted an orchestra. They played recordings for us to conduct which was quite absurd really. So all I ever conducted was a chorus from 'The Messiah" once on a small stage, not even a church choir. But here I was facing the Rome Opera's orchestra. We decided the program which was involving all the American singers and they liked it and what happened was that I had a rehearsal with the orchestra in which I was able to show what I could do. It was coached, of course, by Maestro Ricci and others, and the orchestra knew everything backwards. It was no problem for them no matter what I did because they knew it so well. Therefore, when it came time for the debut, I had already heard the *Don Pasquale,* which was excellent and everybody was interested in to see what I would accomplish. Well, it went very well I'm proud to say. I was a bit shaky at first, but my Maestro sat among the first violins watching to see that if anything could happen, I might fall over or not be able to finish it and he would be there to take over. But, I did it and I got through an overture and then regained my posture and my composure and conducted the rest of the program very well which included arias and duets from *Traviata, Don Giovanni, Manon Lescaut* and many of the standard repertoire.

It was sung by all of these American singers and also recorded by the Italian Radio/Television, the RAI, as we always call it now and it was broadcast several weeks later. And I even still have a tape of it, showing certain faults in what I did, but still, all in all it is a memento of that occasion which frankly in a way, is reason for this book. Because I just noticed several weeks ago on the calendar that it was the 50th anniversary of that concert. I had posters of it and I said: "Well since it is 50 years, I ought to do something." So we arranged a party with a lot of my own musical friends here, who were either at the Metropolitan and some of whom had been involved in staging or in other aspects of opera here or at the University of Washington. We had a celebratory party for me and for 50 years and I am very glad we did. I am very proud of that. Even Anna Moffo sent a fond greeting in remembrance.

So, we all finished and went back to Rome and then everybody went their own ways, as I should say. Some of them stayed all summer. The summer was over, but they stayed into the

Robert Feist and Anna Moffo at a reunion in Seattle when she was the Met Opera chief judge of the Northwest Regional Auditions about 1986.

fall. But, in the course of the summer and fall, we had made trips to the beach, which is called Ostia Lido, right near the antique city of Ostia Antica, which was then the Port of Rome and now is simply a historic city, where you find Roman ruins from the foundations of Rome. At any rate, Ostia Lido is a wonderful beach and all of Rome goes out there all summer long to frolic on the beach and we did too and the water was wonderful. I have several photos of that too. So, besides beach-going and little trips that we would make around town, the year ended with this debut concert for all of us and then we all had to decide what was going to happen. Well, some of the people decided to stay in Italy with their studies privately, several of the fellowships were renewed by the Fulbright Commission. Mine was renewed to my great delight for another year and so was that of the tenor, Bill Harper. Of the others, some stayed, some went away and some returned to America.

ANNA MOFFO SARNOFF

September 13, 2005

Dearest Bob,

Can it really be the 50th anniversary of your conducting debut?

It seems like yesterday that we were both in Rome as young Fulbright Scholarship winners. I'm sure you remember that time as I do - a wonderful experience, and I am so glad that we have kept in touch all these years.

Once again, my heartiest congratulations on this auspicious occasion.

Love,

Anna

Anna Moffo Sarnoff

AMS/pw

A letter from Mr. Feist's dear friend, Anna Moffo on the occasion of Mr. Feist's 50th anniversary.

Left to right—Giorgio de Chirico, the famous artist, Irene Callaway, Robert Feist, The honorable Saragat, Prime Minister of Italy and William Olvis, tenor, at a party at de Chirico's palatial home filled with his paintings.

CHAPTER FOUR
Some of the Fulbrights Become Famous

Among them was the famous soprano, Anno Moffo, to whom I was, of course, very, very attracted all during our first year. She actually already had a commitment in America during the course of our first year to make a vocal debut with the Philadelphia Orchestra which went very well. And during that first year she was also engaged to sing Micaela in *Carmen* in Palermo, Sicily with Vinay, again in Italian not in French. But Anna and I had kept a friendship all these years and I followed her career very, very carefully and wished her all the best when she married the stage director, Mario Lanfranchi, which was at the start of her career in Italy the next year. She was engaged to sing *Madame Butterfly* in a TV production by the RAI. And then she did many RAI productions with Lanfranchi as well as in opera houses, including her USA debut in Chicago in 1957 and then the Met in New York, where she sang for 18 years to great acclaim in a vast repertoire. To our dismay, we just read of her death in New York city at age 73, which no one expected; a great blow to all of her friends and public. It occurred on March 9, 2006, due to cancer. Anna was, of course, a beloved friend of mine from our student days in Rome and everyone knows of her career in New York and all over the world so I can't add more to that.

I will add more about a few of the other colleagues of mine and one Fulbright. Earlier I mentioned the tenor Bill Harper. He actually returned to the States in his second year to go into the service. He was only in the service a year and then he returned to Rome to continue his vocal studies and coaching. Then at my suggestion he went to Germany to find an agent and through the luck of that agent he was engaged as the leading tenor in the German town of Karlsruhe and when he was there I went up to visit him and at the time I was working in Augsburg. So I went over to this city and stayed a few days to hear him in the role he had debuted in, which was the *Masked Ball*. Now to be honest, he should never have been singing that. But it is the German custom to always place people in roles that are above them because they don't have enough of the right kind of tenors It should have been a spinto. Bill was a light lyric, so he should not have sung it. And shortly after that they cast him, of all things, as Canio in *Pagliacci*, another role that only a dramatic tenor should sing. Somehow he got through them and perhaps due to the fact that he had had excellent vocal training in America. He was from the University of Oklahoma and studied with the very renowned dramatic soprano from England, Eva Turner. Eva Turner was one of the most celebrated Turandots of her era singing even with Toscanini and many others in Italy at La Scala. Bill was lucky to study with Eva, and she actually came to Karlsruhe for his performance in *The Masked Ball* and I met her there, which for me was a great thrill. He was engaged shortly after that in Stuttgart which is one of the great opera houses in Germany and luckily they placed him in the right repertoire, roles like *Bohème, Butterfly*, even *Tosca*, a little high, but he did it, the *Elixir of Love* and several lyric roles. In addition to that, he did the world's premiere of the new opera by the famous Karl Orff, an opera that I do not recall but I was at the performance and didn't like it at all. As a matter of fact, I walked out and we talked about it later. Whenever I saw him in Stuttgart, I stayed with him and his wife, a lovely woman, Carolyn, in their apartment and we would hash over many, many things. Bill remained a very close friend. He came to Rome to visit me later when I was teaching there and then he returned to the States, gave up singing and became a teacher. He taught in the elementary or high schools in Fort Smith, Arkansas and liked it very much. He was rid of the stress that had happened during a vocal career and was a good teacher where he remained until our great, great dismay he died just a few years ago suddenly. No one knew about it until I contacted friends of his in Fort Smith to find what had happened. His wife had preceded him in death by several years. The loss of Bill and Anna was very great.

Another one of that era was the bass buffo, Gimi Beni, who had debuted with me, carried on a career for a while in Italy then returned to the States where his career continued in various regional houses, principally in the South because he was based in St. Petersburg, Florida where I conducted a *Tosca* in which he sang the Sacristan. But his career as a bass buffo continued all around the USA even as far as Santa Fe and New York, the New York City Opera. Also, to my dismay, he died approximately five years ago which I heard from friends there and we were sorry about that. Another one of that group, was the aforementioned Irene Callaway.

Irene in the second year in Rome had met a new Fulbright, the bass Peter Harrower, who was very good and they fell in love, became husband and wife and he sang quite a bit of large repertoire, mainly concerts with the Saint Cecilia Orchestra and others in Italy before they returned to the States. Then they were somehow protégés of the great Eugene Ormandy of the Philadelphia Orchestra who used them in various performances. Irene then also sang as her American debut in *Thais* with Leontyne Price at the Chicago Lyric Opera. I don't know the year, but that was her start in America. Irene eventually retired and became simply a voice teacher, but very prominent in Atlanta where they both lived. Peter was the voice professor at Georgia State University at Atlanta, sang very often there and she did with the conductor of that time, Robert Shaw, the wonderful and well-known choral conductor, who was then the conductor of the Atlanta Symphony. I visited them often because they arranged several workshops. They were workshops for young students who came every summer to Atlanta to learn more about staging and singing roles with other young singers. I was always in charge of these workshops, which went on for four years in Atlanta, and I enjoyed it very much though it was tedious because of the fact that Atlanta in August is extremely hot and humid. But I always enjoyed working with Irene and Peter and their students. At some point Peter also became ill with a stroke or an aneurysm and he still did a workshop or so but did not last long and he died, which for Irene and for all of us another shock.

The remaining one of the Fulbrights was Peter Binder who also after leaving Rome went to Germany and became a leading baritone at the opera house in Mannheim, Germany where he remained for a long, long time, way after I had left Germany. He eventually retired and returned to Philadelphia or that area where his family was from, and, as far as I know, is still living there well though blind, as I was sorry to learn.

However, back to the summer and fall in Rome, the year ended, more or less, in September with people remaining or going back to the States I decided to remain and start in the fall in late November on the second season in Rome. Before we get into that second season in Rome, I'd like to make a detour and it's a jump back in time to my youth in America to indicate why all the great singers in the world that I talked about were not all such a surprise to me because I had grown up with many of them for a decade or more in Cincinnati and New York and it is the subject of the chapter coming up. I will discuss my introduction to opera and how it grew in Cincinnati of all places.

The program cover of the Cincinnati Summer Opera Association 25th Anniversary Season, June 30–August 10, 1946.

CHAPTER FIVE
My Youth and Introduction to Opera in Cincinnati, Ohio

I was born there and did all my undergraduate work at the Cincinnati College of Music, which now after many decades has been united with the Cincinnati Conservatory of Music, which was our rival school. They formed the CCM, Cincinnati College Conservatory, a part of the University of Cincinnati. But, when I lived there, it was simply the College of Music and it was adjacent to the Music Hall, home of the Cincinnati Symphony, and now the opera house, where I went every week to usher at performances. This brings me to opera. For some reason, unknown to me, my parents decided to take me to an opera and I was in high school. And the reason could be that perhaps the opera world was so small at the time that we didn't know that Cincinnati was one of three opera companies in existence in America in terms of date after the Met, but soon they had Chicago and San Francisco. But it started in 1921 and it was started at the Cincinnati Zoological Gardens, called commonly the Zoo, which had a huge outdoor area.

With the help of the city and all the people who ran it, it was decided to put up a pavilion, a band shell for bands to play summer music. That went on for a while, and then they announced a season of just light excerpts, solos, operettas and light musical comedy. Well, the people liked it so much that it grew in that same year with four or five full-length operas on the spot, with very little rehearsal, and were not too hard to stage. Well, it caught on so that by next year it was established as the Cincinnati Summer Opera at the Zoological Gardens and by 1922, it was going for six weeks in the summer. It was the only summer opera company in the United States and so by 1941, my parents decided to "try it out."

Now there are many more, of course. Now we can count everything from Santa Fe to those in California and elsewhere. Then, however, there was a summer operetta, light, opera theater and say after 1941-1942, the Europeans could no longer fly back and forth quickly from Europe to New York, so they stayed in their home countries and therefore those who were already in New York took advantage of Cincinnati or their agents did, and sent them to Cincinnati to perform. Now that led to an entourage, to a collection of the world's greatest singers of the era, which we accepted. We took for granted that this was normal all over. Well, we were the *only* city outside of New York and perhaps Chicago that had this array. Well, I had

Some of the famous opera singers who appeared at the Cincinnati Summer Opera, 1946. From left to right: Frederick Jagel, Charles Kullman, Stella Roman, Vivian Della Chiesa, James Melton, Licia Albanese, Kerstin Thorborg, Dorothy Kirsten (left above), Coe Glade (left below), Grace Moore, Kurt Baum, Winifred Heidt.

heard from friends that young people could usher at the opera free. You didn't get paid, but you heard operas. So, I applied and they accepted me and also they accepted many of my friends. So, we had this opera-going clique of people who at my age group in high school ushered at the opera once or twice a week. That went on until something like 1950 or 1954 when I left for Europe. No one in my high school, St. Xavier, went to the opera and I only kept in touch with two high school buddies; Bob Weber in Colorado and Bob Hagee, S.J. a missionary priest, now back in Cincinnati after years in China.

We heard an immense variety. To list them all would be pointless because it goes on and on and on. However, I have in front of me a very interesting program. It was issued in the summer of 1946, and that was the 25th Anniversary of the Cincinnati Opera, a huge volume with pictures of all the artists. I think it is worthwhile to even list some names because of the conductors included over the past 20 years. This did not just start and end with 1946, it goes way back. We had Fausto Cleva, who was the chief conductor all the while I was there and also we had Sir Thomas Beecham, of all amazing cases, Wilfred Pelletier, George Sebastian, Ernesto Barbini, Paul Breisach, and the composer Italo Montemezzi, Giuseppe Bamboschek, Karl Kritz, Thomas Martin, Luigi Dell'Orefice and George Schick, whom I later met at the Met. The singers would I think dazzle anyone because in that period of time, almost all of these singers whom I mention now, I heard in Cincinnati over the course of five or six years. I'm going to list them: Stella Roman, more on her later because she was my favorite. Rose Bampton, Frederick Jagel, Charles Kullman, Kerstin Thorborg, Risë Stevens, Licia Albanese, Grace Moore, who made her debut there as Manon; Kurt Baum, James Melton, Bruno Landi, a fine lyric tenor; Josephine Antoine, Lily Djanel, Frank Valentino, Nicola Moscona, who was at the Met for ages as was the other famous bass, Lazzari. Then we had Nino Martini, the excellent Rossini tenor; Marjorie Lawrence in Wagner; Lawrence Tibbett singing *Rigoletto* and Scarpia; Ezio Pinza, who sang many of his big roles including Boris; John Brownlee and Richard Bonelli, a name that was then famous, not now; Zinka Milanov appeared one season only; Arthur Carron came for Wagner; Martial Singher was a regular as well as Alexander Sved and Salvatore Baccaloni, our favorite, who filled roles like The *Barber of Seville* and others. We had Varnay doing Wagner and doing her first Salome, Franco Perulli, a lyric tenor; the great Italian mezzo, who was my favorite, Bruna Castagna as Amneris and Carmen and such;

Soprano Stella Roman in *Tosca*, inscribed to Mr. Feist:
"To Bob—con grande amicizia, Floria Tosca."

George Czaplicki, a baritone from the New York Opera, who came and conquered Cincinnati. Then they had the other great bass, Alexander Kipnis, Lorenzo Alvary- he actually, I was lucky enough to coach when I first moved to New York from college in 1950. I was introduced to him. He wanted to learn certain songs in the English language as he was Hungarian and sang at the Met in many, many, mostly secondary bass roles. But he also sang in Cincinnati. At any rate, Alvary was a good friend, and remained so throughout his life and even invited me once in New York to be a guest on his radio program which he had created himself and was broadcast throughout the New York area. We had Igor Gorin, Elizabeth Rethberg to do Wagner; Norman Cordon, another bass; Hilda Reggiani, who was married to Bruno Landi. We had Vittorio Trevisan, the old, ancient fragile bass-buffo who did roles in *The Barber of Seville* and such. We had Jarmila Novotna, Josephine Tuminia as Lucia; Hizi Koyke, Grete Stueckgold, who was way before my time, but she was there doing Wagner. We also had Marjorie Hess, Pompilio Malatesta, a buffo; Harold Lindi, who changed his name from Aroldo; Vivian Della Chiesa, who was superb; Dorothy Kirsten in many of her signature roles, *La Bohème, Tosca* and others. Then there was the great mezzo Coe Glade. Everyone joked about Glade with the made-up eyes and eyelashes covered with paint who did Carmen with a wobbly voice, but she in person, did very well. She also did Amneris and Azucena. We had Jacques Gerard, a French tenor doing all the lyric tenor roles; Armand Tokatyan, Leonard Warren, Carlo Morelli, a good baritone; Eugene Conley from the Met and his wife, Winifred Heidt, who sang mezzo; Christina Carroll, who was always heard as Musetta, also Thelma Altman in secondary roles, Gertrude Ribla, who often took over as Aida, or dramatic roles when we didn't have Roman or Milanov. So, the list actually never ever ends. There are a few more I'll name such as Lodovico Oliviero, who was a comprimario tenor; Claudio Frigerio, a decent baritone; John McCormack, the tenor; Anna Kaskas, an excellent mezzo, who later ended up teaching at Indiana University and Carolina Segrera, who was well-known as Tosca, but before my era.

That more or less covers it. The number of people who appeared there also included Norina Greco, Sidney Rayner, who was taking over the roles of Kurt Baum in roles like *Aida* and *Trovatore*, and Angelo Pilotto, who was a mediocre baritone, but much used. He was singing all the baritone's roles if no one else was there. And, the American soprano, Selma Kaye, who was another "take over" artist for *Aida* and *Trovatore*. So, it was an amazing array of singers

INFORMAL PHOTOGRAPHS OF THE CINCINNATI ZOO OPERA STARS, BETWEEN REHEARSALS IN THE ZOO GARDENS, 1945–1946.

Left—Stella Roman and her son Flavio.

Below—Norina Greco.

Above—Soprano Licia Albanese, and tenor Armand Tokatyan.

Right—Nicola Moscona.

that kept that company going for, well, since 1920 and it is still going, but no way like it was then. And that's what I'm getting at as I progress with my book; to indicate that it was not such a shock to get to Italy and hear great singers because I had heard them in Cincinnati, not the same ones, but equally as powerful, in addition to hearing all of the Met broadcasts from 1942 or 1943, which brought names and faces of many more singers into my house.

When I continue, we will go into another aspect of these opera singers in Cincinnati and that connection to Italy before I even went to Italy for the first time. As I said, I was going to all of the performances as an usher, two or three nights a week at the Cincinnati Zoo Opera. Not only did I hear all the singers, but in addition to that, we realized that the rehearsals always took place out-of-doors at the Zoo Gardens and anybody could come. We students who had very little to do in the summer often came. We would sit there at rehearsals, orchestra alone or with the singers and therefore got to know many of the singers that way. In the back of the theater was an open-air-garden where the singers mingled at intermissions and came outside and there it was that I first approached various singers for their autographs and to just chat. And I have loads of informal photos, Stella Roman and others, of course. See photos of others in the garden, such as: Bruna Castagna and Margaret Harshaw, Winifred Heidt, Eugene Conley, Charles Kullman, and Armand Tokatyan. I treasure them because they are informal and we talked all the time. At the same time of this we also were engaged in trying to learn as much about the scores as we could. I, as the pianist, accompanied singers always at the College of Music with excellent voice professors as well as the professors of piano such as my own mentor from high school on, John Meretta. Therefore in accompanying them in lessons and recitals, I got to know a lot of the Italian and French literature and got a good hold on the Italian language in particular.

Having had this chance of meeting so many singers backstage was an opportunity to at least try some of my Italian with the singers I had met and who didn't speak much English, though a few of them did enough to converse with you. But, it was a chance to try out informally my Italian. Particularly because I belonged to a group called "Friends of the Opera," which was an organization that we had formed and in a very casual way of getting together once a week with some important guest. It would be in the garden of the Zoo Pavilion and we would have

Clockwise from Above—George Czaplicki, baritone; soprano, Margaret Harshaw; and Winifred Heidt, mezzo soprano.

Clockwise from above—Charles Kullman and Norina Greco; Ramon Vinay, tenor; Robert Weede, baritone' and Frederick Jagel, Tenor.

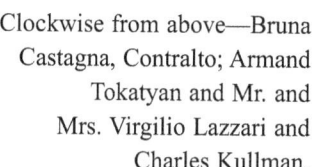

Clockwise from above—Bruna Castagna, Contralto; Armand Tokatyan and Mr. and Mrs. Virgilio Lazzari and Charles Kullman.

dinner or lunch and just talk to them informally. This was an excellent way to get to know them and to try out languages and to their feelings about other singers and conductors. And we remembered many things that they said at that time, one of which was I asked of Stella Roman, what she thought of the conductor whom we knew as George Sebastian of the Paris Opera. And having watched him already, I did not think very much of him and I was a great admirer of Cleva and when I asked her, she said: "Sebastian, he knew nothing—*no nossing*," which was pretty abrupt, but it covered it, as it was what we thought. Also, the conductors who were not Italian such as Paul Breisach from the Met who usually did German works. Occasionally he did *Bohème* or *Traviata* which was never in the mold of the other Italians such as Cleva and so therefore we somewhat shied away from his interpretations which I think was typical. At any rate, through those rehearsals, out-of-doors, and talking to singers, we certainly learned a lot and prepared me for my encounters with all of these great singers and the new ones I encountered in Rome and that's where I'm going to go soon.

During those years of ushering at the opera, the only people who did it with me were people from other schools, none of them from my high school and later not from my college. They were just from various other places who loved opera and we became of group of friends and we would occasionally go to each other's houses and listen to records and things of that nature.

At college, meaning the College of Music at Cincinnati, I had several friends whom I have kept in touch with all these years. Among them must be mentioned Sam and Marianne Carter, since divorced. He is now retired and lives in Amherst, Massachusetts, remarried to Betty, his current wife whom I knew best. Sam did study voice at his college and probably intended to have a career, but it either involved him going to Germany at some point and studying voice there for a year in Munich when I was about to conduct in Augsburg. He even came up there for the first few days or the first week to visit me. But, he went back and ended up getting out of the singing profession, except for singing in church choirs which he still does. He worked as a very important member of the team at Columbia Records, which was very positive for him until he retired.

Clockwise from top left—Frederick Jagel with Stella Roman. Coe Glade. Stella Roman and Mr. Feist. Astrid Varnay.

And the other people of that era in college were several others such as Tabby Henken, a "girlfriend" who has kept in touch with me ever since 1946 to the present, but she lives in California and her husband is deceased. She and I have occasionally visited each other either here or in her California home.

The other good friends were Joel and Janet Ebersole—he a singer and she a pianist and they both live retired in Cincinnati. When I go back there, I visit them each time and we hash over the Cincinnati scene in symphony and opera, which they attend more or less regularly. But, we do keep in touch. None of the other musical friends that I had in college kept in touch, except for a reunion, about six or seven years ago, of the remaining members, let us say, of the Cincinnati College of Music alumni of that year. We had a meeting in Cincinnati and a dinner and it was very much fun to see these people, though I had never kept in touch with them. None of them pursued a really active career in music of a professional level, but kept up with their own instruments or singing, privately or in recitals or in church choirs.

I might as well mention also that I had a break, if one wants to call it that, of a two year stint in the army in the Korean War era. I was stationed in the State of Washington in Richland where the famous Hanford Nuclear Plant was situated and, is still existing. When I was there, I met several people in the city who were members of the local symphony, which was called the Richland Symphony where I had the good luck to be asked by the conductor to be the soloist in the Tchaikovsky Concerto, first movement only, with the hearty approval of our Battalion Commander. I played in uniform and repeated the concerto with the Walla Walla Symphony a month or so later. The one couple, Lydia and Kelly Woods, became very close friends and we are in touch up to the present. Kelly just died about a year or more ago and his wife is in retirement in California. The other couple was Pat and Phil Meyer who live in Morgan Hill, California. She is a cellist and still plays chamber music consistently. So, we have maintained our contact too. They even came to see me once conduct the Oakland Symphony in California when I lived there. When I mention the Army, I may say that I am still in close touch with two of my Army "buddies" who were with me the time in Richland, Washington. They are Bill Fogle and his wife, Marie and Ken Lewis and his wife, Liz. Bill Fogle and his wife live in Cincinnati and have been constantly in touch with me, even when Bill came to Europe on a scholarship and was in Spain (that is his main foreign language) and when I go back to Cincinnati I always stay with them since my father passed away. The other friend, Ken Lewis and his wife live in Prescott, Arizona and I have been down there to visit them once or twice and they have been up here to see me and stay at my house. So, we have maintained this touch which goes back to the Army in 1951 or 1953 and we are still very, very good friends, though none of them are musicians. But they still keep in touch with it and go to concerts or operas.

Mentioning my father reminds me to say, before I forget, that after my mother passed away, and I moved to Seattle to take over my position at the University, my father decided to remain in Cincinnati. He had all of his friends, golf buddies and bowling friends and a whole array of people that he did not want to leave, logically. So, he stayed in Cincinnati, but came every year to Seattle and I went back to Cincinnati every year to see him. So that contact continued even through the telephone. It was nice that he was able to come to Seattle to see me conduct two or three of my opera performances at the University of Washington, which he enjoyed very much. He had only seen me conduct in Europe twice; in Germany and in Cincinnati. That was once or twice when I conducted the chamber operas with the operas of the Peterloon Festival, a Rossini and Mascagni.

But, at any rate, my father's visits to me were very, very welcome and even when I moved to California he came out to California to visit and heard me conduct *Tosca* there. By this time was constantly with his lady companion, who became his very dearest friend, Antoinette. They remained together until he passed away which was in 1990. So, I welcomed her always at my house along with him, and she remained in touch with me after he passed away for another two years until she herself died. But these remembrances are very positive because of the opportunities to visit me here on my home territory, now in Seattle, and also once in California. Many other friends visited me on several occasions in Seattle or in Portland when I lived there and those visits were always very, very pleasant for me to keep up this touch which I also maintained by phone and mail.

Robert Feist in Army uniform in a casual rehearsal with his Richland civilian musician friends in the symphony in 1952 or 1953.

PERUGIA
ASSISI
SPOLETO

Inhalt

ECKART PETERICH ·	Umbrien ist dunkler	4
ROSARIO ASSUNTO ·	Aus dem Skizzenbuch eines Wanderers	10
GUSTAV RENÉ HOCKE ·	Assisi, Franziskus, Giotto	17
GUSTAV HILLARD ·	Visionen eines Heiligenlebens	29
PIETRO SCARPELLINI ·	Hier lernte Raffael	31
HEINZ SCHEIBENPFLUG ·	Flüsse, Quellen, Seen	34
HANS BAUER ·	Die Armbrustschützen von Gubbio	40
HANS VON HÜLSEN ·	Töpferstädte: Tradition und frischer Wind	44
KONRAD HELBIG ·	Umbria verde? Umbria verde!	48
LISE-MELANIE ELWENSPOEK ·	No acqua! Kein Wasser!	55
	Ein junger Mann und andere Anekdoten	56
HARALD KELLER ·	Von der Antike zum Mittelalter	58
ROBERT FEIST ·	Spoleto, Treffpunkt zweier Welten	64
GIAN CARLO MENOTTI ·	Caro Jack (ein Brief)	66
FRIEDRICH MEICHSNER ·	Grünes Herz im roten Gürtel	70
OTTORINO GURRIERI ·	Die Rocca Paolina	74
INGEBORG GUADAGNA ·	Auf der Straße der Geschichte	76
	So steht es nicht im Baedeker	85
	MERIAN-Brevier, -Notizen und -Karte	95

The inside cover of the German magazine MERIAN listing the articles
including an article by Mr. Feist on the Spoleto Festival.

CHAPTER SIX
My Second Year as a Fulbright and Superb Opera

So, after the period of the first year in Rome which I have discussed, we started the second year. This was the second year of my Fulbright Fellowship. And a few of the singers as I said remained and continued their classes and rehearsing and I was still back in the opera house doing what I had always done. And that season was interesting because it was again very diverse, with a lot of things I did not know. For instance, it opened that year, 1955, in the fall with *Giulio Cesare,* a Handel opera and that was surprising because at that time major houses were not doing Handel. Today you find them done all over the place, but not there. So, we had a *Giulio Cesare* conducted by Gavazzeni, whom I admired very much and the cast was not what you would find today at all—because the role of *Giulio Gesare* was sung by a baritone and not by a countertenor or a mezzo soprano. It was sung by Mario Petri and then we had in the cast Onelia Fineschi and Fedora Barbieri, of all people, singing a baroque opera when she was used to singing Verdi. Boris Christoff and Franco Corelli were also in this production and it was staged by Margherita Wallman and it interested her very much. The people involved, such as the conductor and others, had gone up to Germany to see a production of this opera in Munich to get an idea what she did with a Handel opera. Well, it worked except that it would not be acceptable today, because you would have much lighter singers and the singers today would be versed in the baroque repertoire as we know from New York City and from England and everywhere else. So, this was an Italian classic attempt at Handel, not authentic, but pleasing to the public. Following this came another amazing revelation—it was *The Barber of Seville* and again we had the famous Giulietta doing the role of Rosina which I had only heard done by coloraturas in America, *never* by a mezzo. So here was Simionato as she had done her *Cenerentola* the year before, doing the role of Rosina, and was remarkable. The tenor was Tagliavini, famous in all ways but not quite limber enough to do this role well. He was a sensation and everybody liked him. The barber was Tito Gobbi, world famous, so therefore sensational. It was conducted by Angelo Questa, whom I didn't admire particularly, but he was a success. After that came another opera in translation as was typical. I did not mention that in the first year at Rome we had two foreign operas, meaning non-Italian translated into

Italian. One of them was, of all things, *Prince Igor* while at that time you wouldn't have found any Russian singer singing in Italy. So, our opera was done in Italian and at the time I was out of town. I was busy rehearsing the others and all I did was see a performance. I did not get to work on it and the cast was so-so. I remember that Barbato, Christoff and Silveri sang the leads and yet the opera somehow did not ring a bell as it has in many performances I have seen since, especially in Russia. The other opera that I must put in that category of the first year was, of all things, *Tristan und Isolde*. Now this was unusual because just like *Rosenkavalier* they imported an entire German cast from either Germany or Vienna and they did it in German. Conducted by Ferdinand Leitner, who was very good, and I got to know him later when he was the head of the Stuttgart Opera. It had singers who today you'd probably know by recordings. The soprano was Grob-Prandl, whom I do not recall, and Cavelti, a well-known mezzo who sang Brangaene and, of course, Hans Beirer, very familiar to all of those who had heard German opera and recordings as the *Tristan*. And among others was Schöffler as Kurvenal. It was a very good production even though the *Isolde* left something to be desired.

Now, to continue with the second year. After we had finished the opening *Giulio Cesare* we did another foreign language opera which was *Samson and Delilah* which was translated into Italian as was customary. And I had seen it very often in Cincinnati with many famous singers such as Thorborg, Stevens and others. But here we had Gavazzeni conducting an all Italian cast. The tenor was Renato Gavarini, whom no one knew then, at least I did not, and probably no one remembers him. Fedora Barbieri was an excellent Delilah. So, here was my introduction to *Samson* in Italian and it was very, very good except that I missed the French language that I was used to just as was the case earlier in Naples. After that we had a ballet which I am not going to mention. A typical ballet evening with three or four ballets and then came what I call a revelation. This revelation, I still remember, and I don't know why America has not done it since, I think around 1928-1930 in Chicago. It was Respighi's *La Fiamma* (*The Flame*). I think it is probably the best of Respighi for the stage and it had a great cast headed by the wonderful German soprano Inge Borkh, who was very well-known to us and everyone else for her German roles, particularly *Salome*, even *Elektra* and *Rosenkavalier* and many others. With her, doing the leading man's role was Silveri and Elena Nicolai, who was Romanian was the mezzo lead. The tenor, a bit too light for this role, but famous was Prandelli and the baritone, who carried it very well was Silveri—an excellent, excellent baritone, in his prime then. The other two were the soprano Amalia Pini and the bass was a man whom had made his debut with us in Spoleto and he was Ferruccio Mazzoli. This thing ended up by being a remarkable way to meet the cast—particularly Inge Borkh, because she was very friendly, spoke English as well as German and Italian. And it turned out that I saw her very often in those performances and in the rehearsals and she, realizing that I was American, put me to work. She had an engagement through her agent to sing a premiere in America in the opera by Benjamin Britten called *Gloriana* which recently has hit the papers again with a production in England at Covent Garden after an enormous silence because no one thought much of it. So, I went to her room at the hotel adjourning the theater with the score of *Gloriana* because she was due to sing it, of all places, in Cincinnati, my home town, with the May Festival. So, I got to know Inge quite well and I played for her and coached her and taught her this role of *Gloriana* which was difficult. And I do not know how it went in Cincinnati, but apparently very well, but we've never heard of it since until they did it now in London.

The others in that cast of *Fiamma* had nothing to do with me in terms of coaching as I stood out because through her I met the woman who later asked me to search for an agent in Germany. This woman came from a German office and became a coach and a prompter in Rome for productions, but more on her later.

Following *Fiamma* came Verdi, a big Verdi opera which I had never seen. It was *Macbeth*. *Macbeth* naturally required a very, very tough soprano role which was seldom attempted. But now we have lyric singers still doing it and the Russian Guleghina. Here we had an English or Australian soprano, I'm not sure which, called Margherita Kenney, whom I got to know well and she did a very good job. But, what it lacked, was an Italianate quality and the blazing top that the opera demanded. With her as the title role of *Macbeth* was Tito Gobbi in another one of his triumphal performances. The bass was excellent and the tenor, Roberto Turrini, whom we had never heard of in Italy and certainly never outside of Italy. He did it alright, but that role is not demanding. In *Macbeth* you don't see much of him except in the last act. Nonetheless it was my introduction to *Macbeth* and I worked backstage coaching and playing for rehearsals and so forth and enjoyed it.

Left—A visit to my apartment (and that of Kertesz) in 1959. Left to right—Edith and Istvan Kertesz, Gian Carlo Menotti, a secretary, Robert Feist and Thomas Schippers.

Below are views of Spoleto.

Following that came another great introduction and this was Maestro Gui back again from his triumph of before, Rossini. Here he was doing Mozart, *The Magic Flute* and he was famous for all Mozart as well as for the various operas of Rossini, there and elsewhere. His cast was excellent. Doing the role of Pamina was the wonderful woman who had sung Octavian in *Rosenkavalier*, Sena Jurinac, whom I said I got to know very well and until this day we correspond. The coloratura doing the Queen of the Night was world famous Rita Streich, who sang that role all over Germany. The tenor was well-beloved and was well-known throughout Germany, Anton Dermota, a lyric tenor, he was excellent and the baritone who did Papageno was equally famous, Erich Kunz, notable in all ways and Sarastro was Gottlob Frick, a name which everybody would be familiar with from recordings. This was conducted by Maestro Gui, but the interesting thing about it is that it was done in German, the original language. All of these people had been imported for that purpose so they all had no troubles, but Gui knew enough German to conduct it in that style. I must mention here that the same year I went to Naples for some other reason and encountered *The Magic Flute* there too at the big Teatro San Carlo and there was Sena Jurinac again singing the role of Pamina, but in Italian! They did an Italian version of *The Magic Flute* in Naples and she fit in just as well as she had in German. So, in one year she sang this role both in Italian and in German which is quite an achievement, but for her I think quite common. I think she speaks six languages.

Following *The Magic Flute* came one of the highlights of my three years in Rome. This was *Manon Lescaut*, conducted by Gavazzeni again stirring and really overwhelming. Now, I had seen it in New York, the year after college when I was living there briefly, beginning a career as a coach or accompanist and I went to the Met a few times and, of all things, they were doing *Manon Lescaut* with Dorothy Kirsten. They imported Mario Del Monaco who happened to be in San Francisco and they engaged him for one night at the Met to make his debut there in *Manon Lescaut* and it was a knockout.

But here in Rome we had now *two* "knockouts." First of all we had Giuseppe di Stefano in one of his prime roles, that of des Grieux, and the soprano was the woman whom I said I really "fell for," Clara Petrella, dark timbered, luscious voice and absolutely riveting on the stage in every movement. Of course Petrella was well-known for this role as well as roles such as those in *Pagliacci* and the Puccini era. So this production I saw with absolutely bated breath each time, and worked backstage with them. One important factor is that though I didn't play for all piano rehearsals, (the regular coach did that), but when they finally got into a rehearsal upstairs and the pianist was busy elsewhere Gavazzeni said to me: "Mr. Feist, will you play this rehearsal for us today?" So, there I was sight reading (although I knew it already) the third act of *Manon Lescaut* with Petrella and di Stefano singing over my piano playing and I'll never forget that. It was the first time that I had really played for him in a rehearsal and he complimented me which was very nice as did Gui in the rehearsal of *The Magic Flute*.

Well, talk about unusual repertoire, already we had had quite a few, but now comes another Russian work. We had *The Queen of Spades* by Tchaikovsky which I had never seen. It was done in Italian. Again heading the cast as the soprano was Sena Jurinac, in Italian and, the tenor was Antonio Annaloro who had made recordings of that era, a new tenor who was pushed considerably in the upper register, but here more so and overdone and not to my liking, having heard many other Russians since. The rest of the cast had Pederzini, a rather older and worn-out mezzo who did the role of the grandmother. She had the death scene and then she is frightened by the tenor who comes in and demands to know the secret of the cards. The baritone was Mario Petri and others in the cast included Dimitri Lopatto who became a friend when I coached him in his home on many, many operas. Well, this "Dama di Picche" as they called, was extremely moving to me that I preferred it when I heard it later in Russia and also at the Met in Russian. But, I can't say it did not impress me, as it did.

I Puritani came to be another newcomer to my repertoire. I was equally fond of other Bellini which we know from so many recordings by such people as Joan Sutherland, Anna Moffo and countless others. Here we had Virginia Zeani whom I heard in many operas in Rome and she was quite a star and of course, as we know now, she has been teaching for many, many years at the School of Music at Indiana University with her husband who just passed away recently, Nicola Rossi Lemeni. At any rate in *I Puritani* we had Zeani in the lead and the tenor, which is the killing role of all Bellini, was Giuseppe di Stefano again. The baritone Paolo Silveri and the bass, were all were superb in Act One.

The four singers are standing in the wings; the orchestra, of course, in the pit and you hear them singing this quartet which I conducted looking through the window of the hole in the scenery to see the conductor in the pit who was Oliviero de Fabritis, and I enjoyed that. I

Clockwise from above—Giuseppe di Stefano wrote: "Al felice e bravo Maestro Bob Feist con tanti amichevoli auguri." "to cheerful and excellent Maestro Bob Feist with many friendly wishes." Sena Jurinac wrote: "A unserem BOBO mit liebsten Herz and allerbeste Wünsche, S.J. To our BOBO with a fond heart and all best wishes. Augsburg, 1966." Right, bass Lorenzo Alvary, "to my dear friend Bob Feist, most cordially." signed Lorenzo Alvary, 1952.

Giacomo Lauri-Volpi, tenor wrote: "Al Maestro Bob Feist ricordo del Poliuto."

Fedora Barbieri, contralto wrote: "A Robert Feist, molto cordialmente, (to Robert Feist, most cordially, 1955)."

Giulietta Simionato wrote:
"Al Maestro Bob Feist, cordialmente, (G.S., 1955, *Cenerentola);*
To Maestro Bob Feist, cordially."

Above—Robert Anderson, a friend and as Hans Sachs in *Meistersinger*. "To my dear friend, Bob Feist, a good conductor and a consumate musician."

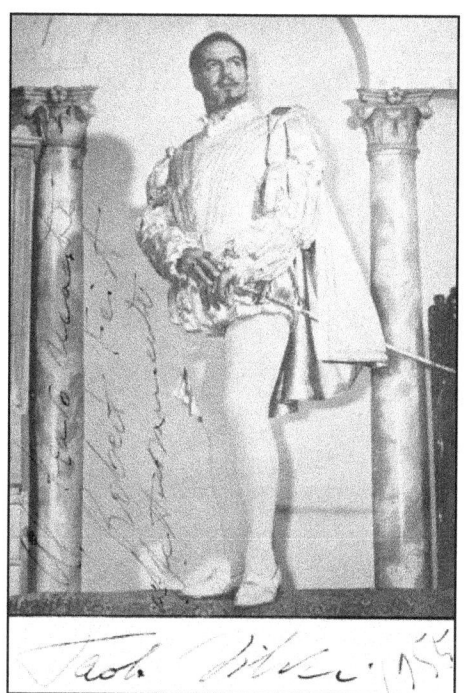

Paolo Silveri, baritone wrote: "Al bravo Maestro Robert Feist, affettuosamente, P.S., 1955." to the bravo R. Feist, affectionately, signed Paoli Silveri."

Frant Guarrera in *The Barber of Seville*. "To my friend and colleague with much affection," signed Frank Guarrera.

Above—Mr. Feist with soprano Anna de Cavaliere and David Mellon after a recital she gave in Lugano, Switzerland.

Boris Christoff, the great Bulgarian bass.

Left—Mr. Feist with famous soprano Sena Jurinac outside a restaurant in Rome after her performance as the Marschallin in *Rosenkavalier,* circa, 1973.

Left: Giulio Neri as he appeared in *Mosé* in Rome, 1956. His inscription to Mr. Feist reads: *Al caro amico e bravo Maestro; Robert, as a remembrance.* Above: Clara Petrella wrote: *A Bob Feist con tanta ammirazione e simpatia;* to Bob Feist with much admiration and kindness.

can say that I conducted di Stefano in *Puritani* even though it was backstage, but it was still a thrill! Talk about novelties, this season was unequaled. Following *Puritani's* success, which of course, included di Stefano transposing down the last act aria so he did not have to scream a high D or a high F.

The next opera was *Pelleas*. I had never seen it but had heard it from the Met in performances with Sayao and others. Here we had very famous names—Micheau, the leading French soprano. The leading tenor, anywhere as Pelleas, was Jacques Jansen. Well, I got to know that opera very well in these performances that I worked on backstage and every performance especially, because I admired the conductor Andre Cluytens who conducted all of them and whom I have admired ever since.

Following this we had one more novelty, at least a novelty for Rome, and back to German repertoire. We had *Die Meistersinger* by Wagner, but not in Italian. They imported again, by way of an agent in Germany, an entire German cast with names that are familiar to anyone of that era or recordings, but perhaps not anyone today. The soprano was Elfrida Troetchel and the tenor was Richard Mattel, whom I do not know anything about from then or afterwards, the baritone who did the role of Sachs, the leading role was Gustav Neidlinger, very famous from then or all over the world. He was superb and so was Erich Kunz whom was just seen before in *The Magic Flute* as Papagano and it was staged by, of all people, Wolfgang Wagner. The conductor was Rudolph Moralt whom I had already heard in Rome and I enjoyed working with him in this case.

Being such a long opera, they needed many pianists to play for the stage rehearsals, scenic rehearsals, and everything under the sun. I played for several of the staging rehearsals because the Italians were either occupied elsewhere or did not know the opera and I was frankly a very good sight reader and could play the *Meistersinger* better than any of the Italian coaches of the Rome Opera. That caught the attention of Wolfgang Wagner who was, of course, one of the grandchildren of Richard Wagner, he and his brother Wieland, who died some years after this. But I used this contact as a means of pursuing another goal; to learn more about Wagner in its home, Bayreuth, and I asked Wagner and he said : "Write me." So, somewhere that year with help of a German woman I knew and studied German with, I wrote to him asking could I attend the rehearsals at Bayreuth, not the performances, just the rehearsals and he replied:

"Very well, we welcome you." So, more on that later when we get to summer, but I knew I had the invitation.

About this period my parents arrived; their first trip abroad. They came by plane by way of Paris, and arrived in Rome and then came all the sightseeing. I was able to get away from the opera very often and take them on tours of the whole city with the aid of friend of mine in his car. The only opera they could catch in Rome was another novelty for both of us. It was Verdi's *Vespri Siciliani* which I had never seen, under my great mentor Gabriele Santini. Well, I had heard some of the rehearsals and played for a few, but here was the dress rehearsal with all of the pomp and circumstance and my great, great soprano lead was Antonietta Stella whom I had admired before in *Un Ballo in Maschera*. With her was the same tenor whom we just mentioned, Roberto Turrini whom we never heard from again. I certainly never did and he did the leading tenor role. The baritone was again Silveri, number two, I guess, in the baritone roster of the Italian theaters. The bass was Giulio Neri who sang the famous aria, "O tu Palermo." Then my parents met us. At intermission, bringing them downstairs, I introduced them to the general manager of the Rome Opera house who couldn't speak a word of English and that was extremely apparent to them and they, of course, could speak no Italian. This is very moving in all cases.

Well, that *Vespri Siciliani* was amazing because I encountered it only a few times thereafter as it is not done too often. Following it came another ballet evening which had ballets by Stravinsky and Monteverdi which I won't go into and I would usually go to the performances but went to see part of it and that was all. But then my parents were still around and we all came back from a trip in time to see *Tosca*. *Tosca* was conducted by Maestro Bellezza, whom I always considered mediocre, but he had Renata Tebaldi. Here is Tebaldi in her prime doing one of her leading roles that she must have done 80 times at the Met and she was indeed sensational and I was glad my parents were there with me to see this triumph. Her tenor was Prandelli whom she had sung with many times and he was not so good in the role of Cavaradossi. The baritone was the same one we have talked about three or four times in the role of Scarpia who had sung in *Samson* and another opera of Verdi's, Gian Giacomo Guelfi, one that I never cared for. He was loud, very loud and very forceful, never had any pianos or diminuendos, but he certainly knocked the roof off as we would say, and his wife was right in the wings and he would always look out at her to see if he was doing okay. I thought that was rather odd, but that is what they do. Some of the wives are allowed backstage and can stand in the wings and look.

Having done the *Tosca* we went on to another novelty. Oh; is this the year of novelties! Pizzetti, probably the leading Italian composer of the modern era then. Santini headed it again. It was *Figlia di Jorio* and it had been done quite a bit in Italy, but this was apparently the first time it had been done in Rome. I did not care for it. I'm not a great fan of Pizzetti. It was not as melodic as I would like, but the cast was quite good. That said, we move then to a very standard work, La Boheme. The *La Boheme*, of course, I knew backwards, you would say, and it was conducted by Oliviero de Fabritiis. Fabritiis again did quite well. The cast was, I would say, surprising. The soprano was Onelia Fineschi, whom we heard in the opening of the season in *Giulio Cesare*, doing the role of Cleopatra. Well, I've heard many better Mimis before and after, so she did not impress me, but was good. Then surprise, surprise, the tenor was Giacomo Lauri-Volpi and anyone was crazy if they thought that he was still living and still singing.

And I neglected to mention earlier is when we kids, students, arrived in Rome and Perugia in 1954 at the beginning of the fall season, the Rome Opera had not yet begun but they did gala evenings to support the damage that was done by an earthquake in Sicily, a Sicily benefit. They did a *Tosca*. I still can't believe that I heard the performance of this *Tosca* because it had not only Lauri Volpi singing Mario, but the incredible soprano whom I had heard of for years, Maria Caniglia. The first 78rpm recording that I had bought of a complete opera in Cincinnati was *Tosca* with Maria Caniglia conducted by De Fabritiis recorded in 1938! And here she was still singing *Tosca* in Rome and very well. Admittedly the tops were strident, but she did the role fantastically. She didn't encore anything, but the audience went crazy and Lauri Volpi sang his aria two times, and among the other parts we had Dadò as Scarpia.

After that as the season drew to an end, we saw a superb production that I had never seen and it was *Andrea Chenier*. Somewhere in the last years at Cincinnati they surprised us by doing it and was done with my favorite soprano and conductor. Now they really had a sumptuous staging that had Tebaldi in the lead, one of her supreme roles and Protti, of all people, doing the baritone lead, Gerard. Here comes the big point. The tenor was supposed to be del Monaco, but he fell ill, not immediately before, but he knew he could not do these

Above—A page from an Italian weekly magazine, ROTOSEI, announcing the first Spoleto Festival. The heading translates as: "Meeting With the Theater of Two Worlds."

Left—At one of the last rehearsals of Verdi's *Macbeth* which opened the Festival. From left to right, the famous director, Luchino Visconti, Robert Feist and Maestro Cavaniglia, both Assistant Conductors for *Macbeth*.

performances and they didn't know whom to get. So, they hired a young Italian tenor called Umberto Borsò who had had quite a long career in Italy, but not at the Met. I think he made the Met for only one opera and that's all. I thought he was superb, one of the great lyric spinto, almost dramatic, tenors and I remember distinctly—we stood in the wings watching him, hoping that he was going to get through it because he had never sung it on a stage and he was actually shaking. You could see that his legs were trembling during his first act aria. But he got through it and made a big impression and returned many times to the Rome opera. So Umberto and I were very good friends and it all happened through this remarkable *Chenier* for which I had played a few rehearsals. The other people were minor and there's really no use going into them. But, it turned out that year had so many novelties that it amazed me that we actually saw in one year—so many operas that none of us had ever seen before.

CHAPTER SEVEN
The Baths of Caracalla and Visiting Germany

The summer season was held out-of-doors at the famous Baths of Caracalla which is in Rome, but is not quite the center of Rome, as any visitor knows. I spent every summer there while I was attached to the Rome Opera doing the same things; coaching, moving people around on the stage and helping with the stage direction and so forth.

Returning to the Baths of Caracalla was a very fascinating experience. This was the summer of 1956. The summer of 1955 we were all occupied, we Fulbrights, preparing for our debuts in Spoleto, so we were not much involved with anything at Caracalla. So, I'm skipping over that. But, during the summer of 1956, I was there every night. A conductor friend of mine, Fernando Cavaniglia, picked us up, Ricci and I, drove us to the theater, parked and I wandered through the backstage area seeing all the ruins, the ruins of what used to be baths, warm, cold, hot saunas, everything of that nature, and of course, the auditorium had been built up in open air, which seated something like 10,000 or more people on a summer night which was packed.

Well this particular summer opened with another total rarity to me. It was really something. It was *Mosè in Egitto* by Rossini, another great Rossini opera and of course, one of his dramatic operas which had been premiered, set in Paris. Then it got revised into an Italian version and it became simply *Mosè* in which it is done most of the time today although occasionally they bring out the French version. Giulio Neri, the famous bass did the leading role of *Mosè* and was remarkable. The entire staging, everything out-of-doors was remarkable in that so much could be put on that outdoor stage and with no microphones everybody was heard in that vast, vast outdoor theater. So, I was impressed and got to know Neri quite well and have his photograph dedicated to me hanging on my wall with a nice dedication.

Following that we had a very well-known opera, one that however is certainly typical for the Baths of Caracalla, it was *Aida*. Heading the cast of *Aida* was the newcomer to me, Cerquetti, who later became very, very famous particularly the next year when she jumped in for an ailing Callas. And with her was Filippeschi and mezzo Benedetti as Amneris and, of course, the usual baritone. In this case it was Colzani, an excellent baritone who we heard years later, particularly in the recording *Girl of the Golden West*. So, the *Aida* was done sumptuously

Upper Left—Mr. Feist after a symphony concert with the San Remo Philharmonic Orchestra with famed violin soloist Salvatore Accardo.

Upper Right—Guests at another recital at the Saragat Villa; l. to r.: Soprano Clara Petrella, Soprano Renata Scotto, both engaged at that time in Massenet's *Werther* at the Rome Opera, and the famous and retired soprano Toti dal Monte.

A recital at the Saragat villa with soprano Anna Moffo and tenor William Harper with Mr. Feist at the piano.

with Radames rising to the triumphal scene drawn in a cart with two or four horses leading him on the stage which caused an uproar with the audience naturally. To do *Aida* at an outdoor theater before 10,000 people is always a sensational event and it was indeed.

After *Aida* we had an *Otello* and the *Otello* had a new tenor lead who I later heard even in Venice, Carlo Guichandut. I thought he was Russian, but I am not certain about that and with soprano Zeani and it was very, very well done and, of course, it suited the outdoor pavilion as well.

Following this came the typical double bill of *Cavalleria* and *Pagliacci*, which, of course, was common at the outdoor theater. The outstanding person in this, for one thing, was the production of the performances by Clara Petrella in her famous role of Nedda, which no one has ever done better, I don't think, and with Filippeschi again in *Pagliacci*. The *Cavalleria* singers I do not recall at the moment, but the work was well received.

Following that came a *Turandot*, the first time I had seen it in an outdoor theater. The *Turandot* had a soprano from Germany. This is typical. So many times when the *Turandot* is done, they import a big German soprano usually known for Wagner and here we heard Gertrud Grob-Prandl and many would know her from her years at the Met and everywhere else in Germany and she was quite sensational, though not Italianate in style. The tenor was Borsò and the Liu was probably, though I cannot recall exactly, Onelia Fineschi. It was a sensational production in terms of staging as well as the *Gioconda* which came after that and which I had never seen anywhere. The *Gioconda* had the soprano Maria Pedrini and the tenor another who occasionally turned up even though he was aging. But the *Gioconda* was fantastic in many ways because we had Fedora Barbieri again as Laura and we had baritones such as Guelfi in this opera.

Concluding the outdoor theater was *Rigoletto* done very traditionally and the cast included baritone Enzo Mascherini also well-known to some Americans, at least I knew him from Cincinnati and so the season wound up very, very well with the big singers which was not a toss-up. You knew you were getting the very, very best. The conductors, who are not mentioned with operas were all leading ones such as Oliviero de Fabritiis, Questa, Santini and Ziino. The *Mosè* had, by the way, on the opening night, besides Giulio Neri had Caterini

Mancini, a dramatic soprano whom I got to know later in Ireland, under Santini. Well, that ended up that summer in Rome at the Baths of Caracalla and when I return we'll talk about that summer afterwards.

I decided to make use of the wonderful invitation from Wolfgang Wagner. I knew the dates (in 1956) in which the Bayreuth Festival would be rehearsed and so I headed up there. I went to Munich first to see a few friends, whom I met. In fact, one of the sopranos from my Fulbright year had moved there intending to try a German career and she was studying in Munich and I saw her. That was Maurine Norton who later got engaged and not only that, but she married and settled there and we've never heard from her since. She was lovely, but I don't know what had happened to her. I just learned she died in Germany in 2006.

Well, at Bayreuth I searched around and found a very nice room in a house. The family was always willing to hire or let out their rooms to anybody who was there for reasons to do with the theater and the festival. It was very close and I could walk, so I spent all of the days at the Bayreuth Festival in the Festspielhaus (the big theater) I did not really go to any private rehearsals or piano rehearsals, only what they did on the stage, generally with orchestra. And it was quite a season because I made the acquaintance of many of them and heard amazing singers such as Silya who was there in her absolute prime and Birgit Nilsson and tenors such as Hans Beirer and Wolfgang Windgassen, Gustav Neidlinger, Ramon Vinay and many others were all on the roster of the festival.

I remember distinctly that *Die Meistersinger* which I had seen in Rome and worked on was here conducted by Andre Cluytens which was an unusual choice but they have since then often had non-German conductors leading their German repertoire. So that summer found me for several weeks in Bayreuth observing, marking in my scores everything about that Wagner repertoire conducted by the leading conductors of that era, Leitner, Moralt, even Knappertsbusch.

So, I learned quite a bit and really enjoyed it. It was warm, pleasant and I got to mingle with the singers outside and the festival began, so I left. I didn't stay for any of the operas in performance because it was sold out, of course, and I couldn't get in and I really did not want to be backstage, nor did they invite me to be backstage.

Clockwise from above— "a Bob Feist con sensi di sincero amicizia e miei auguri per la Sua carriera, 1955. Plino Clabassi."

"A Bob del quale mi onoro di essere amico. Tanti saluti cari. To Bob, whom I am honored to call my friend. Many fond greetings." Feruccio Mazzola.

Anna Moffo; "To Bob, love Anna."

Clockwise from left—
"To a great artist and friend, Bob Feist, with love, Frank Guarrera."
Tito Gobbi, baritone wrote—
"A.R. Feist, ricordo di Tito Gobbi;
"To Robert Feist, remembrance of Tito Gobbi, 1955."
Antonietta Stella wrote—
"A Bob con affetto per mio ricordo, Roma, 1999. "To Bob with affection for my memories."

Renata Tebaldi wrote:
"Al Maestro Robert Feist cordialmente, R.T.: To Maestro Robert Feist, cordially, R.T."

Leyla Gencer, soprano wrote—
"A Bob Feist per ricordo dell *Angelo di Fuoco*, con viva simpatia e cordialità. L.G.: To Robert Feist, as a remembrance of *The Fiery Angel* with great sympathy and cordiality."

Left—Bruno Prevedi, tenor wrote: "A Maestro Robert Feist, con infinita riconoscenza, B.P. Augsburg, 8, 1962. To Maestro Robert Feist, infinite remembrance. B.P."

Above—Miriam Pirazzini, contralto wrote: "Al Maestro bob Feist per grato ricordo, M.P.: to Maestro Bob Feist, as a thankful remembrance, M.P."

Left—Stella Roman in *Madam Butterfly*.

Clockwise starting at right—Giuseppe Taddei wrote: "A Maestro Bob Feist, con viva amicizia. To Maestro Bob Feist with true friendship." Umberto Borsó wrote: "A Bob con affetto per mio ricordo, Roma, 1999. To Bob excellent Maestro with much admiration and friendship." Maria Caniglia, soprano wrote: "A Maestro Roberto Feist per ricordo cordiale. M.C. To Maestro Robert Feist, as a cordial remembrance! M.C."

Above—Italo Tajo, the famous bass and friend of Mr. Feist. This photograph was taken later in Cincinnati where he retired. "To my friend, Maestro Bob Feist, Affectionately."

Below—A translation of the note below reads: "To Maestro Robert Feist with much cordiality, Maria Caniglia, August, 1974.
The photograph below—Mr. Feist accompanied the great dramatic soprano (first complete recording of Tosca in 1938). Maria Caniglia at the villa of the Honorable Saragat in recital in June, 1955.

So, I decided to head down, back to Italy, and I stopped in Switzerland and I went to Lucerne because someone had indicated to me, perhaps an agent that they may want a conductor or an assistant conductor in the Lucerne Opera House. It's a small theater in a small town, famous for its Lucerne Festival in the summer when they bring in great big stars and conductors. I had a meeting with a man who ran it and we had a discussion. I didn't have to play for him, but he knew that I had been at the Rome Opera as a coach and accompanist and he said they would consider it and let me know.

Well, I heard from him some time later, maybe a month or so later, that they thought I was not yet quite ready to take on a position in a German theater as a coach because you really have to know the language and the repertoire of that country very, very well. So, I was not particularly unhappy about this. I went back to Rome and I knew very well, though I had no Fulbright, that the next year I was welcomed at the Rome Opera house. They considered me part of the staff. I was not paid, but I had saved money well enough to know that I could get through that year with outside engagements.

So, I returned and the third year in Rome began in the fall with me taking occasional departures. One of them occurred somewhere in the fall and arranged by an agent I got to know in Rome, who always tried to get me engagements outside the city. I was to go to Tunis in North Africa. They always did a short, two-week season of Italian opera in Tunis and it was very much fun because we went by boat from Naples and stopped in Sicily and then went down to Tunis. My companion on the boat was a tenor called Marchiandi who sang minor roles at the Rome Opera for years and years, but here in Tunis he sang leading roles such as Alfredo in *Traviata*. The other operas that were done were *Tosca*, *Lucia* and I cannot recall the others, but it was a wonderful three-week period in which I was not only the accompanist for rehearsals, but I was also a prompter and I got to prompt several of the operas.

This is interesting because it also happened in Rome and I was always backstage and at the intermissions talking to everyone and the staff. The prompter there came to me and said: "Maestro, would you like to come and sit in the prompter's box with me?" So, I took him up on it and for several operas, just for fun, I would sit with him in the crowded little prompter's box and watch him prompt the singers and see how well it was done. Because I think only the Italians have such excellent prompters. They did not in Germany, by the way. I will mention that later, but certainly they do not have prompters as efficient in giving the words to the singers, just at the right moments.

So, I learned something about that in Rome and then also in Tunis. When I left Tunis we both came back to Naples, but before that we stopped in Palermo again on the island. I dropped the other people and I simply decided to have my first visit to Sicily and it was exciting. I got to see Palermo and I took a short trip elsewhere and I even climbed (well not climbed completely) but I tried to climb Mount Etna and at least drove around it and got to view it and it was quite fascinating. In addition I stayed at this wonderful little town on the coast—Taormina.

I also got to see a little bit of Catania, the second big city in Sicily and I returned another year to see a performance under Maestro Gui and also I saw the stage director called Vassallo who lived in Palermo. He had staged operas in Rome and I got to know him and he invited me to his house and we had some very nice chats. From there I got on a train and returned to Rome and was prepared for the third year at the Rome Opera. But, in the meantime this agent had me do various other things.

I went out of town once with a few singers from the Rome Opera to a small town called Emilia and I was then the coach, assistant conductor and prompter for a production of *Traviata* which was done in the evening in a small town. The tenor lead was Renato Cioni who had made his debut with us Fulbrights, meaning that he was part of the Italian group that made our debut in Spoleto. And here he was starting his career which really, really took off because when I saw him years later he was singing with Callas in *Tosca* at the Paris Opera! So, it is amazing that people move from a small town in Italy to the Paris Opera in the course of five or ten years. Not only that, but in the course of the year, I went to Germany. I went there two or three times trying to get myself booked into a theater. I realized by this time that I could stay in Rome and assist at the Rome Opera without being paid. I could coach singers privately which I did in their home and yet, I thought, I knew very well we had only about 11 or 12 major opera houses and they certainly would not hire me as a conductor or as a beginning conductor. But I knew that Germany had 49 or 50 opera houses scattered all over the country, not only in a city such as Berlin and Munich, but all over.

So, that is what I aimed for. First, along with the help of the German prompter woman who had come to Rome and whom we always used as the prompter for the German operas such as *Tristan* and *Meistersinger*. I got to know her quite well and she advised me by giving me the names of three or four famous agents in Munich, Frankfurt and even farther north in Düsseldorf. So, I knew where I was heading, so I went always to Munich where I teamed up with Maurine Norton when she was still there studying voice and I met one of her dear friends, the American girl, Martha Coleman who was studying too and Martha and I have remained friends ever since. She first came to coach with me, but then she ended up going into management which ended up being her main career in New York with Judson and his associates. Then Martha came under the management of Harold Shaw and stayed with him 25 years, but primarily in the South, to manage his southern clients until she retired.

At any rate, on these trips to Germany I went to the agents telling them my story and the fact that I had been at the Rome Opera for two years and was still there, but really wanted to get into a German theater and by that time I knew enough German to converse. I had studied privately with this woman in Rome, Lisa Elfer. At any rate, my studies were private with this woman who was German, married to an Italian who had died and she taught me all the letters I had to write to Germany in fact. I think her letter to Wolfgang Wagner helped me to get to Bayreuth. So, I kept up with letters and meeting agents. Their view points were different. They all said, yes, you probably have the right background, but you have to improve on your German. But, we have to find a house that really wants to take an American which was, more or less, unheard of at that time. They generally use Germans who have come out of conservatories and that sort of thing and it was very unusual for them to find an American searching for an apprentice job or a young conductor trying to find a job. So, I did not at that time. This was in fall near Christmas of 1956. I did not get the final decision; that came later on a trip. But, I might as well bring it up now, but first let me mention what I did see in Rome because though I was no longer engaged, I could come and go as I pleased. It was amazing. I would come to the main stage door and the staff, the porter, would say: "Hello Maestro, buon giorno, good to see you again." and I would simply go in the stage door and sit with the other conductors in their lounge and talk to them and hear a performance from backstage which was fine with me. And that year was my third year in Rome and it also had some extraordinary things which I will mention now before I move to Germany.

CHAPTER EIGHT
More Opera in Italy and a Trip to Ireland

The season opened in 1956 in December with another total rarity, Mascagni's *Iris* which unfortunately is not as well-known as it should be although it has been done in New York, at least in concert form by the Opera Orchestra of New York and is, I think, a remarkable opera. It was conducted by Gavazzeni and it had my favorite two singers again, Clara Petrella in her role of Iris which was a knockout and the tenor was Giuseppe di Stefano. Filling out the cast was Poli as the baritone and Boris Christoff. It was a wonderful and incredible production. I even took Italian friends to see it and we were all overwhelmed by it.

Following that we had a double bill of an opera by a new Italian and Menotti's *Amelia Goes to the Ball*, which was a premiere for Rome. I had never seen *Amelia Goes to the Ball*, but it was a very enjoyable opera and I got to talk to Menotti and members of the cast. But then came another big one. I had never seen *Simon Boccanegra*. So we had in this cast the great Tito Gobbi doing the role of Boccanegra and the bass role was Boris Christoff and my friend Umberto Borsò turned up as the tenor lead and the soprano was Marcella Pobbe, who later had quite a big career, but this was one of her first big assignments. But the *Boccanegra* I grew to love though I had never conducted it and it has really been one of my favorites of Verdi.

Following that came another Mozart, *Die Entführung aus den Serail*, under a Hungarian, Laszlo Somagi. He would go against this business of "what language." Well, the title was in Italian, but the cast actually sang in German. They had an American soprano who had come from Germany called Marilyn Tyler and who was excellent and the tenor was the great German Ernst Häfflinger—wonderful, (who also died recently in 2007) and the bass was fine too. So this production introduced me to the *Abduction from the Seraglio* and I was glad for that experience as well. Following it came three ballets which I was not interested in. Then came another *Aida* and this *Aida* was under Santini, who was tops all the time. In the *Aida* we had Cerquetti and Simionato. The soprano did a wonderful *Aida*. This was my first experience with Simionato in her role. Here I had heard her do Rossini wonderfully and now she does one of her great, great Verdi roles, Amneris. Well, the cast was terrific because the tenor was Franco Corelli in his prime and the baritone was again Gianciagomo Guelfi, who belted and belted but was effective. The bass was Giulio Neri, of course. So we had a superb cast under Santini and it was a novel experience with *Aida*.

And then we hit another one of the German importations. Well, this importation brought for the first time Georg Solti who was very active in Germany, of course, but they got him to do the *Die Walküre*. Well, I had never seen *Walküre* in Cincinnati or at the Met. And, my God, what they brought in for this through an agent in Germany! We had Birgit Nilsson doing Brünnhilde in her prime, superb in all ways, and as Sieglinde we had Leonie Rysanek. You couldn't do better than this in that era, Birgit and Rysanek in the same opera. The tenor was again Hans Beirer. He had been there as Tristan before and we had Ludwig Weber and we had Sigurd Bjoerling whom I understood was a relative perhaps of Jussi Bjoerling, I'm not sure. The experience of learning *Walküre* in German under Solti was really, really worth it.

To continue, the next opera that popped up was a novelty, a modern Italian opera called *Il Dibuk* about the famous Hebrew legend and was by Rocca. Santini conducted and, lo and behold, they needed a pianist, not for coaching. But since I was there they said: "Would you please do the piano part in the orchestra?" We had two pianos and they had their normal pianist who did one of them and I was the one who did the second piano. So, I spent the whole opera in the pit under Santini, his baton, playing the piano part for the *Dibuk*. The cast was very good. It had the same tenor we had mentioned, Francesco Albanese, the soprano Luisa Malagrida and then there was Dora Minarchi as the mezzo. The bass was Afro Poli, very well-known, mainly as Sharpless. I do not think I cared much for it and it was in a verismo style, but it worked and they liked it. Then to my amazement came a *Carmen* and the *Carmen* was under Angelo Questa with my favorite mezzo again who had just done *Aida* in January and here was February and Simionato turns up singing the title role in *Carmen*. Well needless to say, it was a knockout. But there's always a "but;" it was done in Italian, not in French. So we had Simionato and Giuseppe di Stefano doing another of his wonderful roles as di Stefano sang Don Jose and Enzo Mascherini did the baritone role. And, as I said, Questa conducted. It was sensational in all ways even though it was in Italian. I would have preferred French, but at that time they had not yet gotten to the point of doing *Carmen* in French.

The season continued with the spectacles of ballet. They had in this case, four ballets in one evening. After this came a Prokofiev which I can only mention, *The Angel of Fire* or *The*

Fiery Angel and I will return to that later because it turned up in my repertoire not there, but in Spoleto. Here, however, I do not think I saw it as I was out of town, probably in Lucerne or somewhere else doing an engagement.

After this we had the French *Manon* once again, and must I say, in Italian? sung by the great Victoria de Los Angeles, who was doing one of her main roles and the tenor was again di Stefano who was unequaled in this role. The bass was Clabassi.

Another knockout followed right away and it was the Puccini, *Girl of the Golden West* and the soprano was the woman we had thought was probably at the end of her career, Magda Olivero, who everybody knows ended up returning to the Met at age 65 doing *Tosca* some years back, I don't remember what year. And with her in *The Girl of the Golden West* was Lauri Volpi singing and with all of them aging but many—Olivero and Lauri Volpi, there had been better before and since then.

So, I will go on to the next opera which was *The Elixer of Love* under Santini and here we had Rosanna Carteri, who was superb. The tenor was Ferruccio Tagliavini who was again superb and then the baritone, Giuseppe Taddei. It was amazing and it was very, very good. To conclude the season we had three more works. One, and this would be a knockout anywhere, we had a *Fidelio* in German and it had Birgit Nilsson doing the role of Fidelio and the tenor was the very famous Sebastian Feiersinger, who was again terrific and he had a huge career. The baritone lead, was fine, named Gerhard Nisske. The woman who actually had been a coach and a help to me as a prompter did the staging for this, of all things. Following this came a premiere, an absolute premiere, that no one had ever heard or seen before. And I think I saw only one performance because I had no recollection of this opera at all. Then we returned to the baroque—this time to Gluck with another opera that everybody knows, *Orfeo*. In this case, of course, it was done in Italian and it included Fedora Barbieri as Orfeo and Fineschi as Euridice and conducted by Capuana.

To conclude the season, we had another *Otello* and this time with the same baritone and tenor from the summer production who was Gobbi as Iago and Carlo Guichandut as Otello with Onelia Fineschi as Desdemona. My friend, the stage director, whom I had visited in Palermo, Vassallo, was the stage director and the conductor was a new one to me Emidio Tieri who I did not encounter soon after that. That concluded that season and in the summer of that season another session took place at the Baths of Caracalla in which I was only partially involved because that was the summer that I moved to Germany. During the spring of this year when I missed several of the operas in Rome, my agent had secured for me an engagement in Dublin, Ireland as chorus master to teach all of the Irish the Italian—in the Italian operas and as pianist, coach and backstage handyman for everything. And it was an excellent opportunity for me to work at a good salary and to be flown to Dublin and back and on the way there, I stopped in Germany. I stopped in Munich and then went on to Frankfurt and met an agent. This agent said: "I think I might have something for you in Augsburg. You go down and meet them." and I said: "Yes, I will." Augsburg is about a half hour or three quarters of an hour from Munich on the way to Frankfurt. So, I went to this city and fell in love with it. I was only there for about a day. It is a very old city, about which I will say more in a later chapter. There I went in and met the man who was in charge of engagements. He was the head of all the scheduling of productions and I had to play and sing. I played part of *Aida* and sang the parts of Radames and Amneris and a part of the King and it turned out that he liked it and they engaged me as an Assistant Conductor on the permanent staff of the Augsburg Stadttheater, or the Municipal Theater of Augsburg. I did not receive confirmation until later in Dublin when they sent it to me and I was very happy that I knew I would speak to them I would leave Rome and move everything to Germany.

American soprano Marcella Reale as Tosca, which she sang in Genoa among other cities.

Below—A page from the program dedicated to Puccini on the 50th Anniversary of his death, performed at the Rome Center of Loyola University.

> # PUCCINI
> LUCCA, DECEMBER 22, 1858
> BRUSSELS, NOVEMBER 29, 1924
>
> On the occasion of the 50th anniversary of his death
> The Rome Center of Liberal Arts, Loyola University, Chicago
>
> — PRESENTS —
>
> A Program of Songs, Arias and Duets
>
> Marcella Reale, soprano
> Umberto Borsò, tenor
> Robert Feist, pianist
>
> Auditorium, Tuesday, November 26, 1974, 8:30 P.M.

Robert Feist and tenor Umberto Borsò at the Puccini Memorial Recital at Loyola University, Chicago.

Clockwise from left—Mr. Feist and Ruth Hesse, Preziosilla in Verdi's *Forza* at the open-air Red Gate Theater in 1961.

Mr. Feist conducting a rehearsal in the Augsburg Stadttheater, June, 1960.

Feist with the cast of *Rigoletto* at the open-air Red Gate Theater in the summer of 1959. Left to right—tenor Plahuta, mezzo Kirschweger, Mr. Feist, soprano Williams and baritone Misske.

CHAPTER NINE
Two Seasons at the Red Gate in Augsburg, Germany and then an Unusual Summer

After I knew in Germany that I was engaged for the next year I simply had to go back to Rome, clean things up, pack them and decide when to move—with, of course, a lot of farewells. Now one of these involved going back to the Baths of Caracalla just to drop in as I was not working there anymore and I remembered so many of the things I had seen there for three years. I started working there actually in the summer after I arrived in Rome in 1955 and then 1956 and in 1957 when I left. And I remember really about some things I picked up, but I was amazed at the number of rare things that they did in those days that were never seen in America. For instance, in 1955 they opened the season with Donizetti's *Poliuto*. Well, I never even heard of *Poliuto*, one of his dramatic operas and I worked on the stage and, of course, we had immensely famous singers such as Maria Caniglia and Lauri Volpi who admittedly should not have been singing Donizetti. It sounded more like *Tosca* or *Turandot*, but their fame and their dramatic presence and bouncing high notes they got through it, but of course, all of the coloratura passage work somehow got lost.

Then they had a production of *Norma* which I had heard from the Met, but I had never seen it. Well, here we had *Norma* and with it came the debut of Udovick, an American soprano, who later became a friend. The first name was Lucille and I don't think she had sung before in Rome and her career went to some lengths even to South America. Well, it was a terrific *Norma* and as anyone can imagine, it was a very difficult role to pull off in a huge amphitheater out-of-doors but certainly she did a very good job and I got to know her quite well and saw her often later.

Anther big one that year was *Mefistofele*, an opera which had been done a year or so before. And again it had the Italian bass Neri in the title role. Well, it is always a pleasure to see *Mefistofele* as it is seldom done. The other big novelty that summer, of all things, was an opera by Catalani that no one ever sees. If they hear or see anything it is *Wally*, which is occasionally done, and I saw it in Venice. But here was the *Lorelei* and *Lorelei* is about the fictional woman on the banks of the Rhine River who tempts all of the sailors that had

had shipwrecks. At any rate, it is considered a very romantic, almost verismo opera that is considered by a Wagnerian type of composer. It introduced me to the American soprano whom I heard later in Rome. This was Anna de Cavalieri or, in English, Ann McKnight. This was 1955 and she later sang with us in Rome in the role of Roxanne in *Cyrano de Bergerac* and was most impressive. Here in Lorelei she had the title role and was very dramatic and she did a superb job even in an outdoor theater. It has a famous aria "Ebben, ne andrò lontano," which many sopranos sing.

So, that was the highlight of that summer of 1955 and in 1957. I am about to go to Germany, and in making farewells, and I simply remembered that I had not talked too much about Irene Callaway, who along with Anna Moffo was one of the prime Fulbright students, and she had sung the debut role in *Don Pasquale* with me in Spoleto and then this past year she had been engaged in Bari over on the Adriatic by an assistant conductor of ours to found a new opera company and did *Turandot*. She did the role of Liù which is a wonderful debut role for a young girl. It is not long, but it really shows off the high notes, the style, and she did very, very well. And that summer she was engaged in, of all things, the festival in Aix en Provence and another one on the western coast of France, Deauville, singing Mozart operas.

Well, the date of departure took me to many parts and places in the city to say goodbye to friends. And then my closest Italian friend whom I had not mentioned, Giulio Avancini and his wife, Marisa, who lived right across the hall from me where I and my friends, the Fulbright boys lived. Giulio was an agent for a very big travel company and was gone frequently, but liked music and opera and so did his wife and they and their own family were practically like my own family and we saw each other almost every day coming and going. And they came to the opera to see something I recommended. At any rate that final evening or on the final days, he drove me around Rome on his Vespa motorcycle. We were whizzing up and down the Via del Foro Imperiale, the street of the Imperial locale of the Roman Forum, reminiscing about all the good times we had had over the three years and promising to stay in touch.

So, it was a sad farewell, in a way, to leave so many Italian and American friends, but I knew I was in for a new era and I had shipped some things to Germany. All I had was a big trunk and my hand luggage. So, I went by train, stopping in Torino to have a look at that city. Luckily, to have an idea—because later I was to conduct there several times. I went on to

Munich and then to Augsburg where, with an agent, I secured a dwelling which happened to be simply a room in the house of a family, that so many people do in Italy and Germany and everywhere. I could not afford, nor was about to rent a whole apartment or condo, and I had this room and all of my meals were taken out, meaning in restaurants.

So, I started there in the middle of July in 1957, was introduced to everybody on the staff, and fell right in step quite well. I ended up doing much of the coaching, which was divided between two of us, playing piano rehearsals, staging rehearsals and the usual backstage work—all of this now of course in German which I had learned and which grew in importance and ability as I progressed in the years in Germany. Actually, when I arrived, the summer season was in full swing. they had a normal winter season and then a short break and then in the summer, starting about July they had arena opera just as Rome had had, an outdoor summer festival at the ruins of an ancient wall which was called the Roten Tor, The Red Gate. There was an open-aired stage at the Red Gate going back to, I don't know, maybe the fifth or sixth century and it was built in front of this wall and they did their performances for about six weeks. My introduction to the work was out-of-doors actually that summer and it introduced me right away to a friend who was actually still a friend here because in addition to our German cast we had occasionally Italian performances. The operas were done in German, or course, as was the custom, but when they got guests from out of the country, they would return to the original language and that summer we had, of all things, *Otello* in Italian. And it had the famous American soprano, Mary Curtis Verna, who is still here in Seattle and a friend of mine and I've known her since then. I was a prompter because the opera was done in Italian and I was the only one who could speak it, so therefore, I was translating for the cast and I was also serving as the prompter. The tenor, however, was not Italian. His name was Feiersinger and he was okay. He was a fairly decent, heavy German tenor, but without the Italian feeling and without the real Italian high notes you wanted. But, they did this *Otello* several times and it had a big success as everything out-of-doors did. The other operas there is no point in mentioning as every summer would have different operas and I will mention them as they come along in the succeeding years.

So then the fall season began and to do this briefly—it was the type of repertoire theater where an opera would be done, repeated off and on through the entire season. Then another opera would come up three weeks later and that would be repeated on and on and on. The casts would occasionally change, maybe the soprano, maybe the tenor.

But the season began with an opera that I had not worked on—*Fidelio*, and I prepared the singers for it and it had a very fine dramatic soprano who was our leading one and her name was Marion Lippert. Lippert later sang in Northern Germany, Frankfurt and elsewhere and she even arrived at the Metropolitan Opera years later. I might as well comment on that now as she had been engaged in the meantime in Italy; she sang Macbeth. She sang in Rome and Naples and then she was singing *Turandot* at the Met, one of her leading roles and she did it apparently very well.

I was in New York at the time, she was singing *Tosca*—or was it Munich?—and I heard her do the *Tosca* with James King, the young American tenor at that time and just yesterday I read of his death at age 80 in Naples, Florida. He was a friend because I remember playing for his recital debut, or let's say, his audition recital in Cincinnati, for the American Opera auditions which sent the winner to Italy to make a debut with the theater in Milano. That is where I caught up with him in Milano as I was returning to Europe in the summer of 1961 and we remained friends.

But then time passes, and I had lost track of him until I read about his death, which was quite a shock. He had a wonderful career as did Marion Lippert, but not to digress any further. As the season progressed we were all very busy with the whole array of operas—many old like *Bohème, Tosca, Traviata* and others that were new to me such as *The Merry Wives of Windsor*. This was an opera by Nicolai that I had never seen and two of my wonderful new friends, two sopranos, had the lead in this opera and they were Norma Willmann, and in English it is Williams, and the Swedish Gunnel Ohlsson. They remain friends to this day. The opera went over very well because it is very well-known in Germany although it isn't here at all. The season progressed with a whole variety of operas that I mentioned and I, of course, was not involved in conducting any of them that first year. The only work I did was backstage, playing for rehearsals and so forth.

The only out-of-state activity happened at Christmas. I had already begun to miss Italy and to think about what they were doing at the Rome Opera and I read somewhere that the opera season was opening as always in December, late December with *Norma* and with the great

Maria Callas. So I flew to Rome and then went to a friend's home and spent something like ten days there.

Well, of course, they welcomed me at the opera house backstage as always as if I were a member of the ensemble, but, of course, I was simply a guest. I was able to stand in the wings watching everything that happened and observing Callas as she sang the first act with, of all people, Franco Corelli and the great mezzo Barbieri. Then it happened, as the world knows, and has never forgotten. The intermission came and it went on and on and on and all because Callas refused to go on. She said she was ill and her voice was not there and she could not sing anymore.

All of us backstage were amazed because we thought she sounded fine—the same as she always sounded, maybe strident on top, but no real difference. However, she refused to go on, and the audience was getting very impatient and it was really somewhat of an insult because the President of the Republic always came to the opening night of the opera and sat in the Royal Box. And that year finally they realized that Maria was not going to go on so they just left and the theater was closed and the audience went home without hearing the entire *Norma*. Quickly things happened up in the office and they engaged a substitute for the next performance and that was with the well-known soprano Anita Cerquetti, who had been singing this same role in Naples. So, here she was commuting from Naples to Rome and back to sing *Norma*, a grueling opera, but she did very well and it put her on the map and she became quite famous in succeeding years for all of those sorts of heavy Italian operas of that repertoire. And, of course, Callas recovered and we heard her later in different theaters and in different roles.

Well, after this little vacation, I came back to Germany and re-entered my job which was always backstage. However, I made a lot of friends in the city as well, not only the singers, but members of the population that I always encountered. And it turned out that during that year I didn't get to conduct. In the summer, which was then the summer of 1958, they were doing *Rigoletto* out-of-doors and they simply said to me: "Look, we know you conducted a debut in Italy, but we think you should make your debut here. We can only give you a brief rehearsal with the orchestra." Even though the opera was still in progress, meaning it had been done several times, they arranged for a reading rehearsal with me and I was glad to take it over. It was done by the singers who were very well-known to me, except that right on the day of the performance, we found out that the baritone, who later made his debut at the Met, was ill. So, a guest baritone, Misske, whom I had never known was engaged and I had to go into rehearsal with him at a piano in the studio. Then he went on the stage and sang and he had never sung with me or that orchestra and that was quite a task for him and for me, but it came off well.

The soprano was Willmann and the tenor was the wonderful Slovenian tenor, Plahuta, who became a good friend of mine. So, my debut there happened with *Rigoletto* out-of-doors and then we went back to the normal routine in the winter. This went on for years and years and years. The only change that occurred is when we engaged a new conductor for the next year and this was the Hungarian Istvan Kertèsz who was apparently, so they said, a refugee from the Communist's overtaking Budapest. Many stories about that exist, but he came in to us and had an audition which required him to conduct two operas and he conducted *Bohème* and *Fidelio* very well—impeccably and I was impressed.

Then he went away and we found out later he was already doing a guest performance of *Turandot* in Hamburg. So, the whole story of his entry into Germany is interesting. If he came in as a refugee, how did he already have an engagement at the famous Hamburg State Opera House? I really don't understand, but that is neither here nor there. He came to us and took over as first conductor which they then called Music Director. He was given that famous music title, General Music Director, and the man who had had the position was an old German called Anton Mooser who was simply called the Municipal Conductor which he didn't like at all. Nonetheless I got along initially, and for years very well with Kertèsz because he luckily had worked with an Italian Maestro in Budapest and learned the Italian style and traditions quite well and he did them that way in Germany. I prepared the singers to put them in that same background. He did the usual Italian repertoire and also had to branch off into certain German operas as well which over the years meant *Rosenkavalier, Salome* and some Wagner. But, initially, it was mostly Italian and Mozart. We did a lot of Mozart; *The Magic Flute, The Marriage of Figaro, Don Giovanni* and so forth.

Along with this came the summers in which I was never occupied except for the outdoor season and the out-of-doors season kept me there for a few weeks and then I was free. I usually went back to Italy just to see friends and roam around to see what they were doing at any opera house, out-of-doors or indoors. It was a good chance for reunions.

Left, Robert Ardrey and Robert Feist.

Below—The title page of Robert Ardrey's book, *The Social Contract*, dedicated to Bob Feist.

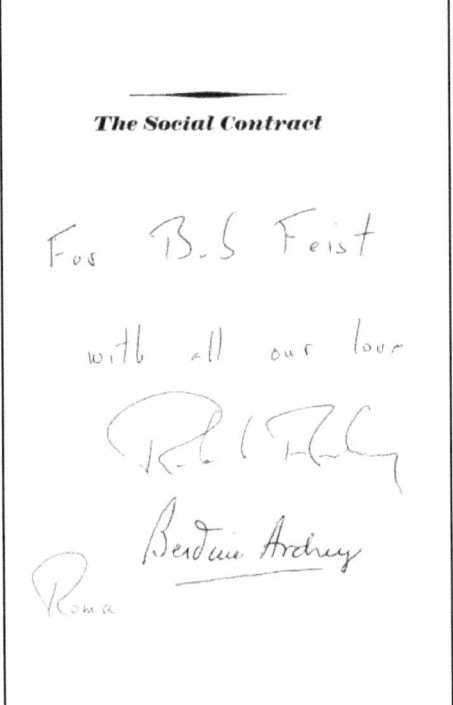

Left middle, Mr. Ardrey in his office and Robert Ardrey and Berdine on the terrace of their Rome apartment in Trastevere. We were friends for many years.

A reception given for Norma Williams and Feist after the recital for the commanding officers at the U.S. Army base in Flak Kaserne near Augsburg.

The Ballo in Maschera, Augsburg Stadtteater, Jan., 1959.

So, along those lines, it so happened I ran into frequently my former mentor Maestro Gavazzeni who lived in Bergamo but conducted at La Scala mostly and he conducted also in the arena of Verona. Well, I saw him in so many different cities and operas. It would be hard to remember them all. I do remember seeing him once doing *Norma* with Gencer at La Scala'which was very good. I saw him doing *Forza* there which was very good and saw him also at the arena of Verona doing an *Aida* after which we met when he was leaving the arena at the stage entrance and I had just come from a visit to Greece and he asked how Greece was and wanted to hear about it. As for the other cities, I saw him in Florence conducting there. I saw him in Venice, because in Venice he conducted a rare opera by Donizetti that I had never seen before or after, *Maria di Rohan*—with Scotto. The summers took me to various places, but not to America for years. I just enjoyed going back to Italy or roaming around Europe seeing places I had never seen before. And, the one year, which was the second year in Rome, I saw not only old friends, but several more operas that I had not encountered before as was the case with *Lorelei* and *Poliuto*.

In Germany, in my second season, I was assisting Kertèsz in *The Masked Ball* and at the usual time, after the four performances, he had to go somewhere else to conduct and therefore asked me to take it over. So, this was my house debut. In the theater in Augsburg I did *The Masked Ball,* in German. I know it backwards in Italian, but now I had to gain a sense of the text in German that he had prepared in a very Italian style. So, all of the arias were very Italianate and it went over very well and the cast was excellent with the great Marion Lippert as the soprano and the American baritone Dunlap as Renato and my friend, the Slovenian tenor Jerney Plahuta. That was a success and I did it five or six times that season. So, that brought my total up to *Rigoletto* and *Un Ballo in Maschera* in Augsburg until other things came along in succeeding years.

What came along in Rome in between was in September of 1956 at the end of my second year in Rome's Caracalla Theater. And during that summer I had wandered around a bit to Italy and when I returned to the help of an assistant conductor in the theater. He was a very good friend, Maestro Cavaniglia, and he got the idea to introduce me to the director of a secondary opera house in Rome. It was Teatro Eliseo, right on the main Via Nazionale where many, many, young singers were making their debuts, who were not ready for the Rome Opera. It was like a city opera, you might say. So, I worked there during the day. This was a month's long season coaching, working backstage and they said to me: "You know you should take over an opera." And I think they suggested *Traviata*. So, in September of that year, 1956, I did rehearsals which was a big help even though I knew it very well. The cast included a soprano whom I think was Spanish, Delores Beltran. I never heard of her again. The tenor was a friend of mine who had been with me in Tunis on that tour, Angelo Marchiandi and he went on to sing for years and years in Rome, and the baritone was one whom we never heard from again. The performance went very well and I was very happy about it. All of my friends came. And it so happened, I might as well mention it now, the following year which was 1957, I went back there and worked in their spring season which occurred at the end of the Rome Opera season, so this would be in June of 1957. And again they suggested another *Traviata* which I did that June of 1957. This time with the same tenor, Marchiandi, with a different baritone and with a new soprano. The soprano was from Finland, Maria Eira, whom frankly I never ran into again anywhere. But it was a very good experience to have that on my list again. And, of course, I may mention here that all of these occurred before I really enter into the German era at Augsburg, before I ever did *The Masked Ball* or *Rigoletto*.

Below is a letter to my parents from Elsa Picozzi, daughter of a famous conductor and wife of Fulbright stage director, Professor Riccardo Picozzi:

Rome, October 2, 1956, Via Depretis –

Dear Mr. and Mrs. Feist,

It was a great pleasure for us to witness the first performance of Traviata, *conducted by your son, Bob, at the Teatro Eliseo, a few nights ago. He really did wonderfully well considering he had practically no orchestra rehearsal, but many debutants in the cast to make things more difficult for him. He had the whole performance strongly in his grip and my husband feels sure that when he will have a chance of conducting again he will do better and better, and even this first experience will be very useful for him. We are so glad of his first success, for we are very fond of him, and he is such a hard-working boy always willing to do more. We know how much you will enjoy the news and how hard it will be for you to be so far away.*

With sincere regards from us both,

Riccardo and Elsa Picozzi

Above—The East Berlin opera house, Staatsoper.

A monument to the Soviet war dead in Treptow Park, East Berlin, Germany.

But to return again to the German theater in Augsburg, this is picking up where I left off. After my first year there and the second year, that is when I did *The Ballo in Maschera,* we are now in the year 1958. The first year found me out-of-doors at the Red Gate and then indoors with *The Masked Ball*. During the course of that year when I still worked backstage, as usual doing everything, there was this call from Italy and the call recalled a meeting I had had in the summer of 1957 when I was still in Rome, from Gian Carlo Menotti. At that time Menotti was in Rome planning his first year with his new festival called "The Festival of Two Worlds," or Festival dei due Mondi." After looking all over Italy for a small town he decided Spoleto was the perfect city for such a festival. Of course it was a city which in September all of the winners of the Italian competition and Americans and Fulbrights make their debuts.

Well these festivals were going to take place in June of 1958 and when he phoned me in Rome where I was still living, he wanted someone to accompany the auditions. He couldn't find a pianist. So I agreed and went down to the "home" of the Symphony Orchestra of Rome and played for the auditions in this Teatro Argentina, a famed theater because Rossini's *Barber of Seville* had been premiered there. Well, during the course of this period there was a day-long audition period and many, many singers, unknown to all of them, although I thought I knew one or two, auditioned for Menotti, and I played for them all. I sight read all of the scores they gave me and at the end of it I did not know then who was going to be chosen for the festival. But Menotti and Thomas Schippers, who was his new Musical Director (and remained that for years) came up to me and I remember Schippers saying: "Well, who are you? Where did you come from?" I said: "I've been living in Rome as a Fulbright Fellow for three years." and he complimented me and said: "Would you like to join us in Spoleto for the Festival?" And he said next year, it would have been 1958. And I said: "Well, yes." He said: "We'll contact you," and they did. During the course of that year, 1958, which was the season 1957-1958, they did contact me in Augsburg by phone or letter and asked me could I please get permission to leave the city and the theater for a period of about six weeks or so in Spoleto and my manager at the theater agreed to let me. Well, this was quite another wonderful choice. I left sometime late in May. The theater was doing an opera that I had actually prepared on the piano and it was a rarity Dallapiccola's *The Prisoner*, which I liked and it had never been done and they did it with the American baritone John Robert Dunlap.

A view of the Augsburg Theater.

Above—Mr. Feist with the American tenor Eugene Tobin after a performance of *Otello* in the Augsburg Theater around 1960.

Left—Swedish coloratura soprano, Gunnel Ohlsson.

Robert Feist with his mother (left) and father (right) and Ann Cathcart (center) at a party in Augsburg in 1960.

Robert Feist's close friends Dr. Josef Lederle and his wife, famed soprano, Sena Jurinac.

Norma Williams and Jerney Plahuta, Bob's friends and colleagues in his apartment in 1961.

While the performances were going on I left and I went to Spoleto and got a room there with a family and began working. I was an assistant as was a usual choice and what I did was prepare the opening opera which was going to be *Macbeth*. The *Macbeth* was staged in the Teatro Nuovo where I had made my debut in 1955 and it was done by a very interesting soprano called Vartenissian (and baritone William Chapman) whom I had never run into. But it turned out she had a brief career, but even recorded the "Verdi Requiem" with Serafin. During the course of the preparations, Schippers called me down from the stage and said: "Well Bob, I have to hear something in the auditorium. Would you please take over this scene." So, without any preparation I had to conduct the banquet scene of *Macbeth* and I did it from scratch, sight reading it, and it went quite well and they thanked me and Schippers was very complimentary. The performances went very well and as it was a new festival, it was reviewed all over, even in foreign countries—in Germany, France, England and mainly because of the presence of Schippers and Menotti.

Many singers were introduced during that period and not only were they introduced but he brought several ballet groups, one of which was Jerome Robbins and his ballet from the New York City Opera and the other was simply called "Chamber Ballets of John Butler," another well-known choreographer of the N.Y. theater. It was a theater that was right down in the center of Spoleto next to the square, the piazza where the cathedral was and it was called the Teatro del Caio Melisso.

Well, the ballet performances went quite well. I must say it was not difficult music. We had enough rehearsal time and even though it was modern it was not that difficult for the orchestra to manage it. So, now I had under my belt even some more premieres, Italian premieres like ballets in this festival and I was very happy with that.

By the end of the season we had had many parties, some in Menotti's own apartment with members of the company, the cast and all outside visitors who came for all of it, and that pleased me quite a bit—to meet them and to become part of the international group which continued into the next year I think I will mention that right now. Because at the end of that season, I went back to Augsburg and had to do my work as usual at the outdoor theater, The Red Gate and in that season we had again not only Italian operas, two or three, but they were always sung by invited guests from Italy. Well, among them came Mary Curtis Verna, soprano,

Clockwise from above—Robert Feist with the great dramatic soprano, Marion Lippert, backstage after the performance of *The Girl of the Golden West* at the open-air theater, the Red Gate, Augsburg, Germay.

Mr. Feist with the cast of *La Bohéme* at his last performance in the theater at Augsburg in 1964.

Soprano Norma Williams with Maestro Feist on stage after a performance of *La Bohéme*.

Right—Marion Lippert as Tosca. The inscription below to Mr. Feist from Ms. Lippert has been translated from the German:

"To my dear Bob, this greeting in great thankfulness, as well as my best wishes from my heart for all happiness for you as a man and artist after many happy collaborations.

Marion
September 1, 1962"

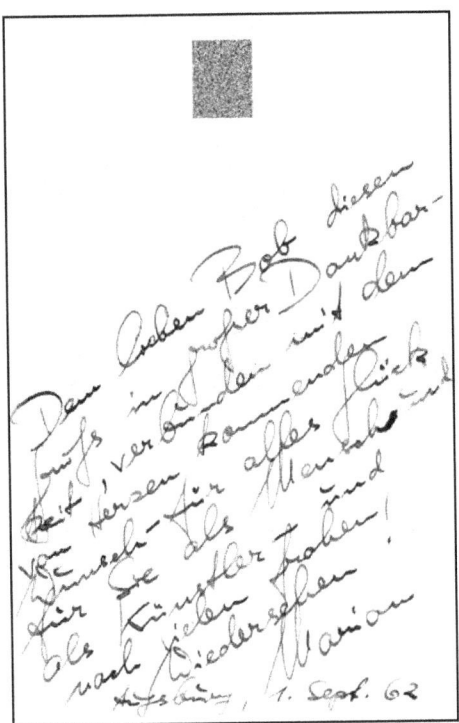

who had sung the year before, and this time she was to sing *Aida* with the tenor Umberto Borsò and Miriam Pirazzini as Amneris. Along with this we did Verdi's *Nabucco. Nabucco* was very seldom seen in Germany at that time and was done first by our local cast of singers. This included a debut by the Dutch soprano, Antoinette Tiemessen, who sang very often with me in succeeding years, but at the time of the Italian season, in the outdoor theater, the soprano role and the others were sung in Italian. In this particular case it was Anna de Cavaliere, whom I had heard in Rome before doing *Cyrano* and also *Lorelei*. The other roles were sung by our own local singers who had just sung it in German, but now they relearned their roles in Italian.

It so happened that I had met prior to this, during the first or second year, a lot of American teachers at the American schools at the Army base. It was a very big Army base that was typical in Germany, (Reese Casern or in German Flak Kasern), at that time, and these two teachers of the American Elementary School became good friends and I often brought them to the opera. Well, they decided that summer to have a big party on one of the off nights at their home and among those invited were Mary Curtis Verna, Umberto Borsò and, of course, the soprano who did *Nabucco*, Anna de Cavaliere, and her husband Fred. It was a wonderful evening in which, to my surprise, they all agreed to sing and Mary Curtis Verna and Borsò sang the wonderful *Andrea Chenier* duet which probably echoed off the roofs in that apartment where they were the guests. We had a great time and everybody enjoyed that immensely. The artists soon after that left and the performances were over. They only did two or three of the operas and they left and we went back to our normal outdoor season with operas in German. When that was over, we began the next winter season at the opera house and the number of operas done that year I cannot recall. There was the standard repertoire, but always sung in German and there were some novelties as well. Now we come up to the summer of 1959, at which point there was a new event that occurred.

During the course of the spring I had a phone call from the Director of the Menotti Festival, a woman, Anna Venturini whom I knew very well. She called from Rome to see if I could contact the conductor Istvan Kertèsz and I said: "Yes, he's our Music Director." Well, he was one of the winners of the competition that was held in Rome for conductors. I believe it was called Previtali Competition, or something like that, Previtali being the Conductor of the Santa Cecilia Orchestra. They chose several winners, among them Kertèsz. I said "Yes,

I knew him." They said: "Could you ask him if he would like to come to Spoleto in that summer of 1959 and conduct the Festival Premiere of Prokofiev's very rare *Angel of Fire* or *The Fiery Angel*, as they often say. Well, of course, I asked Kertèsz and he jumped at it. He was honored to conduct in this festival and it turned out that naturally he needed an assistant, so I was laden with the task of learning the piano score to *The Angel of Fire* and learning it for myself for the rehearsals that would occur in Spoleto. He was to come later after me. So, I went down by myself and obtained an apartment for two with a nice balcony and kitchen and everything. When he was finished with his work in Augsburg he joined me and I worked with him and the singers and played all the rehearsals for *The Angel of Fire*. This was not an Italian premiere. The cast was excellent with the great Leyla Gencer who had sung at La Scala and I heard her very many times. The baritone was Rolando Panerai, a very famous baritone, so the performances went very excellently. I had very little to do with them except backstage to get the singers on and off. But, I enjoyed the summer very much visiting with Kertèsz. His wife, Edith Gabry, joined us for several weeks and we had our usual succession of parties and so forth.

In addition to that work, I again had a ballet evening and this was actually not just ballet. It was ballet and some short operas. It was in that small theater once again and the works were the following novelties; one was the now well-known *Hand of Bridge* by Samuel Barber in its Italian premiere. The other opera was a new one for Italy by Lukas Foss called *Introductions and Goodbyes*. This opera proved to be very difficult, not so much for me, but for the singers and the staging which had them coming and going all over the place. And, we tried it and we tried it with the orchestra and finally one day Menotti came down to the orchestra pit and said: "Let's talk about this." We went back and talked and he said: " You know we cannot get this done on time and I think we're going to have to drop this *Introductions and Goodbyes* for now and substitute something else." In its place they determined that a ballet was easier. Right now I do recall which ballet it was but it went quite well and was not that difficult to conduct or to dance.

Eventually the Foss opera did turn up. I've seen it on programs elsewhere, so it did get performed. So, we did the Barber and this ballet many, many times in this small theater and it went very well. The public liked it and we had many, many festive occasions because of it.

Beside, of course, Menotti and Barber himself and many other well-known people were there along with several other important critics and composers and musicians from the Rome area and elsewhere in Italy because the orchestra was made up of people mainly from Milano, a chamber orchestra in Milano, The Angelicum.

So, that took care of that early part of the summer of 1959. The performances of the famous Prokofiev *Angel of Fire* continued its success and critics came from all over and I must mention something here because the first sign of a disagreement I guess with Mr. Kertèsz. First of all I may interject to say that the orchestra playing for *The Fiery Angel* and the *Macbeth*, in the year prior, was not a chamber orchestra, but it was the Trieste Philharmonic from the major city of Trieste, which was engaged for that summer, only for the Menotti Festival (that eventually stopped and other orchestras were brought in including an Eastman Orchestra from New York, but at the time it was the Trieste Philharmonic).

Now back to the beginning of the disagreement. A critic from a very major German paper, *Die Welt* in Hamburg had been there and had reviewed it very much in detail, which I did not know then. When I returned to Augsburg, a critic from the local paper whom I knew, gave it to me and to my amazement, the critic mentioned very briefly *The Fiery Angel* and Kertèsz, but wrote extensively about my own work with the opera and the chamber ballets that I had conducted. This surprised me; the fact that he really did not rave about Kertèsz.

Well, over the years we had several other "disagreements," but that was probably the first. Another I can mention came somewhere that year. There was the decision on the part of the management to do a rare opera by Rossini and this was *La Cenerentola*. Well, *La Cenerentola* I knew very well. I had seen it and worked on it with Maestro Gui in Rome with the great Simionato. But, apparently it was quite new at the time in Germany. Much of Rossini had been forgotten in Germany and a critic in Munich of a leading newspaper, Panofsky, had actually taken the score, translated the entire opera into German including the recitatives and Kertèsz and our own opera company accepted it without even questioning it. Then I started to work on it with the singers and compared it to my own Italian score which I had marked from Rome. Well, the amazing thing about it was that this critic in Munich had actually altered the recitatives to suit his own German translation. He altered the music, the notes, everything about it—so it didn't even sound like Rossini.

So, I brought this to the attention of Kertèsz. He did not know, because he did not know the opera and he said: "Well, change them." So, we rewrote the recitatives with the original piano score of Rossini with the right notes and the right harmonics and tried to fit the text to it or we changed the text so it would fit. We never heard anything about it from the critic in Munich, of course, but he knew we had changed his concept considerably. The performances of *La Cenerentola* went very well and it was done in the major theater with a very good cast except that we did not have a mezzo doing the leading role of *Cenerentola*. Well, of course, I remember I had seen Simionato and was very hard to get her out of my mind when we did this opera of which I conducted several of the repetitions in the opera house. I enjoyed doing it and we did very well, but I regretted the fact that we did not have a coloratura mezzo.

To go on now. In the course of that season of 1959-1960 and other years, I acquired a long repertoire. They always occurred with my taking over the baton for Kertèsz or for another conductor probably Anton Mooser, the German in residence there. So, in this fashion, having already played the rehearsals, conducted the singers, I knew the operas very well. So, I would take over usually with no rehearsal and conduct things such as *The Tales of Hoffman*, which is not easy in any way; *Tosca* for which they did give me an orchestra rehearsal and that helped quite a bit, with a very good cast. This was with Marion Lippert, the dramatic soprano, Plahuta, the tenor, and two different Scarpias, the American Robert Dunlap and the other American who had just joined us, Robert Anderson, a bass baritone who had come from Heidelberg. So, the performances of *Tosca* went very well and I enjoyed doing them.

Bob Dunlap then moved to Wiesbaden on their permanent staff and soon after made his Metropolitan Opera debut as Sharpless in *Butterfly*, the same night as Scotto's debut in the title role. Soon after he moved to southern California, where he taught voice and I had a reunion with him in Santa Cruz around 1990. He died a few years later.

In addition to this came another interesting situation involving the United States. The Metropolitan Opera had decided to create a national touring company. I think it was called the Metropolitan Opera National Company. It was meant to introduce young singers to audiences all over the country. They would travel with an orchestra and alternate the casts at times and they would spend the year doing *Bohème* and *The Marriage of Figaro*. So, I met the directors in Munich at an appointment sometime that year before I ever did the *Bohème*.

Risë Stevens was basically in charge and the conductor was Robert La Marchina who later ended up conductor at the Met and also conducted for the opera in Hawaii. The other person involved was the famed and excellent scout for the Met and this person was a colleague and a friend of Rudolph Bing. His name was Roberto Bauer. He was German, but for ages and for decades in Milan and was the scout basically for the Metropolitan Opera for Italy and Germany. He traveled around considerably, heard all the singers, made his recommendations to Bing personally and many of these singers made their way to the Met. I had met him under the recommendation of someone, I do not recall who, perhaps a singer that I knew in Rome. I met Bauer at his home before these auditions occurred and he was very kind. He was impressed with my knowledge of opera and what I had done. We would hear records of famous old singers including the final recording of a castrato that he had and it turned out that Bing was coming to Milano to hear a new group of singers. So Bauer called me from Germany and asked me to please play for these singers and I agreed. It was all sight reading because I did not know until I got there what they were singing. It was quite an array of people that I played for that year which I think was June. Among them was Marcella Pobbe who made her debut at the Met and others of note. One was a baritone whom I had often seen, Mario Sereni, who had a long career at the Met and who recorded Gerard in *Chenier* and also others such as Mario Zanasi. Later on, when I would see them in a performance, either in Italy or at the Met, I could visit them and they were glad and remembered that I had played for them at the audition. This day the audition took place in Milano in a church or small auditorium and Bing and Bauer sat in the audience and heard all the singers and then eventually made their decisions. It turned out that I had dinner with them. Bauer had arranged that we have dinner at his own apartment. We sat out-of-doors on a terrace and his servant, maid and cook prepared the meal and we had our dinner together talking about the auditions and the singers. At this point I cannot remember whether the discussion went on in English or in German. Bauer was fluent in all. I do not think Bing was fluent in Italian, but anyway we had an interesting conversation. Bing got to know me but it did not good as I was never invited by him to the Met.

    Some of the singers did go to the Met. Certainly Sereni did because I kept up with Bauer for many, many years. In fact one year I was invited to his Christmas party which he had every year and at that party many famous singers who owed their career to him, or their career at the

Met, appeared including Franco Corelli. It was the first time I had met Corelli, who came late, was a little bit distant to everybody, and did not go around being the happy-go-lucky person. Nor was he that way at rehearsals as I had noticed at the Rome Opera, where I saw him many times. But it was interesting to meet him and the other singers at this big Christmas party.

Now how does this fit in with *Bohème* in Augsburg? Well, it turned out that Bauer and his American conferees such as either Stevens or La Marchina, or one other person who was in charge of the staging, would go to various theaters in Germany and hear the singers performing. He let me know and said: "Would it be alright if they came to hear a performance of you doing *Bohème*?" Talk about guts, which it really takes, I agreed to do my first *Bohème* without an orchestra rehearsal. There was no time for it. So, I relied on my tradition, my ability and the Bohèmes I had heard and I did a *Bohème* with no rehearsal and it went very well. In fact, all the singers were pleased, much more so than they had with the German conductor because it was more Italianate which I had always done. After the performance was over and the applause and so forth, I agreed to meet with the visitors at a nearby cafe-restaurant where we used to hang out after performances and it was a very informal sort of thing. We met in the bar, but at a table and discussed it. They were both complimentary, but Bauer could not really overdo himself and say how much he thought it was excellent because he was in the presence of La Marchina, the conductor who was a little bit aloof and not exactly complimentary.

The result of all this is as everyone may imagine—fruitless because when the Metropolitan announced their national company for their tour of America, they did not invite me at all and frankly I was glad because at that point I was conducting operas in Germany. And I was hearing all the ones I did not know perhaps and the idea of running across the U.S. to every small and large city, with the same singers and a small orchestra to do either *Bohème* or *The Marriage of Figaro* frankly did not appeal to me. So, had they asked me, I would have declined. It fact in retrospect perhaps they did ask me and I declined.

So, that was the end of my personal connection to the Met. La Marchina did make it to the Met and a year or so later he appeared at the Met doing Menotti's last opera which was called *The Last Savage* and it starred George London and I don't think it lasted long. It did one run at the Met and never came back the next year and I don't think La Marchina did either.

So much for that. The years went by and any significant events only occurred when I left the theater periodically. I conducted other operas there with or without a rehearsal including one out-of-doors opera at the open-air-theater, *La Forza del Destino*, with no rehearsal—my first *Forza del Destino* without any rehearsal and as my farewell—*Turandot*, but we'll get to that later. In the meantime an agent in Milano called whom I knew quite well, having visited her before. Ada Finzi was the prominent agent for opera and symphony with an office in Milano was very kind and helpful. She was asked me if I would like to come down to do a concert with the San Remo Philharmonic. San Remo is a small but pleasant Riviera town right near Monte Carlo, Monaco, Nice—all of them. It was also the home, as I found out later, of Franco Alfano who had composed *Cyrano de Bergerac*. Well, it turned out that I went down there and did a symphony concert with the very famous (later on) violinist called Salvatore Accardo. We became instant friends and the program included the "Paganini Violin Concerto" which he played very well. I did the Bizet "Symphony in C" and several contemporary works, Creston and also Delius. The work itself was very pleasant the orchestra very responsive and not only did Salvatore and I get along very well, but the management liked us.

Then I went back to Germany and it turned out that over the course of time, other invitations came from Italy. I had met through another conductor, the Director of the Italian RAI which was the Italian radio/television orchestra or management which is in Rome and each major Italian city had a RAI orchestra, a radio/television orchestra. These concerts were taped and broadcast later. And, it turned out that for the first time after I had met the director, Giorgio Vidusso, he was working in Rome and not in Milano. We called him Maestro, though he was no conductor. He was simply the business manager and he knew all of the singers and conductors in the world. He phoned or wired me asking me would I like to make a debut in Italy with a Sicilian orchestra. It was not in a main city, it was in Palermo in Sicily. Well, I agreed. It was famous and why not. He purposely chose an American program thinking it would be interesting involving Barber's "First Symphony" which was not easy and was unknown in Italy, and the "Copland Piano Concerto" which is a hard nut to crack for any pianist or conductor or orchestra. In addition I was doing "Rossiniana," a Suite by Respighi of scenes from Rossini. When I got to Palermo it was in the middle of summer, July or August and seemed to me that the temperature was 100° and we were rehearsing and recording in an auditorium or hall that was not air-conditioned and it was miserably hot. Before that had happened, I had stopped in Milano to meet the pianist, a woman who was going to play the Copland. This did not turn out well. She didn't like it and she had trouble with it. She said: "I can't do this so, I think you should get someone else." Well, naturally I talked to Vidusso. He said: "Let's drop the Copland, it can come up later. Let us only do the Respighi and the Barber." And I did it. We had sufficient rehearsal time. We all sweated and it was done in this hall of 100° and they did a very good job and I remember afterwards coming to my hotel and the manager of that orchestra in Palermo said: "Well, I have to tell you Maestro, that you have conquered the orchestra," which to me was quite a compliment even though I never returned to Palermo to conduct.

And the next few occasions of engagements out of Germany I returned several times to the city of Torino in Northern Italy, which at the time, by the way, maybe still had the reputation as being the best symphony orchestra in Italy. Because it was in the North, it was a big business city, the headquarters of Fiat, and so forth. But it was the city where the people had much more interest in being precise and their recordings were always excellent. Well, I faced them two, three or four times. The one I will mention first is the fact that at one of the concerts there included the Copland Concerto. But, it had another pianist who said he would learn it and he did learn it and played it very well. We had sufficient rehearsal time. It was very difficult even for that orchestra, but did perform it. I also included on the program a novelty for Italy, the "Symphony in G Minor" of Lalo. No one knew that either, and there were a couple of sections that had to go on without a rehearsal because there was not enough time to rehearse everything because of the difficulty of the Copland.

Other works that I engaged in—in Torino, I will mention later after I've spent some time on another big project that took me away from Germany completely, But I went back to Torino several times and to the RAI Orchestra in Milan which was also very good. But, one of the occasions that brought me from Rome in 1966 was the first time I conducted in Milan. It was one of their two chamber orchestras, Angelicum, and Pomeriggi Musicali was the other. This was the Angelicum and it was a very good orchestra and again I chose a difficult program and it included the "Apollo" by Stravinsky and other works, all American except Sandor Veress. This program included the wonderful short work by Ives called "The Unanswered Question," probably unknown in Italy at the time and that went very well. In addition to the "Apollo" by Stravinsky, I just mentioned, we played Krenek's "Elegie For Strings" and that went well. And finally, a work for two pianos and orchestra by Veress, a composer who lived in Switzerland and was quite well-known though I do not know many of others of his and this was called "Homage to Paul Klee," the famous German painter. It was very descriptive. It depicted six or seven paintings of Klee's in musical terms and was excellent. The two pianists were very well-known in Italy as concert pianists and as professors, Gino Gorini and Sergio Lorenzi, both of whom remained good friends and I performed with them later. In fact this particular "Homage to Paul Klee" we later did in a concert in Lugano, Switzerland.

The other concert that took place in Milano occurred a year or so later and it was in the other concert hall where the Pomeriggi Musicali worked and it was another orchestra of equal ability and they had their permanent conductor. but I was invited as a guest and that program also included several rarities for Italy. One of them, unusual for a rarity, was "The Overture to the Wasps" by Vaughan-Williams and a world premiere by an Italian composer, his name is Fellegara and I have not heard or encountered him since. To be honest, it was a surprise to me that at the time this was going on at La Scala which was very nearby, right across the street from the Galleria, where this concert hall stood. Gavazzeni was conducting *Boris Godounov*, I think in Italian, or perhaps in Russian, and he knew of my performance with the Pomeriggi Musicali and he actually went out of his way when he was free one afternoon, walking to the concert, and came over with his wife to sit there and hear this whole concert. Later he came up and complimented me very much and even wrote me a note about it. So, I was very happy that finally, after all those years, a mentor there actually had been able to see me work though not in an opera, but at least in concert.

Another departure from Germany of interest occurred in the summer of 1963. This occurrence was the 150th Anniversary of the birth of Verdi which was celebrated all over Italy, of course, because it marked a decisive moment in his life and the Italians celebrated it very often. Knowing of this I talked to a German critic in Munich who by then was a friend and he had come to my performances in Germany and had heard me do *Bohème*. He gave me a stunning review saying it was the best *Boheme* he had ever heard in Germany! This was Antonio Mingotti, basically Italian, he moved to Germany, became fluent in German and became a critic of the *Abendzeitung*. I knew him and his wife very well. When I would come to Munich, to hear anything at the Munich Opera, I would be a guest in their home. But, he was given the task, or the project, of doing a film for the German TV.

It was their Second channel, meaning their cultural channel, on the life of Verdi. He was to write the script, go along with the crew to Italy to film it. Well, at that age—he was not a young man, and he did not want to go through this, so he asked me, and he asked the directors of the German Radio, Deutsches Television, if they could turn it over to me and they agreed. Well, I wrote the script according to where we were going to go and it was corrected or altered by him or by the staff. I met the people who were taking it to Italy and there were several photographers and the stage director who did the filming.

We set out that summer of 1963 from Milano and we covered many of the sites in Verdi's life. This was for the Television Deutsches Fernsehn which was based in Mainz, Germany. It started with narration and also included scenes from all of the Verdi sites; his home, which was outside of Bussetto, his Villa Verdi and in Milan his wonderful Casa di Riposo, the House of Repose or retirement for all opera singers and musicians who had been impoverished and needed a place to live. It was like a retirement home. We filmed there, interviewed several of the people who were there.

We had always with us a woman who was engaged "off the street" and she simply came with us and always pushed a cart, like a vending machine and we filmed her as we would find an Italian vendor on the street selling food or bananas or whatever. We filmed her in front of the Verdi Conservatory of Music and in front of the opera house and the other locales that were frequented by Verdi in his lifetime. It gave a nice informal touch to this proceeding. Surely his villa, because of Verdi, was beautiful because the word was that his adopted children—the people who inherited his estate (because his children had died, not at birth, but soon after) carried the name Verdi, but with another name attached, and this family was very nice because they let us film their own house and the entire Verdi Villa; meaning we went through the whole house, the whole area where he lived. The room where he composed all of his operas, the dining room, his bedroom, everything in the villa was filmed for eternity and it was a fabulous experience to direct it. I was not a director, I was simply there to assist the director who spoke no Italian and I was translating everything in Italian into German for the photographers and staff of the German TV. This took quite a bit of time, but it was always pleasant.

Sometimes the days would go on and on and on. And I remember—one night, I said: "I've got to get out of here," and went to the woman who was the official translator. She was Italian, and we went around town having a glass of wine and something to eat because the filming was driving us crazy, but that is what happens when you film for TV. I think that covers, more or less, the film, which covered everything except that we had no musical events. They used in the film excerpts from his operas, of course, but we were not present at any of those events. We stayed in a hotel in Milano and also in Bussetto where we shot the opera house which is called the Teatro Verdi in the city in which he grew up. To be specific, I have mentioned it because it was associated always with his name. Verdi was born in a very small village called le Roncole and that is where his villa stands which we filmed. Bussetto is larger and that is the town where he did a lot of his studies and where he became an organist and a choir director after childhood. So, Bussetto is where the opera house stands which is called the Teatro Verdi. So, we saw all the Verdi sites. We did nothing in other cities such as Rome or anywhere else where he was active, but it was all centered about his youth, his growing up and his retirement in Milano where he lived there in a hotel for a performance. And then he gradually weakened and he passed away there. His villa was called Villa Verdi and that is the villa everybody visits when they go to Bussetto to see where he lived. Well, the taping was finished and the show was televised nationally in Germany on Deutsches 2, the Second German TV Channel and I saw it and I was very happy as were my friends. I have not seen it since and I do not know where I could locate it. Mingotti was glad of this installation of this idea to me and was very happy with the results as well, After this we returned to Germany and we all saw the film on TV. That brought me, more or less, at the beginning of my last year in Augsburg. I didn't know at the time that little by little I had decided I really had had enough of the German scene. I've not commented too much on other performances that I saw, but I frequently went out of town, on business or just for a vacation, so I saw operas in Frankfurt, Heidelberg, Vienna and Munich and many other cities. And, that is where I encountered most of the great German singers. Munich was the closest to us, maybe 35 or 40 miles by train. I could go down there and see an opera, maybe stay at the Mingottis and return the next day. Or with friends, I would drive down and they would drive me back.

It was in Munich that I first saw the rarest of operas unknown to me—all of rare Strauss' operas; *die Aegyptische Helene, Daphne,* his *Elektra* and *Capriccio, Intermezzo, die Schweigsame Frau, die Frau Ohne Schatten and Liebe der Danae* in 1989. All of these operas you seldom run into, I saw in Munich with very good casts; people like Rysanek, Beirer, Nilsson, Neidlinger, many, many others as Munich was then one of the leading German houses like Hamburg and Düsseldorf, Cologne and Stuttgart and it still is.

By the way, Kertèsz left the Augsburg Opera when I had finished the TV film on Verdi. He became the Music Diretor in Cologne, but soon conducted all over the world until his shocking death by drowning, off the coast of Israel, on a break from conducting the Israel Philharmonic. It was about 1970 and was covered in all the world's papers, a great loss to all in many countries.

Above—Mr. Feist with Maestro Tenaglia, head of the archives of the Ricordi Publishers after inspecting all Verdi manuscripts for the German TV film *Viva Verdi* in 1963.

Right—Mr. Feist taking a break while filming the TV documentary *Viva Verdi* at Verdi's villa near Bussetto.

Clockwise from above—Jaroslav Horáck and Dalibor Jedlicka in *The House of the Dead* by Janacek with dramatic sets by Valdmir Nyvlt and staging by Ladislaw Stros. Another scene from *The House of the Dead* in the 1964 production in the Prague National Theater. Soprano Libuse Domaninská as Katja Kabavova, by Janacek, Prague National Theater.

CHAPTER TEN
The Rockefeller Foundation Grant

This turned out to be a major decision on my part to start for other territories and other repertoire. I had seen in all the news in Italy that the Bolshoi Theater in Moscow was coming to Milano's La Scala for a few weeks of performances, the first time the Bolshoi Opera had gone out of their country. The Bolshoi Ballet, of course, had come out. The Bolshoi Ballet Company had gone to America and everywhere else, of course, but not the opera. The La Scala Opera had already gone to Moscow and performed many operas under Gavazzeni and others, but not vice versa. So, I realized they were coming to Milano in the fall. Not only that, but I was interested in other Eastern repertoire and saw an interesting notice that the Edinburgh Festival in Scotland was going to host as one of their prime attractions, the first time, the Prague National Opera was coming out of Czechoslovakia to perform in Edinburgh.

Well, I thought it was a very good excuse, a reason, to make my request. I had met on a prior occurrence in America, in New York and then in Germany, the representative of the Rockefeller Foundation. It was called the Martha Baird Rockefeller Foundation who gave these awards and you had to have a good reason, like my Fulbright. I told them I felt that I had to have a better understanding of the Russian, the Czech and other Easter European countries as well as the French. I knew some French opera, but had only heard one or two operas in Paris and wanted to see what the repertoire was really like all over and their theaters. Well they agreed to this and they gave me a commission and told me to keep in touch, to indicate my expenses and my itinerary. They liked the itinerary very much, and it began in the fall in 1964. It took a little bit of time to adjust to this idea because it called upon my resignation from the Augsburg Theater which they accepted and all the requests I had made to other theaters in Germany had come to nothing.

So, I looked forward to this wandering period and had it planned out very well. It started with the trip to Edinburgh in September of that year because the festival took place then. I flew up visited a friend in London, then went on to Edinburgh and got a nice hotel room and immediately when the Czechs arrived I met them at the theater while they were rehearsing and it was a great pleasure because they were extremely generous and kind to me and interested in the fact that I wanted to know more about their country and their repertoire.

We generally spoke in German, some spoke English, but I knew no Czech and never learned it. I embarked on this by attending all rehearsals and all performances that the Czechs did in Prague. Besides, of course, being a tourist, I saw the entire city. I saw the castle I saw everything that was royal about it and I saw all the quaint parts of Edinburgh, and heard a wonderful concert by the Pittsburgh Symphony under William Steinburg in the presence of the Queen. The Queen was there at that time and it was a wonderful occasion. I had never been in her presence and they did a program that interested me very much.

Well, whole weeks went by with very, very much velocity. It was a lot of study. I had the scores, I went to every performance, marked everything, met the singers and they invited me to visit them which I had intended to do. "Well," I said: "I will be back in the fall to see you all." They were very glad.

On the heels of that, I went back to Italy by way of Germany, where I had rented my apartment out to another soprano who was coming into the Augsburg Theater, but left the furniture there. Then I went on to Milano and in Milano the Bolshoi arrived, the entire contingent, orchestra, chorus, singers. They had quite an array of Russian operas, not only *Boris Godounov* which I had seen and knew, but also the wonderful final opera of Prokofiev, *War and Peace*, which quite intrigued me from every point of view. They also did Tchaikovsky's *Queen of Spades* and *Eugene Onegin*, of course. I had seen *The Queen of Spades* in Rome, but in Italian, now it was in Russian which was a different story. Not only did I go to every performance as a guest of the Bolshoi and La Scala with free tickets to every performance, but I was allowed to meet the people, the members of the cast. So, I was occasionally backstage or in the rooms in which they would invite you. And the main person that I wanted to meet was the chief conductor of the Bolshoi Opera, that was Svetlanov. To this day he is my favorite Russian conductor and one of the finest I've ever seen, though he died a few years ago. And he talked to me very nicely and went through the scores with me, the score of *War and Peace* and several other operas, explaining things. And then he said: "I invite you to come to Moscow and then we can talk more and you can hear more performances of the Bolshoi." I was very, very thrilled. I was overcome by their kindness and generosity to me.

So, while I was there I said: "I think I will try another outlet for my daily activity." And I went to Rome where I knew of many American universities and the one that attracted me was the Loyola University of Chicago, which had an American program for Americans in college in Rome at the Cultural Art Center and it was called the American Center of the Arts. It was a noted Catholic university, one of the four Loyola Universities in the USA, and as a Catholic it interested me very much, and it was the largest of several third year USA colleges in Italy. I talked to the manager or let's say the dean, and I indicated my past experience and wondered about the faculty. He said: "Well, I will tell you about it." As this dean said, at the Loyola University, they had no music. They had a professor of art and art history and literature and all the other subjects that were taught in their normal programs in Chicago, but nothing abut music. But he said "We need it. So, if you would want to—you can come in here and take over and begin a program in music history which would be symphony and opera." "Well," I said: "Fine, I would like to do that as long as I have permission to absent myself if I have engagements." So, I got that set. I knew where I was going to be the next year after I had finished all this traveling.But, back to that, I returned to Milano to see a performance or two, but I had finished with Bolshoi. Then I went up to Germany and from Germany I flew to Prague, Czechoslovakia. They welcomed me. They remembered me because I had the Rockefeller Grant and Rockefeller means everything. It is just a big name. So, I had the permission to go to any rehearsal and performance that I wished. So, I practically lived in the Prague National Theater and the other one which was called the Smetana Theater and now the name has been changed to a concert hall. But they performed in two different theaters and I was there all the time, rehearsals and performances. And to name the vast array of Czech operas that I heard would go on and on and on. I'll list them separately and have them inserted into the dialogue, but at the present moment, I can just say that I saw about four or five Smetana operas, four or five Janacek's, a few of Dvorak and other modern composers that we don't generally run into.

The one I will mention because it came up later for me, was the Martinu opera *Julietta* which was his last. And the singers there and the conductor said: "Take notice of this, because this is a very important work." It was unknown in America, and would you believe it—I introduced it to America a few years later! It took a while though, however.

Maria Tauberova, leading soprano and Ivo Zidek, leading tenor in Bohuslav Martnu's *Julietta* performed at the National Theater in Prague.

The same singers in a dramatic pose. Mr. Feist conducted *Julietta* many years later in its American premiere at the Meany Theater at the University of Washington in Seattle, Washington.

The final scene in Tchaikovsky's *Pique Dame (Queen of Spades)* with Aurab Angiaparidze as Hermann in a 1964 production at the Bolshoi Theater in Moscow, USSR.

During my years at the University of Washington I conducted 18 operas, some well-known and some were rarities. For instance: Handel's *Ariodante* was a West Coast premiere from which I received a congratulatory letter from the Handel Society of New York. Also, the *Clemenza di Tito* was a first performance in Seattle, also was Puccini's *La Rondine,* never done here in Seattle. Also Britten's *Midsummer Night's Dream* was a first performance in Seattle and also the *L'heure Espagnole* was also a first for Seattle. Then came a one-act opera that was a premiere here at the University, Donizetti's little one-act *Campanello* and Rossini's well-known *Italiana in Algeri.* But I think, most important was the American premiere of *Julietta* by Martinu. That is the opera I had seen in Prague and everyone said: "You've got to see this," and I did. Well, it created quite a stir because it had never been seen in America. We wrote to the English National Opera in London who had all the materials and parts and scores and they sent everything to us, vocal parts, orchestra parts and so on, because they were thrilled that someone in America was finally doing it as they had done it before. Well, it received excellent reviews here and I was very, very happy to do this American premiere of a great opera by a Czech composer.

So, the entire period in Czeckoslovakia was spent in the theater and in restaurants to eat and they invited me, various singers and conductors, to their homes. They had parties and I was not a guest of honor, but they welcomed me as a good friend and I liked that.

To name them all, they would be unfamiliar to most readers; Domaninska; a wonderful soprano who did *Libussa* and things like that. The tenor Ivo Zidek, who was their leading tenor, both of them had also sung at the Vienna Staatsoper on occasions and so many, it is hard to recall or pronounce their names, actually and yet, the whole period added many more names to my list of favorites including several conductors as a matter of fact. One that I liked particularly was Bohumil Gregor and others.

But it was an elevating experience and I loved Prague though it was under the Communists and everything was desolate. It had never been bombed, so everything remained intact from the Middle Ages on. The only thing that was dreary was that there was nothing in the shops to buy except Communist tea and articles which did not interest anybody and they put up with it. The people were surprisingly friendly despite what they were living through which was Communism. And the squares, the wonderful piazzas were excellent and superb and I've seen them again as I returned to Czechoslovakia a couple of years ago.

Clockwise from right—Alain Vanzo and Jane Berbié in *L'Heure Espagnole* at the Opera de Paris. Albert Lance, tenor in *Tosca* at the Paris Opera. Alain Vanzo and Mady Mesplé in *Lakmè* at the Opera Comique.

Right—The Ball Scene, Act I of Prokofiev's *War and Peace* with Yuri Mazurok (Andrei) and Tamara Milashkina (Natasha) at the Bolshoi Theater in Moscow. Below—Pavel Lisitzian as Napoleon in *War and Peace* at the Bolshoi Theater in Moscow, USSR.

Clockwise from Above—
The Prague National Theater was known for their dramatic scenes. These sets were designed by Svoboda with staging by Kaslik in Dvorak's *Rusalka*, Act II in 1960. Rusalka soprano Schbertuva as Rusalka at the Prague National Theater. Ladislav Mraz and Drakomira Tikalova as seen on the stage in Dvorak's *Rusalka*.

After that visit I returned to Germany briefly and checked into my apartment to see a friend who was taking the apartment and decided it was time to go back to America for a visit. So, I flew by way of London to New York and I spent approximately two weeks in New York. And there I met the soprano I had known from Germany, Mary Curtis-Verna, who welcomed me to her house for a visit and also gave me tickets to the Met very often and I saw quite a few performances at the Met. In fact I saw her do *Turandot* and a few other operas. We also sat together for *La Forza del Destino* with the soprano, I think from Bulgaria, Raina Kabaivanska. She was very well-known in Italy and was quite young. Well this girl had been given an awful lot of roles at the Met. I also met George Schick who was in charge of artists—new artists or bringing in artists and knew of my background and let me go to all the performances and rehearsals and I had hoped that would lead to something at the Met, but it really didn't; the reason being at this time—there were no Americans welcomed as conductors. At any rate, the performances were always conducted by Europeans and as had always been the case. I found out similarly that my connection to San Francisco had reached a stalemate because in Rome I had met Adler, who was the director. I went with him to a concert. I wrote to him and later came his invitation that if I wanted to come to be chorus master or assistant conductor or something like that. That was not enough. I was to go back to the States as an assistant chorus master or at the Met as a coach which they did suggest and I did not want to go to the Met as a coach. I would have preferred a conducting post.

Similarly, around that time, Dallas had invited Maria Callas to sing *Medea* and *Norma* and something else and I was in touch with people there and they also extended an invitation to me as an assistant conductor at the Dallas Opera for a season—just for the season with Callas and that would be a few weeks. But, I certainly did not want to just go there for a few weeks to be a coach. I would have preferred conducting, but they did not offer that. The only other place left was, of course, Chicago which was very well established. And in Chicago I had met Carol Fox, the Artistic Director, who was very nice. We corresponded and I asked about assistants, and there were several, and one of them was Rescigno, who was then their music director and that didn't last long because by the time I mentioned, he had left the Chicago Opera and formed the Dallas Opera with another who was part of their original triumvirate.

So, once again, the major opera houses in America offered no inclination towards me. So, after seeing everything in New York at the Met and agents, I saw the Rockefeller people who were very thrilled with what I had so far done. All of the descriptions I gave in writing and they were applauding what I had accomplished. I visited my parents in Cincinnati and went back and flew to Germany. After a brief stay there, I went down to Italy to Torino for another engagement with the RAI and that was, of course, as I said, best orchestra in Italy. And it was a very interesting program and it involved a few other works, new to them and then I went back to Germany again.

But this time only briefly, because the next stop on my list was Paris. I was welcomed there as well. A very good friend of mine offered me his apartment and I stayed there just while I was shopping around. And through another friend in Rome, I obtained an apartment for myself, sublet to me, and I had it for the whole period of some three months in Paris. It was perfect. It was in the 16th Arrondisement and convenient by subway-Metro as you say-and I went to the Paris Opera and was welcomed with open arms because of the name Rockefeller. So, here I was in the middle of the Paris world and had open doors to me for any performance or rehearsal at the Paris Opèra and the Opèra Comique. The Director of the Paris Opera at that time was the well-known Georges Auric, one of the composers of the famous French group "Les Six," who welcomed me and I had learned enough French that we could converse in French. I had, in my last year in Germany, taken private French lessons with a girl and I knew enough to get by and in three months improved considerably, because the French will speak English, though they prefer not to. Therefore I got along using whatever French I knew. So, in Paris I encountered many operas for the first time.

Well, I went on from there. I went to Lyon, Nice and Bordeaux. In Bordeaux I ran into German friends of mine and from my German home town of Augsburg and they were then working in Paris. This man, Ernst Braun was in charge of a company that had a branch in Paris and I visited them often, went to operas, and there were there in Bordeaux and there we saw a wonderful performance of *Werther* and it was sung by an Australian singer called Albert Lance. His real name was Lance Ingram and he changed it to Albert Lance. And it was thrilling to hear *Werther* sung in French by a very excellent cast and also being with the Braun family was very important to me and I got to be friends with Albert, the tenor and his wife. From there I went on to Toulouse, which is a beautiful city as well as Bordeaux. And there I heard a new opera which was new to me completely and this was Massenet's *Herodiade*. I loved it. I don't understand why it is not done more often. You seldom run into it anywhere. Frankly I've never run into it in America. But the opera was superbly done and Rita Gorr was in it. But that made the trip worthwhile. So, I had seen operas in Paris, Lyon, Bordeaux and Toulouse.

And then I went on a trip back to Germany and stopped in Strasbourg which is on the border in the Alsace-Lorraine area and it was a performance of *The Tales of Hoffman* which was very good, but I didn't meet anyone in the theater. I was just passing through. It had nothing to do with my Rockefeller Grant at all.

While in Paris I saw everything else. I saw all of the city's cultural delights, the museums, the Louvre, the Rodin Museum and all of the city squares and the Champs Elysees and got to know the city and its language quite well and that took all the time when I was not in the opera house. I met some of my friends including my French friend, Claude, who was a friend of my very best friend in America, Bill Fogle, whose apartment I had briefly. So, my tour in France was something like three months long and filled with delights and an incredible amount of repertoire that I learned for the first time in French: Opera Comique and Etchevery was the main conductor at the Paris Opéra Comique and he became a very kind friend going through scores with me and explaining all French traditions which is a very, very great help. Jolivet was one of the many contemporary composers whom I happened to run into by going to concerts that were given by the French radio, the Radio Television Orchestra. Of the things that I heard, I was very impressed by an oratorio called "Le Couer de la Matiere," which I thought translated as "The Heart of the Matter," based on the American novel of that title. But, it wasn't. It was simply an oratorio that Jolivet had conceived himself, and I was thrilled with it. I met him and he became extremely kind to me and I said that I wanted to hear more of his works. So he said: "If you go to the library, the Maison de la Radio Museum, they will let you hear anything and I did. They pulled out all of the tapes of Jolivet's productions or suites and I was able to hear them all and several of them I marked down for my own benefit. It turned out later that I actually conducted them elsewhere. I did an Italian premiere of his concerto for trumpet and orchestra and also his suite called "Les Amants Magnifiques" which I conducted also here at the University of Washington.

As for the oratorio, the "Couer de la Matiere," in it was a baritone whose name was familiar to me, Louis Quilico, a Canadian baritone, famous at the Paris Opera where he was permanently engaged. I invited him to my apartment and we chatted very much and we became good friends. It so happened that he, the next year, was moving to Rome because he was probably engaged already to sing an opera in Naples. While in Rome I visited him with a student of mine, a singer, and he coached this kid in something from *La Bohème*. Then it turned out that he said he was singing in Naples shortly in a rare opera and would I be kind enough to come and I certainly did. I went frequently to Naples So, I went down there to the San Carlo Opera and he was singing a complete rarity, the opera *Saffo* by Pacini of whom I had never heard a note and it was fascinating—not only his work in it, but the soprano was Leyla Gencer, who sang all of these rarities with exquisite taste all over Italy. So that started our friendship and I kept in touch with Louis Quilico for years including seeing him once in Cincinnati doing *Rigoletto* much later.

As for Jolivet, he and I continued a correspondence and it was very fascinating and I have included some letters here from him where we discussed the current scene of opera around Europe which I have translated. He was very grateful for my work on his behalf by introducing his works to the Italian public and he became an extremely kind friend as long as he lived and his letters indicate this friendship and I do cherish them. I was also invited to his home for dinner with his wife and his daughter whom I occasionally took out on dates to see musical performances. But, of course, over the years these contacts just passed away. They could not go on forever.

But I will include here some letters from the great Andrè Jolivet.

(Translated from the French by Mr. Feist)

23 Sept 1969

Dear Robert Feist,

How happy we were to have received your news and to be in contact with your brilliant career. Bravo, bravissimo.

You are on track to become a conductor truly international and I am also very sensitive that we have wished you well and we have not forgotten anything about your programming in Turin some days ago which was fine. Thank you. *(He is talking about the program I did in Torino with one of his works as a premiere there)*

When are you coming back to Paris? Christine *(his daughter)* and my wife here are hoping very much to see you very soon. This is joined to our wishes that you will play a good role in our very friendly remembrances of you.

Jolivet

27 October 1971

Dear Robert Feist,

Yes, Europe is a museum and it is also a cemetery especially since they have tried completely, stupidly to copy the USA and those things have subordinated or stopped the artistic creations that we had and the financial rentability of our works. It is certain that in your big country things will continue to grow and the activities will become more and more interesting and manifest themselves with enthusiasm and sincere connections.

As far as the Far East is concerned the style of the music is beautiful even if it is somewhat hidden of complete discernment in the choice of works and interpreters that we hear. I believe as you do that you have a real interest in attaching yourself to our country. What you have done a little bit around the world will simply give people much consideration. To speak about this from a distance does no good. So we will have to wait for a French encounter. Good luck, but choose very well your point of departure. Here everything is bad. After the sickness of my wife, Christine had an accident and she is now in a hospital.

Keep me in contact with all of your projects.

Very cordially yours,

Jolivet

15 May 1971

Dear Maestro,

Finally this morning I was able to hear the disk that you have sent to us. Bravo! The voice is beautiful and there is no reason to exaggerate the appendages that the verismo composers make. They are a la mode and they are not exportable. And that brings me to the point that your orchestra is of a sobriety and a profundity that is completely classical. I am very much pleased to own the language of your wonderful qualities as a conductor. Continue your career in the Orient and the Far East. Europe is dead. In Paris—Bruck is no longer seen. Courtinot is on the point of retiring. The Opera and the Opera Comique are closed. The only chances for the lyric theaters are in Marseille, Toulouse and Rouen. Why don't you send all of your resume and the disks to those cities. These are all signs of a decadent regime in which we are living.

Continue to give me your news.

Very cordially yours,

Jolivet

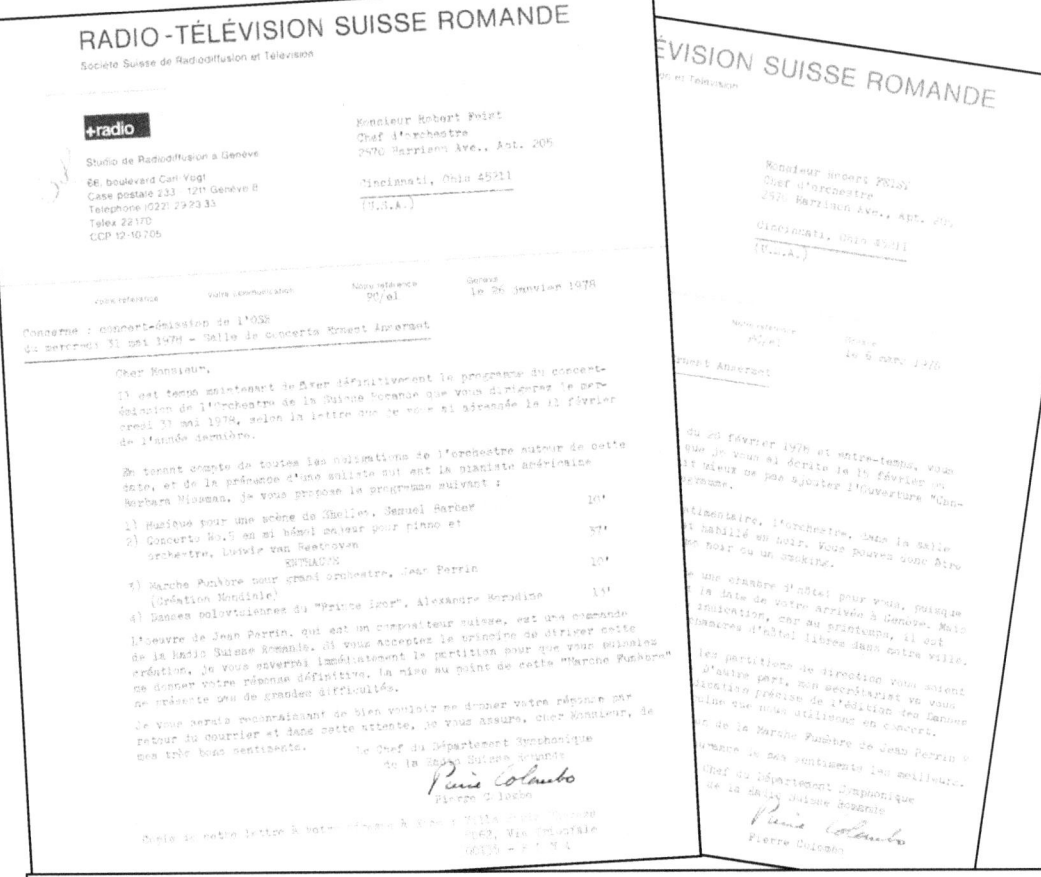

RADIO-TELEVISION SUISSE ROMANDE

le 26 janvier 1978

(Part translation by Mr. Feist in which the letter says: "It is time now to fix definitely the program of the broadcast of our orchestra which you will conduct in May of 1978." And then he goes on to say:)

...if we keep track of all of the obligations of an orchestra here and the presence of a soloist who is the American pianist, Barbara Nissman, I propose the following program:

1) Musique pour une scéne de Shelley, Samuel Barber
2) Concerto No. 5 en me bémol majeur pour piano et orchestra, Ludwig van Beethoven.

ENTRACTE

3) Marche Funèbre pour gran orchestre, Jean Perrin (Création Mondiale)
4) Danses polovtsiennes du "Prince Igor," Alexandre Borodine

I would be very happy to see you and to give you a response to your next letter and I assure you, Monsieur, of my very best sentiments.

The Chief of the Départment Symphonique de la Radio Suisse Romande,

Pierre Colombo

THE LAST GREAT ERA OF OPERA / Robert F. Feist

The Russian Museum from an "Inturist" postcard.

Eastern Europe and Moscow

Then came the big one. This was Eastern Europe. I arranged through a travel agent in Paris and I flew from Paris to Warsaw, Poland, just to stop and see it. I was only there two days because it was quite arid and quite dull. Most of it had been ruined in WWII. The buildings that were up were quite modern and looked very, very Russian. I heard there was a rehearsal of a rare Polish opera, and then I didn't need the Rockefeller name at all. I saw a little bit of the city, met a mutual friend who took me to meet their family and I did.

Then I set off for Moscow which was the highlight of the trip. So, I was in Moscow for approximately a month. Again the name Rockefeller opened all the doors because I met the Director of the Bolshoi, the chief conductor whom I had met in Milano, Svetlanov. He welcomed me and he also had become the Chief Conductor of the USSR Symphony Orchestra. So, I could go to any rehearsal at the opera. I saw many of the operas I had already seen and several new ones. And when I went to his symphony concerts I sat with the orchestra and I went backstage to talk to him about them all. He invited me to lunch one day with his first cellist who was fluent in English and German and did all the translating as I did not speak Russian. But, they were extremely kind to me and it turned out they were interested in my background in American music and they thought it would be good to have me come and conduct in Russia. By the way, the same thing happened in Czechoslovakia. But, the conclusion to these conversations did not turn out well and I will say right away why.

America, at the time, was in its cold war with the Soviet Union. They wrote to me and said: "We do not feel at this time that a program of American concert music would be acceptable to the authorities in Russia or in the Soviet Union." So, they could not arrange it despite letters between us and the conductor through his interpreter. Therefore it stopped, but I still had hopes for Prague in Czechoslovakia until later, quite a bit later, that problem was solved not to my advantage, but that is another story:

A Later Reconnection With Russia

The Russian whom I met in Moscow asked me if I intended to see other parts of Russia (or the USSR) and I said: "I had no time," though he urged me to try to visit Leningrad, as I would have liked. Well, to my surprise, it occurred much later, in 1978, when I was in the USA again and I had many meetings all over. It so happened that through a friend I had an invitation to go on a cruise, a famous final cruise of the *Kungsholm*, a well-known cruise ship.

It immediately attracted me and the cruise managers hired me on the spot as one of three guest lecturers on this arts cruise. The others; (I've forgotten their names) one a well-known professor of history, the other of art and painting in the style of his mentor, Andrew Wyeth. So we left NYC in the summer of 1978 and sailed directly to Iceland and spent a day or so in Reykjavik which was interesting and still warm. The trip took many days We went to the tip of Europe (Norway) to celebrate with a party marking the "land of the midnight sun," and then stopped in Tromsø for a shopping visit and then saw other ports and many fjords along the coast, all with stunning vistas. In Bergen I was able to go up a small mountain or hill and visit the birthplace of the famous composer, Edvard Grieg—memorable! Then more fjords and on to Oslo for a longer visit and then a long, gentle trip on the North Sea, but not stopping in Sweden or Denmark—only Helsinki for another memorable day. Then the ship went on to what is now St. Petersburg for a few days and I saw all the tourist sights, palaces, historic buildings and theaters.

Far left—At a party on the *Kungsholm* as they reached the North Cape.

I even saw a performance of *Traviata* in Italian in the Maryinsky Theater. From there we went back along the North Sea, then a canal leading to Hamburg where I had been much earlier and actually saw an agent there. On to Le Havre, the famous French port, where he took a trip up the river to visit the famous Rouen and its cathedral painted many times by Monet—all fabulous. Then we all went back to the boat for a non-stop cruise to New York, during which we lectured and I accompanied a soprano in recital and played a piano duet with another pianist on board.

Having spent all this time in Russia, I was seeing operas and it was excellent. I retreated to my hotel very often eating Russian food, which was excellently prepared in the hotel, and using a cab to go everywhere. I saw the entire city including the graveyards where the famous conductors and singers were buried and seeing the Red Square with all its glory and the tombs of Lenin and others. So, I think I saw everything of interest in Moscow. (Text is continued on page 145).

The new Warsaw Opera house, due to open at the time of this photograph in the fall of 1965.

Saint Michael's Church near the Kremlin in Moscow.

Introduction to the Letters from Russia

As for the Russians, this began not in Russia, but in Milan. As the Rockefeller grantee I had free access to any performance at La Scala given by the Bolshoi Opera their first visit out of the country. Their ballet, of course, had been all over the world, but not the opera. La Scala had already performed in Moscow, but the Bolshoi had never been out of the country until they came to Milan that fall. And, I purposely went there for that period and had access to any performance with free tickets where I could take friends which I did. The repertoire that you will see on the list is of all performances that I saw during the Rockefeller Grant. Among the conductors that I met, seeing him, Svetlanov, was the most important because he was then the chief conductor of the Bolshoi Opera.

And that is what brought on the letters, because when I left Moscow the letters began and there are only a few as you will see. But there is a reason why they are so important to me. As for the fact the American Embassy took a great interest in me as it had elsewhere and that is the reason why these letters were tranferred. First of all I must commend the American Embassies, particularly their cultural attachés in all foreign countries, for the immense help they give American soloists. And, not musicians only, but for the exchange of artists between foreign countries and the USA. I had had this experience elsewhere including Teheran. When I conducted there the cultural attaché was extremely helpful in arranging all things there for me and also in Czechloslovakia where the cultural attaché in Prague became a friend and very helpful. I visited him at his home and his office a lot. Many attachés in other countries in Eastern Europe were very helpful.

But the one in Moscow, Louis Wiener became a very helpful friend and he knew the Bolshoi conductor, Svetlanov, who was a great, great conductor. I don't think he realized then as we do now that he was the greatest. I've seen things on TV, portraits of Rostropovich and other great Russians. There were pictures of the history of these fine conductors. But they had not gotten around to doing one on Svetlanov who everybody thinks was better than them all. Svetlanov was welcomed by me through the cultural attaché who got in touch with him and he met me and let me come, as I said, to any rehearsal or performance at the Bolshoi or at the State Symphony Orchestra. After one of the concerts he did or rehearsals he invited me to dinner and with us at dinner was his own first cellist, Seva Lezhnev.

Lezhnev was his interpreter. He spoke fluent English and he could translate anything. The whole dinner went on with conversations that went from English to Russian and back and forth with the translator. Svetlanov was so impressed with what I had learned through him and what I had already learned in my career, especially in Italy, that he continued to ask questions about and wanted me to come back. I had mentioned that I wanted to conduct in Russia and other eastern European countries to do American works that they didn't know and he approved and he welcomed the idea and continued to push it hence the letters with Wiener in which you will see all his own attempts to get me engaged.

Svetlanov went so far as to suggest they accept the works I had proposed of Americans. He thought they would be excellent. Wiener did what he could do, but we could only go so far because there was always this big black image of Communist Russia hanging over us and that was "Gosconcert." This is the name of the big agency which handled all incoming and outgoing artists. If it was Rostropovich going to America or if it was someone like Bernstein coming to Russia, it had to be done through Gosconcert, the equivalent, let us say, of Columbia Artists Management. And as you see, I would have to have my agent in New York (which I didn't have at the time) contact Gosconcert with the proposal that they hire me to conduct American music in Russia, which of course, Svetlanov approved of very much. All of the extra notes and P.S.'s written by Lezhnev, his cellist, indicated the same. They were looking forward to it. This was a period that I thought would eventually work out to my benefit. Well, as we can see, it did not. We were in the times of the so-called "Cold War" and this Cold War influenced decisions on the part of management, particularly Gosconcert which as you will read was impossible to break down. You could not get me or other Americans invited to Moscow or elsewhere in Russia to perform because of the unwelcome feeling between the Russians and the Americans. This obstacle, this wall of the Cold War existed to the extent that they really did not welcome American artists until the end of Communism in 1989 when it all stopped and fell apart.

It was a shame and I noticed in Svetlanov's letters that he regretted it. He wished I had come and I wished I had come. But the letters I prize very much because he was one of the few great, great conductors I encountered and he gave much of his time to me personally. I could say that for Gavazzeni, Gui and very few others.

The same thing occurred, by the way, later in Czechloslovakia, which I intend to call it because that was what it still was then, because I was there twice. I was there in the fall and I was there the next spring after Moscow and got to know everyone at the Prague Opera House and the symphony orchestra. The conductors and the singers threw parties and invited me to their homes where I chatted with all of them in German, of course, because I didn't speak Czech. Some of them spoke English, but not many. I even stayed with one man and his wife because there was, as we say, no room in the inn. I remember all of those things because they all wanted me to come back and conduct. Even the conductors and the extra conductor, Jan Hus Tichy was probably the best known.

There so many others that I saw constantly. I can remember my birthday of that year in 1967 or 1968. I was looking at all the program of the whole country and they were doing the rare, rare Janacek opera, the one that is called *The Makropoulos Case* and it was being done not in Prague, but up in the northern part of the country in a small town, Ostrava, and I said I want to go. So, I wired them and then I went on a train arriving in town that afternoon. I was impressed by the fact that the opera director and the conductor welcomed me before the opera, gave seats to us and afterwards they took me to dinner in a hotel to honor my birthday on the day of the first time I saw *The Makropoulos Case*. The conductor of that was Zdenek Kosler. Some of his things had been seen by me here on this national culture telecast called "Classic Arts Showcase." So, I will never forget that either and the fact that the Czechs all wanted me to come back. If fact it progressed to the state that I was invited to come in the fall of 1968.

As luck would have it I flew from Australia after the second season there conducting the Australia Opera to Manila and then on to Tokyo where I had a hotel reservation and everyone knew it, including my agent. When I got to the hotel in Tokyo there was a telegram from the agency in Prague, which is like that in Moscow that invites foreign artists, and it was very simple. It said: "Unfortunately at this period of time we have just been invaded by the Russians, they have taken over our city and we cannot invite you for any American music at this time. But we hope the situation will change." Well, the situation did not change for a long time and that was my one big chance to get to the Czech Republic and conduct in Prague and it went down the drain along with the hopes for Moscow. But anyway I had no letters about that from Czechloslovakia.

The letters from Louis Wiener and Svetlanov will cover Russia and that just about sums it up and I hope the letters are of interest to all of my readers. Thank you for even taking the time to peruse them.

Letters from Ernest Wiener, the Cultural Attaché at the American Embassy in Moscow.

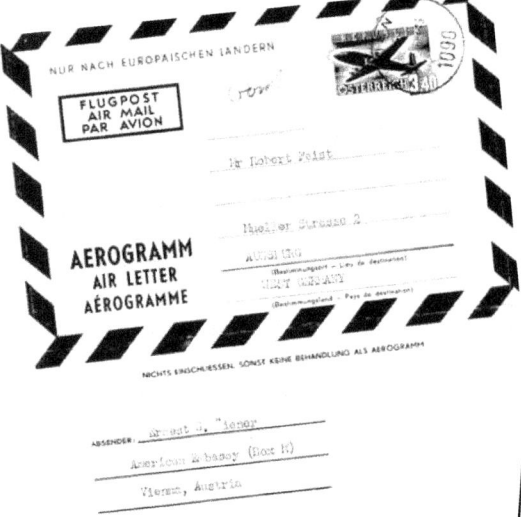

Moscow, July 18, 65

Dear Bob,

Moscow has its usual summer binge with visitors. Only it seems worse than last year. The Film Festival, 500 American chemists, Harriman and millions of others. Anyway it is a good excuse for not having answered you earlier. Also, Peggy and I took a very pleasant and interesting trip to Iran. We went to Baku to meet up with the Juilliard Quartet and Alan Hovhaness, we then took a boat across the Caspian, stayed in a very nice hotel in Ramsar, took a harrowing trip by bus over the mountains to Teheran, then by plane to Ispfahan, Shiraz and Persepolis and back by train via Yerevan, Armenia. The old mosques are simply beautiful and the whole place has a remarquable flavor all of its own.

After coming back I suffered for couple of weeks with a nice case of diarrhea, and according to the British doctor here, a bacteriological infection from it lodged itself in my right knee which has been keeping me in bed all of this week. It looks like few more days of rest and big shots of pennicilin etc.

I trust that you received the pictures from the Bolshoi which I finally obtained after considerable telephoning, never actually having talked to Chulaki himself - to whom I did write a letter on your and mine behalf after you left. By cautiously exploring the situation with Goskontsert about your arrangements with Svetlanov I got a rather discouring answer, but I have not yet been able to get together with Svetlanov himself. I'll do it as soon as I am on my feet again. Both the Russians and I would be interested in your article for the Met News.

Your experiences in Czecho sound wonderful, I am thinking of visiting there perhaps in the fall.

We have our daughters with us from Wien, the boys will be leaving for college at the end of the summer and "the old folks" will be in Moscow all alone, so I hope you will come and see us again.

I'll Let you know the developments after I have seen Svetlanov.

With best regards,

Sincerely,

Moscow, Sept. 26, 65

Dear Bob,

Thank you for your letter and your article, it was fun to read both. I decided to hold on to the article, our friends might not appreciate some of the statements.

I finally met Svetlanov at a concert he was conducting last week. There was an excellent performance of Mendelsson by Igor Oistrach and terrific Chaikovski 5th. He was very happy that you received his letter and was discussing your program with some people present. I gave him the name of your agent and he was sure that things will work out with Goskontsert. As you have probably seen in the papers, the Soviets are curtailing the spectacular parts of our exchange program but the quieter things go on. They just don't want to be caught holding hands with us in public as the Ambassador very aptly put it. But I am hopeful for the long run. We are not retaliating in kind and the Philharmonic is going to New York.

Right now they are going through the whole program and one can hear some wonderful music around here. Anyway life is pretty hectic and I am looking forward to Decmeber when I plan to take of for a month;Vienna, Berchtesgaden Prague etc

Anyway I will keep you informed on the developments for your return and as I said Svetlanov and his friends are taking it for granted. I'll see how Goskontsert feels about it.

With best regards

Sincerely

Tonight I heard Svelanov again conducting among other things Khatchaturian with Rostropovitch playing the cello, it was great!

Red Square in Moscow.

Moscow, May 17, 66

Dear Bob,

In a month from now I will be leaving Moscow for home leave in the US. On the way I expect to collect our daughters in Wien, then visit Opecho and finally take the boat from Genoa on July 6. No final word yet on my next assignment: either Washington or Brazil, I am told.

Several days ago I had the Svetlanov at my apartment for a film showing. We spoke about you and Svetlanov, who remembers you fondly, said: We won't be able to do anything this year but I think that we can get Mr Feist over here next year. Let us hope it works. At any rate I wanted you to know that this was the latest I heard.

With best regards, and who knows, we may meet somewhere again,

Sincerely,

Moscow, March 7, 66

Dear Bob,

Just a quick note to say that I saw Svetlanov the other day and gave him your regards. He had nothing to say. I find the same true of Goskontsert. As you probably know the Russian team is now in Washington negotiating the new cultural agreement. This was an important decision on their part and is definitely a positive sign. I think that we have to wait for the conclusion of these negotiations, perhaps 3-4 weeks and then there will be some more movimiento in the cultural scene.

Life here has been rather difficult over the past several months, but the writers, actors and other intellectuals do maintain contact with us and the strange reservoir of good will toward things American seems to survive all the official propaganda.

With best regards and hopefully, one of these days, more positive news

Sincerely

Mr. Feist pictured in front of the huge Moscow University.

Dear Mr. Feist,

    Finally I have a chance to thank you for very kind letter I've got from you. It was nice to know that you are well keeping and all your affairs are all right. I was touring much as well as the State Symphony did. Just only several days ago I came back to Moscow.

    Thank you very much also for very kind attention in searching the score of Villa Lobos' Symphony. If it is not very trouble to you, ask please, somebody else (I mean some publisher) for it though perhaps it might not be published yet. I only know that the piece was played in Rio de Janeiro under conducting of author himself and that was very good singer (woman) with a Spanish name (I forgot which). Also there is tape recording in our radio home and that is all. Now we are in contact with our state organization named "Gosconcert." It is the only organization which has the right for inviting all foreign artists to perform in our country.

    Please let me know immediately with whom (your impresarios, or organization) Gosconcert must contact for sending official invitation of you. I think it is a little early now to check finally the time of your coming but I think it should be wonderful if you will come here in January.

    As for programs, all of them in my opinion are perfectly good, but it seems to me that your Ist and III programs would be best to play here. I think we'll be able to play here two programs at least. But all of that must be checked with Gosconcert and you'll be informed as soon as it will be.

    As for rehearsing time please don't worry. I think it will be given enough for you. Also very important thing is about music material. All material (all parts for all instruments) you must bring with you (or sending before your coming—as it is comfortable to you, except maybe the Gershwin Concerto).

    All of us were very pleased to know that you liked your seeing Moscow and I hope that during your next visit you'll be able to hear and see much more.

    I also look forward with hope to meet you soon. All of us are waiting for you here, but not only as a good friend and also on the musical field.

Sincerely yours,
Yvgeny Svetlanov

P.S. Best wishes and regards from my wife.
(Director of the Moscow Orchestra. Translated into English by Seva Lezhnev, cellist for the Moscow Orchestra, Moscow. 2/9/1965)

Forgive me please so long silence, but there were so many troubles in my life. Sometime I'll explain you it. I think of you very often and want to see you very much. I hope that you'll be in Moscow as soon as possible and we'll be able to meet you not only as very good friend but as very good musician and conductor. I'm sure you are too. Let me congratulate you with coming of Xmas-days and the New 1967 year. My very best wishes to you and let me wish you good health, much of happiness and hopes that we'll meet each other in this 1967 year.

Thank you very much for wonderful gift you sent me. The Russians use it too and always as I use it I remember you very friendly. The smell is really wonderful.

Always your friend waiting for you,

Seva

P.S. Mr. Svetlanov asked me to give you his best wishes and regards and much happiness in the New Year. He also thanks you for letter (postcard).
(Postcard from Seva Lezhnev, Moscow)

The greatest Russian symphony conductor of that era, Yevgenyi Svetlanov, with his interpreter and cellist in his orchestra, Seva Lezhnev, in front of the University of Moscow, May, 1965. A statue of Tschaikovsky is in the background.

My dear Bob,

Mr. Svetlanov asked me to translate and write his letter in English which I did with much pleasure. Now I use this opportunity to write some words to you from myself. Our orchestra was not in Moscow during all summer. We have had summer season to play Sochi at the Black Sea and just came into Moscow one day where I get your letter, very friendly and kind. It was very good to know that you are O.K. and you've got "War and Peace." I hope it will be useful for you sometime. We came all very tanned from the south though rather tired cause it was not vacation you understand. It was too hot and dampy there. I don't like such a climate at all. Now we have a month of vacation. I hope to rest somewhere near Moscow till about October.

I hope to see you in Moscow as soon as possible. My wife and I recall you very often and she joins me in sending you best regards and wishes of a good health and much of success. Hope to hear from you soon and anxiously awaiting for your coming here. I've translated your letter to Svetlanov and found all your programs and pieces really wonderful and very interesting both for our orchestra and public and chosen with very good taste. Hope to play it soon.

That is all news for today and I'm waiting for you.

Your best friend,

Seva

Then next on the list, as the geography indicated was Bulgaria, the next country. There when I arrived, it turned out that they were full, meaning there were not hotel rooms available. Luckily I had been on the plane sitting next to an American official from the American Embassy and he was going there on business. And, he said: "Look Bob, I have a double room in my hotel. You can share it, otherwise you will never get a place to stay there." So, that was very, very kind of him and he shared this hotel room in Sofia, Bulgaria and I saw only one thing. I went to a performance once of an opera that escapes me right now, but it was not particularly impressive. I was only in the city one day and a half and the heart of Sofia was very beautiful and interesting, not having been ruined by the war, not at least that I saw. So, I departed, but I did not have any fond memories of Bulgaria.

Bucharest, Romania was the next stop on the list and Romania has been called "the Paris of the East." I did not know any Romanian and I could not use Italian, so I got by with German as usual. Well, I saw a performance of a rare opera which I had heard of, but had never seen (see list in addenda). And my stay was brief even though the photos I have of Bucharest reminded me very much of any other, let's say southern Italian town. It could have looked like Italy, Spain or France in the structure and the architecture, I admit I found it appealing, but there was not much to see. I didn't even see a museum. I saw the main streets.

So, the Bulgarian and the Romanian stays were not long, nor not terribly productive. So, there is very little to write about to the Rockefeller people.

The next stop was Yugoslavia. The former Yugoslavia, when it still had all of its members or other states and was still under Tito. I went to Belgrade, the capitol and there I saw a performance of a nondescript work that I cannot really recall. It was a ballet, I think, a ballet by a Bulgarian.

And it was dreadfully wet with rains and floods and so the whole town of Belgrade was not festive at all.

So, then I said it's time to go back to Czechoslovakia. I went by train and stopped on the way at Bratislava which is now the capitol of Slovakia. At the time, it was all Czechoslovakia. In Bratislava I heard an opera or two and roamed the city. I was only there one day and one night and then continued on my way to Brno. Brno I had visited in the fall when I was there for three weeks. Brno was really the hometown of Janáček. So, the Brno Opera became a focal

Top—Prague Castle can be seen at the top of the hill, Hradcany in the background with Mr. Feist overlooking the famous Moldau River (Vlatava in the original Czech).

Above—The new opera house in Brno, Czechloslovakia (now called the Czech Republic) due to open at the time of this photograph in 1965.

point, when I saw Janáçek's *The House of the Dead* and then I met the conductor, Frantisek Jilek. He was absolutely kind and friendly to me and gave me all kinds of pointers about the operas that I knew from the Czech Republic and I enjoyed the stay there very much. I had seen all the places where Janáçek lived and worked.

I went from there back to Prague where I was welcomed for the second time, but it was the May Festival, the "Prague Spring" where they invited many conductors and singers and everything else. I had difficulty in getting a room. Luckily for me, one of the singers I knew, Dalibor Jedlicka, a bass, said: "Bob, you can stay with us since there is no other room." He gave me permission to stay in his home; they had a guest room and I stayed there, which was very, very kind of him and his family welcomed me. Luckily, a few years ago, I was back there and I called them and talked with them on the phone.

So, this time, in Prague, it was more or less a repeat of what I had seen before. I saw many of the same operas, some new operas, but they all impressed me very much and the people were wonderful. It remains for me one of the main cities of Europe that I'm fond of and that I think I know quite well after that visit. I knew this cycle of the Rockefeller agenda was over.

I left by way of Pilsen, which is more or less on the border of Germany and was famous for their beer, the Pilsner beer, and there also I saw another unusual opera by Smetana that I had never seen before.

From there I continued on to Germany starting with Nuremberg, which I visited for a while and then came back to where I had lived in Augsburg. Well, this was late spring and I knew that I was going to have to move. It started about this by deciding to store all of my belongings including furniture in a storehouse in Augsburg, and leave my apartment to be rented by somebody else. So it was no longer under my name. There after that, I realized I would have to have it shipped to Rome which I was going to do later. So, I visited many friends.

Loyola University: Rome Cultural Center (of Chicago).

Two best friends of Mr. Feist; on the left, Frank Guarrera, long-time Met Opera baritone and Ralph Wells, a student of Guarrera and Feist in Portland, Oregon, who died suddenly on June 18, 2008, of a stroke and a brain tumor.

CHAPTER ELEVEN
Back to Rome and I Begin Teaching

Among them was my very best friend in Germany who was my doctor (surgeon) who had performed minor surgery on me. He took care of me for years and I visited him constantly even from Rome, Dr. Josef Lederle. He was the chief surgeon there and I had been at his house often for musical events and for an evening with dinner and wine. Not only that, for a few years prior to that, there had been a concert there conducted by Kèrtèsz and the guest soloist was the famed soprano from Yugoslavia, really Bosnia, by the name of Sena Jurinac. She was world famous, as I said, for her Octavian in *Rosenkavalier* and many other operas. But she happened to be at a party that Dr. Lederle gave after her concert and Kèrtèsz brought her and we met. I said:"Don't you remember we met in Rome at the Rome Opera when you were doing *Rosenkavalier* in 1954?" And, she was really, really kind. So, after a short time, I don't know how long, they became engaged and she married my friend Josef Lederle and moved there from Vienna and her career went on. She went always by train from Augsburg to Munich, to Vienna and back and kept house in Augsburg as any normal wife would have and for her, it was quite amazing. She was a charming, dedicated woman and a wonderful wife for Josef or as we called him, "Sepp." He died in the fall of 2005 and I and Sena and his other friends were saddened. She was recently profiled in *Opera News*.

The move to Rome was not difficult. I went down first to look for a place and I found an apartment that I wanted. It was very near the University and I arranged for all of my belongings to be sent to another storehouse in Rome and they were there and they stayed there for some time while I took advantage of this rented apartment of the top floor of an apartment house which was already partially furnished. It was sufficient for me at the time. And then I began my period in Rome teaching. This was in late summer of 1966. Before I was ready to teach, I found out from friends that I had known that an invitation was coming to me. In Paris I had met the man who was the artistic director of the opera in Sydney Australia. I met him through the tenor from the Paris Opera, and Lance and he had been asked to try to find me through Jurinac that he knew from Vienna because he was a Viennese-born man, Stefan Haag. So it turned out that little by little he got in touch with me, either when I was in Germany or had just arrived in Rome, saying that he had been asked before he began his European trip searching for singers, to keep a lookout for a conductor for the New Zealand Opera. Well, it turned out that through the recommendation of Lance, the tenor and Jurinac, Haag met me in this coffee shop and suggested it. I said: "Let me think about it, but tell them I'm interested." Lo and behold, soon after that I got a wire or a letter inviting me to take over the New Zealand Opera which would begin late that summer and into the fall. Well, I couldn't very well reject it. But, I had to straighten this out with the director of the Rome University. I mentioned it to him and he said: "Well, take advantage of it. You will simply postpone your beginning here until the winter quarter. You do not have to start in September when the students arrive. We would announce that you would be coming and you would begin your teaching in January." Actually I knew the tour would be over late in the fall, but it would be too late to teach an entire course that fall. But it would give me time to settle in and decide what the teaching would involve. So, I agreed and I wired New Zealand. They sent me all the details about the forthcoming tour and when I would arrive and where it would take me in that country.

I will indicate all the wonderful details of this first visit of mine in the southern hemisphere. I had never been there before and it involved not only New Zealand and Australia, but also Asia and the Middle East. On that note begins my trip from Europe by plane to America. And this time I first stopped in Boston.

CHAPTER TWELVE
Trips to New Zealand and Australia Conducting Many Operas

I chose Boston because it was the home of the son of my famous friend and great soprano, Stella Roman, about whom I have not talked much, but she was my idol, with my first experience with her in 1943 in Cincinnati doing *Tosca* with Lawrence Tibbett and Charles Kullman. I was knocked out by her voice and her personality and remained that way for the next—oh, I don't know—ten or twelve years, because I heard her there before I left for Italy. It was an amazing experience. I got to know her because I saw her backstage in the first year getting her autograph. I had then seen her every performance and every rehearsal and she was very friendly and charming. We spoke English and she would send me a photo of her with an affectionate greeting in Italian.

Over the years she sent letters and some of her own paintings because she took up painting. What amazed me was the last year in Cincinnati when she called because she was singing with the May festival again for the third time and she was doing the "Verdi Requiem" and wanted to know if I could get someone to tape it. Well, I could not, but I heard the performance and it was excellent. And I have always inquired since why she fell into oblivion. In fact, in New York, Bing did not rehire her as she told me. He would have offered her Nedda and Gutrune and that's all. So, she disappeared. She sang yet for one or two seasons in Cincinnati after Bing had taken over and in San Francisco where she was equally a star, as in Cincinnati. But no more at the Met and after that we never heard any more about her except a letter I sent to George Jellinek, due to his radio broadcast on the Met Broadcast Series and asked him why we never heard anymore of Roman. And he explained it very nicely as she had made no recordings and that was true, and only recording artists are the ones we kept hearing and hearing about in person until recently, when I found here in the record stores three CDs of Roman on Eklypse Disk of her Hollywood Bowl concert in 1950 and a complete *Forza del Destino* under Bruno Walter from the San Francisco Opera (or the Met) in 1943, or 1945 with liner notes from the well-known *Opera News* critic John Ardoin. I suggest any reader to try to locate these superb CDs in their own area. So, it turned out that this Boston trip involved her son, whom I knew and grew up with in college. He was in Cincinnati studying medicine, Flavio Romanul. We had been friends forever, but I've lost touch recently. But, I knew he lived in Boston and he had started a practice there. So, I flew to Boston first and was welcomed at his home and spent a few days with him and his wife and children who were very, very young. We even called Stella in her home in Los Angeles where she had retired and talked to her very charmingly on the phone. I had a lot of time to talk to Flavio about that.

I really did not find out more about her lack of recognition in America. She had sung all over Italy, making her debut there in 1932 or 1933 in *Chenier*. She sang in the Rome Opera for years. She was the first Empress in *Frau Ohne Schatten* at La Scala when they did the Italian premiere of that Strauss opera. And she had coached it with Strauss and she coached *Rosenkavalier* with him as well. But, it so happened that in America, after her departure from the Met, they more or less ignored her—no great accolades of any kind because there were no recordings. Yes, she did a couple. She did a "Missa Solemnis" I think, with the Philadelphia Orchestra. She made two unfortunate recordings of *Aida* and *Il Trovatore* in Rome with the Rome Opera with secondary conductors and really third-rate other singers. I never realized why she did this. I don't know who paid for it or arranged it, but she should have done it because she was more or less over her prime and should not have attempted it at that point. They have done her no good. But, all I remember, is her glorious voice and soaring top notes which domineer everything in scenes of *Aida* and yet could be reduced to a glorious pianissimo in the "O Patria Mia' of *Aida*, such as no one else had done, as one can hear on the 1994 Eklipse CD or the CD of *Forza* labeled "The Forties."

I admit that often that Milanov returned to the Met and all we have heard is Milanov in extremely positive terms as if there had been no Roman—it was all Milanov. And I think again because there were no recordings of Roman for people to measure her by. I myself was not a great fan of Milanov. I had seen her in person in Cincinnati in Aida and *Il Trovatore* and she did not measure up to Stella at all. She had trouble with coloratura and her voice could become harsh. In its best form it was fine. But, it turned out that for years and years from the Met—all we heard was Milanov. Exceptional perhaps, the importation of some soprano from middle Europe or Yugoslavia, one of whom, Daniza Illitsch did an *Aida* and cracked on a high C in the "O Patria Mia," but she never came back either. So, the story of Stella more or less ends there except for my continued correspondence with her and seeing her later in her Los Angeles home when I was in the Army and also in New York in her very final weeks of life and that I will mention when we get to that point.

By now we are back in Boston. I visited with Flavio and his family and realized his son was becoming a fine pianist. After quite a career of that he decided to try conducting and he became a conductor in Germany as I had but in the Opera House of Essen. It turned out that on one of my trips, in 1998, I was in Essen and heard an *Aida* there and looked at the list of singers and conductors and he was listed as one of the conductors, but I missed his performance. He was doing at that time. The *Dialogues of the Carmelites* and I never found out any more about him from any other source. Perhaps his career went on or perhaps it did not. Also, I had lost touch with his father, Flavio. I will pursue this some day and will try to check up on how they have all survived.

But now onward. From Boston I went on to see the Rockefeller people to tell them about what I had achieved and what I had actually done on that year of exploration. I visited other friends in New York and also my parents in Cincinnati, who incidentally had also made another trip to Germany to see me in 1959. They had first come in 1956 to Rome and to Paris. But here in 1959 they visited me in Germany in Augsburg and saw me conduct. Then we took a road tour around the southern part of Germany to Munich and all the way down to the Alps where we took the wonderful cable car that took us up to the top of the Zugspitz overlooking the entire Alps, which was a remarkable experience. They cherished it as did I.

Here it was now 1966 and I'm back again. This is only my fourth visit to Cincinnati in all those years! So, it was a nice prolonged visit because I was there studying the score of *Die Fledermaus* at home before I continued the trip. And the trip went on from there by plane to Chicago and then to Los Angeles where I stayed with some very, very good friends that I had known in college. I went from there on the plane to Sydney and then on to New Zealand. In Sydney we stopped briefly and I sent a few cards and letters and then we arrived in Wellington, New Zealand, which is the capitol. Wellington proved to be the first of all the cities I saw in New Zealand. It was extremely interesting because I found out later that country itself had an immense amount of sheep. They jokingly said there are 2½ million people here in the whole country and about 22 million sheep, which may have been true. But, everywhere you went throughout the countryside, you saw farmlands with sheep.

Well, I met the ensemble and the orchestra of the New Zealand Symphony, which if I recall correctly, played for the tour. The tour simply covered the entire country—all the main cities. We went by train, plane or by car and I remember taking much of the time by bus or car to see much of the countryside. So, after the introductions, meaning the first performances in New Zealand, where I stayed in a hotel in Wellington we went on. After Wellington, the first move was south because there are two islands. First we went to South Island and that took us to Christchurch, another very big city.

After that we went down to Dunedin. Now New Zealand goes farther down with other cities, but we didn't go that far. In Christchurch, the entire company, on a day off, were taken on a plane trip up to a wonderful mountain where they had a hotel and restaurant and everything. I have photos of that which was memorable. That was the whole orchestra and cast on this excursion to the mountain. Then we performed in Dunedin and we stayed actually, several of us in the orchestra, out of town along a lakeside which was very pleasant. All of the countryside was gorgeous. Unfortunately, we never got down to the very tip of the country and the famous lake, well it's really a gorge, and it looks like it is surrounded by a wall. It has a lagoon which has a name, which at the moment I don't have in my head and I didn't get to see that.

So, after the excursion into the southern part, we flew back to Wellington and from Wellington we went north. We stopped at several towns to give performances of *Fledermaus* and on to Auckland. Auckland was the main city, the biggest and the most commercial. On the way there I stopped in the famous Rotorua, which is a hot springs resort. It has bubbling hot springs all over the place in which I fell and dropped my camera and therefore ruined all the photos I had taken. Well, that's the way it goes if you're not careful at hot springs.

The performances in Auckland went quite well. Only once along this trip, somewhere in the middle of North Island, I had given over the baton to my assistant conductor who had been with us on the whole trip and he conducted a week of performances in this small town and then later joined us and stayed to the end of the trip. In Auckland I conducted something like a week or two weeks of opera of *Die Fledermaus* and I think that was all I could take because I'd had enough of it. But, I saw all of the country, had an excellent orchestra and met many friends. In the cast were two singers from Covent Garden in London, Victoria Elliot and Peter Grant and the others were all excellent local singers. So this experience was an introduction to that part of the country which now has grown enormously in popularity and number of inhabitants. Far bigger now, I understand, than anyone would have dreamed.

On my way back to Europe I stopped first of all in Sydney again because the Australians who had gotten me this position wanted to see me. And the manager, the one who was introduced to me in Paris, was by birth a Viennese and they were glad to hear about the New Zealand experience and said: "Look, that went so well, we would like you to join us next year here on our Australian Opera tour." At that time the Australian Opera, which was called the Elizabethan Trust Opera, due to the people who funded it, the Elizabethan Trust, used to use the orchestra of the ABC, which was the Australian Broadcasting Commission in each city that they went. The conductor would have to re-rehearse the entire orchestra that was new to these operas in the repertoire. And I realized that I was going to have to face that.

However, in the meantime, I had time off after our conversation. I saw a bit of Sydney and grew to love it very much and then flew back to Rome.

And here I must say these excursions took me around the world. I did it three times and every time I left Sydney, I chose different Asian cities to visit as a guest. I could arrange my travels as I pleased. The first time the plane just stopped at Perth, but I did not get out. So, I never did see Perth in Western Australia. However, then I had chosen Singapore. Now this was a beautiful experience because Singapore was then and is now a very clean, neat, well-behaved and English-speaking city. So, I saw very much of Singapore including the downtown area, the zoo and I must tell that there was much to see about Singapore because I never will forget. In Singapore the plane went on to Bangkok, which I had chosen.

At Bangkok was another eye-opening experience because I was there several days and saw everything that tourist would see; not only the downtown area, but I took boat trips on the canals, the streams that surround the city. There you saw people living and working on the sides of the river and children bathing in that very dirty, fluid stream. But, in addition to that, there was the beauty of seeing all the temples. There are so many of them and that whole area is filled with Buddhist monks walking around dressed in their normal garb. And then going into the temples and visiting them and seeing all the statuary and people worshiping these and outside where there were statues and relics and things of that nature. Anyone who has been to

Bangkok will know of what I speak. I did not go out of the city. I stayed more or less within the city and met a couple of German tourists. We became friends and I enjoyed that experience very much. In fact, I returned to it—I think two or more trips.

On that trip, the next stop (and it was always up to me to plan ahead of time, and unless I'm very mistaken) the next stop on that trip was New Delhi, India. New Delhi was a totally new experience, English-speaking yes, except for those who did not understand it and, of course, I had the advantages of seeing much of the history of that country, in addition to all of the poverty. I don't know when I've seen a more poverty-stricken country or city than New Delhi. On the way to the airport and back, people on the sides of all the roads to the airport were asking for money or help. These things do not leave your consciousness. In New Delhi I saw all of the monuments and churches and ruins. I saw people washing their clothes in the rivers and that sort of thing. But, the main attraction was to get out of town to see Agra. Now that is the site, of course, of the Taj Mahal and I couldn't avoid that—I just wanted to see it. It was a flight, not terribly long, maybe an hour and a half. At Agra I had a very, very nice hotel, first class hotel and they had planned for me the next day to go over to the "Taj." Well, they said: "Look it's evening and its even open now. If you want to go over, you can look at it now." So, I took a cab over and got to the entrance which was somewhat a framework that is of marble and is just an archway that you go through and you get this towering look at the Taj and the end of a long, long pool, a constructed pool, not a lake necessarily. It was all walled, but the view was astounding. I was amazed because then and the next day I determined that this was the most beautiful architectural structure I had ever seen anywhere. The harmony and beauty of that magisterial structure is indelibly etched in my mind.

I went back to the hotel, had dinner, slept very well and the next morning took the official tour to visit the Taj Mahal at Agra. And again I was astounded. But this time I walked alongside of this entire pool. I do not know if they call it a pool or a lake. The term for it is not clear to me, but it is a huge pool and surrounded by beautiful statuary and lamps and so forth. I walked along the whole length of it where you are looking up at the real Taj Mahal itself, an enormous structure that looks like a combination of church and palace which was built for the wife of the Taj, the wife of the emperor of the time. So, I saw all of that and was glad that I had not missed any of it. It was the best thing I have ever seen in India.

Then I went back to the hotel and I think I stayed that evening, and the next day went on from there to Bombay, which was planned. Bombay was short. I think I was there a day and a half and I remember only that the city was immensely crowded, but so was Delhi. Going in a taxi, when you came to a street corner, you would stop and wait until hundreds of people crossed the street in front of you. And hundreds were waiting on the sides of the street on the sidewalks. This was my main impression of Bombay.

I wanted to swim and I asked and they said: "Well, you can go to the American area where there is an American Embassy and all of its staff members." And I was able to go there and there were dressing rooms and a wonderfully large pool that was somewhat warm and it was more or less right on the Indian Ocean. You could see the ocean from there. You could sit and order food out-of-doors or drinks and swim and have a very pleasant day, which I did. Then I went back to the city and actually getting back to the city there was the usual staring and facing all the traffic. I did no business there. There was no music that I wanted to hear and that more or less ended the Indian aspect of this part of my tour.

At the airport I got into a discourse with the staff of the airplane and I told them I had a very bumpy flight from Bangkok which upset me very much and I said to them: "I really don't want to get back on this plane because I became sick even coming here. And now I have to go to Rome." And they said: "Look sir, we'll give you some medicine (which was a type of Valium really) which will calm you down. When you get on the plane you take it, and this flight should be very calm. We suggest that you get off at the next stop, just for a visit. Do not go on all the way to Rome. We are stopping in Teheran." So, I said: "Well alright." Teheran, at the time, was under the Shah. So, I had my first visit to Iran and it was very, very, quiet and pleasant. In fact, I saw it, of course, years later which I will explain in detail then. It was like a major American city; people spoke English, people in taxi cabs spoke English. They would drive you anywhere you wanted with no trouble and there were no beggars nor hitchhikers. I saw all of the famous sites, the palace of the Shah, the jewels of his wife, the museum, all of the things that tourists always get to see. It was very impressive and I was very quiet, relaxed mood and I enjoyed it very much. I knew, not then, but later, that I would return to Teheran and then I saw much more of it the next time.

But, I finished my visit and flew on from there to Rome where I was met by a friend and I went back and I stayed in a hotel because I had not yet decided where to move. I had not yet taken an apartment. Well, I stayed in the hotel briefly while I looked around for an apartment and I found one which was furnished. It was up on Monte Mario, one of the big hills surrounding Rome, very near the American University, the Loyola University campus. They knew I was arriving late because the fall quarter had begun and I was not due to teach until January. So, I used the time to really rest and to visit all my Roman friends and to make a side trip to Florence, and on to see opera at Naples and other places.

So, that period was a period of relief for about, I would say, a month or more. At Christmas, I spent it there and I went up to Switzerland to see friends of mine from Germany who were teaching in an American college, then called the American College in Switzerland, but it was changed to Fleming College, the name of the woman who founded it. My friends, who hosted me, turned out to be my best friends in Switzerland, an American couple called Nancy and David Mellon. He was the director or the Dean of this American College. I stayed at their home which was on a hill outside of the city of Lugano and very beautiful. So I saw all of Lugano and that city and they became my hosts every time I would go from Germany to Italy or from Italy to Germany. I would stop in Lugano and visit them as happened this time.

Then I went back to Rome and was ready to start my first year of teaching. Well, the first year of teaching was not a year. It started in January and ended in May because I was already starting in the middle of the year. It was the winter quarter and this was at the University of Loyola in Rome at the Arts Center which had been in existence for a long time and I was ready. Every year I really had a very large class. It could be anywhere from 49 to 60 and I lectured on symphony or opera and played a lot of recordings to introduce students to this art form. And I also insisted that they go periodically downtown to either the Rome Opera or the Academia di Santa Cecilia for a symphony concert by the leading orchestra of Italy.

So, there is very little to say about it. The teaching went very well. If I had to go away occasionally, I could do so without any trouble. As it turned out, going away occurred earlier than I thought. It was going to be in May and that meant I would be cutting the year, the spring quarter off a little bit, because I had to get to Australia in time for their winter season. And that began somewhere in June. So, I had to leave in May and the reason for leaving in May was that I had to stop for a symphony concert that I was giving in Torino again, and it went very well. The RAI was the orchestra and I was very happy to do this concert.

From there I flew back to America once again to my parents in Cincinnati, briefly, had a visit and then was on my way to Australia—Sydney this time. And that is where I met other people from the company, but they were not there—they were in Canberra and that is the capitol. So, I joined them there.

The season was already in session and I went to a performance of *Don Pasquale* that was very good and with the leading soprano, June Bronhill. She was very famous because she had left Australia many years before for London, where she sang opera and musicals and all sorts of theatrical work and made quite a reputation. (In fact, recently her death notice appeared in *Opera News* magazine on her long career). It was a great pleasure to meet her and the other members of the cast. But right away we went up from Canberra to Brisbane in Queensland. That was one of the five cities that was touched by the Australian Opera every year.

And it so happened this year was the first one in which the Australian Opera used an orchestra that was started from scratch. They had for years, as I have said, used the Australian Broadcasting Orchestra in each city requiring the conductor to simply re-rehearse every opera in each city they went to, which became very tiring. So, they made an arrangement with the union and simply hired many, many musicians and the conductor only rehearsed them for the first performance with every city that occurred in. And it so happened when they got to Canberra, I heard a *Don Pasquale* that had already been in session.

Now in Queensland, meaning Brisbane, they were doing *Tosca*. They asked me to simply take it over. It was going on already several performances and I agreed because I knew it very well. And I jumped, actually, as I recall with no rehearsal or maybe a brief rehearsal with the orchestra and did a *Tosca* with Reginald Byers who sang very often with me and a Hungarian baritone and the soprano who had never really sung the kind of repertoire formally, Maureen Howard, but she did sing many other operas with me. That performance went well.

During that particular season, a period of three or four weeks in Brisbane, the opera that I then introduced, which had been arranged, was *The Flying Dutchman* and the other was *Rigoletto*. Well, the story about the Fliegende Holländer is such that it returns us to the discussion of Roberto Bauer in Milano because the Australians had asked me if I could find

A quote from *Opera News*
February 17, 1968
Robert Feist, young Cincinnati-born conductor with wide European experience, is now in his second season in Australia, where he is leading many performances for the Elizabethan Trust Opera Company. On March 8 he will conduct the Australian premiere of *Don Carlo,* in Adelaide; his schedule also calls for *Tannhäuser, La Fanciulla del West, Die Zauberflöte* and *Tosca*. Artists to be heard during the sixth-month touring season include Antonietta Stella, Tito Gobbi and Ken Neate.

a soprano who was able to undertake the role of Senta in *The Flying Dutchman*. And I asked him for advice. He knew everybody in Milano and he suggested the American soprano called Marcella Reale who had already sung for years in Germany and Austria and Italy. He asked me to listen to her, so I went to her place and played through various arias with her and she had already heard about this, so she did the Senta aria and I thought she was excellent. It was a lyric voice tending on the spinto, but really just good strong lyric and I thought she would do well. So, Roberto Bauer agreed with my decision and so did she. She was happy to have this chance and the Australians took it immediately. So she flew to Australia with me, not at the same time, and we met and rehearsed together in Brisbane.

Now it so happened that as in the case of the *Tosca*, *The Flying Dutchman* was already on the stage and. it was conducted by a conductor who came from Perth, a symphony conductor who actually previously had been in America conducting at my own home university, meaning the University of Cincinnati, which was then called the College of Music Orchestra. He was doing *The Flying Dutchman*, being a German, I thought he was the expert there. I heard it and Marcella sang very well as Senta, but then he went off to conduct a symphony work and I took over *The Flying Dutchman* with rehearsals. However, I had two orchestra rehearsals and we did several performances in Brisbane before we moved on to another city. In addition to that I conducted another *Tosca* or so.

Don Giovanni also appeared in that season in Brisbane and Marcella Reale undertook the role of Donna Anna which actually was done in English in this production. I did not conduct it then. I did one later on in Sydney, but not then. And *Rigoletto* came up. Donald Smith was the tenor and Raymond Myers was their leading baritone at the time. He did many operas with me. In fact he did the role of the Dutchman as well in *The Flying Dutchman*.

The leading bass was in the *Don Giovanni* and also in *The Flying Dutchman*, a bass that they had had for years. His name was Neil Warren-Smith. But here the tenor was Donald Smith and he was excellent. He had a long career in London at both Sadler Wells and Covent Garden, often taking over roles from people like Corelli and he was really a superb tenor. The production was fine and I enjoyed it and we had very, very good results.

Then the opera company moved by plane, as is the custom there, and the orchestra, chorus and singers all flew at the same time and we flew down to Melbourne. Melbourne was the second biggest city we touched upon after Sydney, but we didn't get to Sydney until the end. So we did these operas there and the other works that I was scheduled to conduct premiered there. So, the opera was one of the three or four in the repertoire in Melbourne and we enjoyed it. There was very little sight-seeing to do. We saw the city, of course, on days off, when I was not conducting, and also we all had trips out of the city, around to see the countryside.

The same happened with the next stop, which was Adelaide, another city that was considerably British, but Melbourne is considered to be the most British of these cities in its heritage and style, more or less quiet and intellectual. Adelaide was a little more fun and we had time off so I could go to a health club and swim and workout and to keep more or less, in shape. The Adelaide season was again about three weeks and we did the same operas there, all successfully. We added one more and this was another opera that I was in charge of and it was Puccini's *Turandot*. The *Turandot* is not very hard to do, but we had a cast that was excellent. We had a soprano who had been with them for some time called Morag Beaton and she did it very well; some trouble with the top, which was tight, and which was customary with many sopranos, but did it very well. The Liu, Rosemary Gordon, was an Australian of, I think, German heritage and she was a very excellent lead but Morag would have been better suited to the role such as Donna Elvira, which she also did, and roles tending to be more dramatic than Liu. There was again Donald Smith, the hero of all these operas and he did a very good job as Calaf. So, the *Turandot* turned out to be a success and he did that throughout the tour in the other cities as well.

Soon after that we returned after a break in which we had time off in Adelaide. I was able to go down to the coast of the Indian sea. I don't recall which sea it was, but Adelaide is on the ocean and a favorite vacation spot. I could look it up on the map, but I'll just say it was the Indian or Pacific Ocean. So, we went there, just a few of us and went swimming and water skiing, which was fun because I had learned it there and did it a few times. I had done it first in Italy but reprised it there and it was a good vacation.

But finally we ended up in Sydney on the tour. The opera house, of course, the one we all know was not yet built. It was in the process of being built. It was started but was not at all finished. It wasn't finished for many, many years. So, we performed in her Majesty's Theater, one of the big, old theaters that would have been a movie house at one time, but it was fine

Clockwise from above—Mr. Feist with the famous soprano Antonietta Stella at the new Sydney Opera House still under construction in 1968. Mr. Feist feeding a wallaby and enjoying holding a cuddly Koala bear at the zoo in Sydney, Australia.

for opera and we did the entire repertoire there, which included the *Rigoletto, Tosca, Turandot, The Flying Dutchman* and *Don Giovanni*. Somewhere in the course of these productions, all of which I conducted and enjoyed very much, they asked me to take over a performance of the *Don Giovanni* because apparently the conductor had to leave. So, I did one *Don Giovanni* in Sydney as well as the other operas. So, it was quite a struggle undertaking so many works, though I was not really the prime conductor for *Don Giovanni*.

So, the season ended with a bang. There were many parties during the course of the tour and after the final night, there was a big farewell with many of the people. But, I knew I was coming back, because they asked me. They said: "well, they liked what you have done and would like you to come back next year?" I said: "I agree." So, we decided on the repertoire which would be the next year and that concluded that and then I left again for Rome. As I had done before, I chose another route, a route that took me through Asia and places I had not been to. Well, they had just had an earthquake or a tornado I don't recall which, and it had happened in Manila. Manila was my next stop. I had never been there and friends urged me to go to Manila which became for me then, another regular base. So, I flew to Manila having talked to them by phone and they said come anyway. So, I went, and heard a performance of the orchestra, the Manila Symphony, and met the wonderful woman, An American woman, who was in charge, more or less, of the symphony, although she was not the artistic director.

This was a wonderful lady called Carlyn Manning, whose husband had been there for years and welcomed her as his bride when they went there later and he was in charge of one of the big auto producing companies from America that settled in Manila. They lived in a very wonderful and expensive home, that was on the outskirts in a quiet residential neighborhood. But, I was in a hotel where occasionally I felt the reverberations of aftershocks from the earthquake and you could feel the movement on the 8th floor of the hotel and you could see the chandelier shaking, but it did not interfere with our rehearsing the symphony concert, just one, and it went exceedingly well.

I was very glad to do it and they welcomed me wholeheartedly, especially the orchestra's concertmaster, who became a friend. I will always remember the orchestra and they did their very best. It was quite a good orchestra. There were parties in between, and time to sight-see around the city including areas that were very unpleasant. It is not all a glorious city. The main street which had all the embassies, right along the ocean side and was quite nice and others area were not. But I had a chance to exercise and work out in the health club and visit other people.

That ended that season, as I said, in Manila, which was just that one concert. This time I flew from there straight on to Bangkok; there was no Singapore this time. I was in Bangkok just a couple of days as I was before, looking around, seeing the temples and the pagodas and all of that. It was a very pleasant stop on the way. In Bangkok the plane went on again and this time, oddly enough, it just stopped briefly in Burma I never expected that, so I got out for one minute and put my feet on the ground in Burma, which now, of course, has now changed its name to Myunmar. But I did at least see the airport.

From there the plane went on and this time there was no New Delhi involved, but we went right to the mid east and we stopped in Beirut, Lebanon. Beirut was then calm and quiet. Nothing was happening politically or warlike. So, the visit in Beirut was pleasant and I had a special trip that took me up to the mountains where they had had for years, a festival outside of Beirut in Lebanon. It was Baalbeck.

After visiting this historic site with ancient ruins set in the mountains, I went back to Beirut and spent a day or so. My hotel was actually next to the hotel where all the members of the German airline were staying, and that was *Lufthansa,* and we visited occasionally. From Beirut I went on to a neighboring, more or less, neighboring area which was Tel Aviv, and in Tel Aviv again things were quiet. The so called "Six-Day War" that had ensued was now over. It was the first time one could visit calmly and quietly. So, I was in Beirut first, then went on to Tel Aviv where I took side trips that took me to Jerusalem which I saw in its entirety and part of it belonged to Jordan at the time. It was divided. Israel had much of it and Jordan had another piece of it. We saw Nazareth and Bethlehem—all very interesting to me, as well as the historic Christian and Jewish sites in Tel Aviv itself—a very interesting trip.

From there we went on to Rome. There was nothing in between that. I was going to see friends and people were going to pick me up. So, I moved into my apartment. No, I'm sorry, it was not then, if I think back carefully. My furniture was still stored in a warehouse in town and I took an apartment of a friend of a friend. He was in the business world. This was an apartment, a very nice one, in a, more or less, new section of Rome, only a only a few miles from the University itself, near the Piazza Balduina, halfway up this big hill, but very heavily populated and very quiet.

So, that year began for me, in the fall, in September. This was the second year, the one that started in the fall and it went very well. The same situation as before with teaching, more or less, everything I knew about opera and symphony to big classes of students who were also taking courses in art and art history with another professor and learning all about the cultural world of not only Italy, but of the world. All the professors were excellent, from Chicago or elsewhere, clergy or laymen. One who became a famous lecturer on the Met Opera broadcasts in our era was M. Owen Lee, a priest and friend.

There were times of departures as usual, but this year went along fairly consistently. We had classes until December, at which time there was a break, and then we would resume in January and continue until May or early June. During this year I got to know many of the faculty better and I also got to know quite a few of the students; those who were, more or less, receptive and intelligent. I invited, occasionally, a few to my apartment for a drink or a pasta dinner. There was conversation which made them happy because they got to know more about my history and the history of Europe So, I kept up with quite a few of them; I think, perhaps, six or seven. Over the years they remained in contact with me by letter, cards or phone, chiefly perhaps my only musician student, who lived in Rome and visited often for years, and is now famous, Carlo Pezzimenti.

Now we are actually in the winter of 1968. The year of 1967 had been in Australia, the first tour until fall and then I did the fall quarter at the university. And when we came along to 1968 another departure occurred, always in concurrence with the directors of the Rome Center at the University of Loyola. This was to accommodate the second tour that I did in Australia, which was the most important one. It involved my departure from Rome somewhere in early January as I had to start rehearsing in the summer—which for us is winter, in January in Sydney. So, I flew, more or less, directly from Rome, in January, to New York, and then on to Cincinnatti. Someone else took my classes over that year—the entire period from January until May when I was not in Rome at all.

The second tour to Australia turned out to be even more eventful than the first. And I had several important works to do. Among them, or the most important of them was basically the

Clockwise from above—Conductor Feist rehearsing the Manila Symphony. Conductor Feist and solo violinist, Oscar Yatco at a performance of the Manila Symphony in a huge outdoor park in 1970. Mr. Feist on the stage of the new Manila Cultural Center of the Arts.

Australian premiere of Verdi's *Don Carlo*. They had thought about this and wanted to do it the year before, which would have been the 100th anniversary of its world premiere in Paris. But we didn't get it done at that time.

We postponed it. So, we came up with the 101st anniversary for Australia And so, when I got there, I knew that I was facing two operas, *Don Carlo*, in a premiere, and the other was *La Fanciulla del West*. This premiere of *The Girl of the Golden West* took place in Australia and it was in the year 1968. The order of the premieres for the performances, I don't recall exactly. We rehearsed very, very much in Sydney and that was where all the orchestra rehearsals took place.

There was much time in between to get out of town and go to the beaches and see all of the city. I lived in a motel that was quite near King's Cross—which was the center or focal point of all the activity, somewhat like the Times Square of Australia. Therefore we didn't immediately premiere those operas there, we simply embarked on a season, and the season started in Canberra which was, of course, the capital.

Then the tour took us to Brisbane, then Adelaide and Melbourne and finally Sydney. We ended up there always. The operas that year included not only *Don Carlo* and *Fanciulla*, but also again *Rigoletto*, *Tosca* and another Mozart opera, *The Magic Flute* as well as Wagner's *Tannhäuser*, which I knew was going to catch up with me sooner or later—though I had done one or two of them in Germany. And so, little by little, the season progressed. We moved from town to town by plane and did the performances usually within a three-week period of four, the largest being in Melbourne and also in Sydney. I had time, in between, when I was not working, to use the various health clubs in the city to keep myself, more or less, in shape. And usually, after a performance, several of us would go out to a neighboring restaurant, which would be open at that hour which was quite unusual at ll:00 p.m. at night; and we would have our late dinner there.

Again we had a very good assembly of singers and I'll mention first of all that we did the *Turandot* with Morag Beaton, and Donald Smith was the tenor and we also did *Rigoletto* again with the same cast, and we did *The Magic Flute* Now this year we had another conductor who was engaged as our symphony visiting conductor. They had no general music conductor or principal conductor in either of those two years in Australia. That came later with Richard Bonynge. So the two years that I was there, I was simply one of the two or three conductors.

The first year had been with a German, who did *The Flying Dutchman* and this year we had Carlo Felice Cillario who was known for all of his performances in Italy and especially the final performances of Maria Callas in Paris and in London.

The repertoire was divided, I thought very strangely, because I did *Fanciulla* and *Don Carlo* and he did *Tannhäuser* and *The Magic Flute*, both in German which was not his language. He also did *Tosca* initially and I took it over later. But, there was no use quibbling about it; not being familiar with the German language, he conducted it as one would, not knowing the language he is conducting. It was alright, but I do not think he was ideal because many of the tempi he used in *Tannhäuser* were certainly not the sort that you would hear in a German production.

Getting back to the casts; I mentioned the *Fanciulla* cast, which had Reale and Smith and Alan Light, and it was very successful. When we got around to *Don Carlo*, it took place strangely enough in Canberra. It was because of the fact that the soprano engaged was the very great Antonietta Stella, whom I may have mentioned earlier and had become my favorite.

In my mind and in my heart she replaced Stella Roman from my youth as the greatest spinto soprano. I had heard her so often in Rome for years doing all of those roles—all the Verdi roles, even *Butterfly* and *Tosca*. So, here she was in Australia. They had imported not only Stella but Marie Collier from Covent Garden, who was an Australian but had a big career in London. Tito Gobbi even joined us for several months and also Marcella Reale and a few other guests. So, it was a prominent season, I would say. Well, when we got around to doing the *Don Carlo*, it was rehearsed very well from scratch because no one had ever sung it except Stella and that was back in Italy. She was the Elisabetta and Alan Light who would sing the Grand Inquisitor. The King Phillip was the bass whose name mentioned when I was talking earlier about *The Flying Dutchman*, where he did the bass role. This was Neil Warren Smith, the leading Australian bass who then or later sang several times in London and Covent Garden. He was the King Phillip and was excellent.

Reginald Byer, who had done many things with me; *Rigoletto* and *Tosca*, was the tenor lead of *Don Carlo* himself and was fine. Raymond Myers popped up again who had done *Rigoletto* and other operas. He was the Posa In addition to that we had an excellent; well, we had two, actually, Ebolis. One was Lauris Elms, because she had gone to London and became a very prominent figure there recording several operas with Joan Sutherland. And, as a matter of fact, she was a very good Eboli. But, we had to have two for just programming reasons, and the other one was the soprano Morag Beaton, who had sung *Turandot* with me.

So she sang alternately with Elms as Eboli The only one in the cast that I hadn't mentioned was the Count Lerma by Ian Campbell, now Artistic Director of the San Diego Opera! What a small world! I even went down from Seattle to San Diego to visit him and hear several operas there, plus meeting Richard Bonynge, Joan Sutherland's husband. So, the cast was excellent and the performances went very well and received great acclaim.

I suppose mainly because it was a first production for Australia, and because the cast uniformly sang well and I would say also due to the presence of Stella, who was introduced to the press personally, and with me as her translator and interpreter, and she fit in very well. She just played along with us. We went hiking together when we were up in Brisbane. We went down to the ocean and took hikes along the beach with Cillario and with Myers and with Reale and we had many good times together. I even have pictures of us at the zoo holding kangaroos and koala bears. This is very much fun to look at. In addition to that, Stella also was just a fine artist to work with and to have lunch with or have a drink after a performance and we often reminisced about her own career. This was her first time there in Australia and her first trip which then took her to the Asian cities.

She went to Korea, and, I think, Japan after that. She did not sing originally the *Tosca*. The *Tosca* which premiered, I think, in Melbourne, was sung originally by Marie Collier, a native Australian, and Tito Gobbi who was very, very well-known, of course, all over the world. The tenor was Donald Smith, as usual and Cillario conducted it. He did a few performances. I do not remember how many and then his term was up or his contract. So, he left and I took over the *Tosca* and I had as my cast first of all, a few performers with Marie Collier and with the new baritone, who was Raymond Myers, whom I had done many things with. Then later it changed again because Marie Collier had finished her contract and went on to visit her relatives or something in Melbourne and Stella moved in.

Well, this was a supreme moment for me because for me to conduct that famous woman, whom I had heard so often, right in front of me doing *Tosca* and the rest of this superb opera as long as she was there—which lasted throughout the whole season, was a thrill of course.

She also did at the same time all the performances of *Don Carlo*. So, I don't know in general how many I did—quite a few with her and we became very good friends, a friendship that continued after I returned to Rome.

So, we had moved around from city to city and ended as usual in Sydney with these performances and there was a lot of acclaim and a lot in the press and parties and so on. I was very glad that I was healthy and well through the whole thing and we all got along very well with no strife whatsoever.

The only thing that happened was that at the very end of the tour in Sydney, after the departure of the conductor, Cillario, I had to take over from him, a performance or two *of The Magic Flute*, which I did having already known it in Germany. And I also took over two performances of *Tannhäuser* There was no rehearsal for me. I just jumped in and we had a cast change. There were two different baritones; one was Raymond Myers and the other was John Pringle, who jumped in for the last performance. The bass was Donald Shanks. The soprano was, of course, Marcella Reale, who had done all of the *Tannhäusers* on this tour and in addition to that we had a very, very well-known Australian tenor. This was Ken Neate, who actually just popped up recently in an issue of *Opera News* for some other reason. But he had had a huge career. He had gone from Australia to Europe and he studied in Paris with a very well-known teacher, as did Lance. He came to Italy, made his debut, sang many operas all over Italy, including a very wonderful TV production of *The Girl of the Golden West*, which was just now mentioned in *Opera News* and which I happened to see when I was in my first year in Rome.

I saw part of that *The Girl of the Golden West* with Frazzoni and Mario Petri. It happened that Ken Neate moved on. He sang in Paris and elsewhere in France and then he moved to Germany. He took on not only the heavier roles, but some of the roles that he had missed in his younger days—even learning some of the Italian roles in German which was the case of the time. Ken Neate and his wife of the time, who came with him, was a great pleasure, and we kept our friendship up for many, many years.

So, the season ended. I was glad to do the *Tannhäuser*, though it is not my favorite work, and I did not like the production very much. But we ended it with *Don Carlo* or *Tosca* and then the season was over and it was time, if anybody wanted to stay around, to have parties and such. I saw many old friends that I had met in the city including people in the American Embassy. The man who was the American Ambassador and the American Cultural Advisor and I were invited to parties-we all were-at the home of the Italian Prime Minister at the Italian Consulate. This included the Italian Ambassador and also, of all people, the Brazilian Ambassador who had been a friend of mine from a prior experience. All these were in Canberra, the capital.

So, there were many parties at many embassies and it all made it very worthwhile and very important for all of us. In fact, the Australian experience remains so strong in my mind because of the fact that very recently the people in the archives, a conductor, assistant conductor and others found it was important to cherish or to keep a catalog of outstanding performances on CD.

Luckily they asked many of us if we had had any tapings done. In Sydney I asked people to come to mike and to tape performances from somewhere. One was from the orchestra pit. Another was from the box on the main level of the auditorium. So, I had tapes of my *Tosca*, *Fanciulla del West*, *Don Carlo* and *Tannhäuser* and maybe something else. Well, they called from Sydney and asked me did I have the originals and I looked around and I did. I had the original reel-to-reel tapes which are more authentic than something dubbed. so, I sent them down and they were produced.

They were produced on the label of the Australian Opera and they are now out on CD, but I don't think they are at all purchasable. They were meant only to be in the archives for the Australians, who wished to hear them They can maybe get a copy if they are subscribers to the Australian Opera. The general public cannot buy these.

Luckily, I have two of these operas that I cherish very much; particularly the recordings of *Don Carlo* with Stella and the *Tosca* with Stella, which is quite superb. Even though occasionally, as in *Don Carlo*, the voices are too far back from the stage and the orchestra and you don't hear them as clearly. But in *Tosca*, they're right there in front. The main benefit of the period that after I left there, we were getting these recordings. But they came much, much later. We had no idea this was going to happen.

My flight back to Rome again involved some stops in Asia. I stopped in Tokyo to meet the American ambassador there seeing if there was any chance of conducting there, but there was not. Then I went on to Hong Kong for a brief visit and went on from there to Bangkok briefly and then I think the next big jump was from there to Italy. I don't remember any other place in between.

So, this brought me back to Italy Basically at the end of that would have been a school year, 1968. By the time I got back there it was July or August and then we were preparing to go into the next fall teaching season, which would have been the fall of 1968. I just checked my CD of the *Don Carlo* which concluded the season in July, 1968. So, I got back to Rome probably in August of that year and resumed teaching in September.

Robert F. Feist.

CHAPTER THIRTEEN
Teaching in Rome and an Invitation to Perform in the Mid-East and North Africa Introductions To The Letters from Maestro Gavazzeni adn Letters from Maestro Gui

The next years went on very calmly and normally. I had my normal set of classes in Symphony and in Opera and the only absences that occurred was when I went off somewhere to conduct, all of which was allowed, and which kept me in the circuit in Europe. Among the absences that I took from Rome was the first experience in Naples conducting at the Teatro San Carlo which was famous for ages. It had been run by Rossini for a period in his career and where many of his operas were premiered and it was a jumping off place for countless singers who made their debuts there. It is a gorgeous opera house, perhaps more beautiful than any other in Italy—sitting right in the center of town, next to the royal palace and across the street from the Galleria, a gallery famous for it arcade and shops which were celebrated in a book by John Horton Murray, called *The Gallery*, which I had known since high school.

In San Carlo I had met the management earlier through Maestro Gavazzeni, going down there for business They called and wrote to engage me and in November of that year I made my debut there in a program they thought would be appropriate. It was all American. It involved the engagement of an American pianist, Chodak, who played the "Gershwin Concerto." I did the Symphony No.1" by Samuel Barber, which was difficult as it had been earlier in Palermo and shorter works. Well, the concerto, the whole concert was so successful they invited me back several times. I admit that the orchestra made up of good musicians would tend to be a bit sloppy or not paying enough attention. They often had their coffee cups under their seats and they would take a sip of cappuccino or caffé and they were always looking forward to lunch time to have their "big pranzo," however, when they pulled themselves together at the rehearsals, the performance was worth it. The next time that I went back was a year later for a different sort of concert involving a guitar, but I will get to that later.

During the course of the school years, nothing particular happened of great excitement in the school. But in 1970 something occurred that has been every since fixed in my memory because Marcella Reale was awarded the "Puccini d'oro" or the Golden Puccini 0prize for singing in Italy—an award given very occasionally and with that came a recording. I was chosen to be her conductor and the recording was, of all things, to be done with the Rome Opera Orchestra, which was a great thrill. We did it in a recording studio in Rome and we had several sessions to do it in. The recording was meant to be all verismo and some unknown verismo. There are some familiar arias by Puccini from *Boheme, Tosca, Fanciuilla* and there were many, many unusual works that had not been heard before. Perhaps they had been recorded in 1920 by someone and forgotten, but here they were again. Recording of arias by Cilea, Giordano, Zandonai, Mascagni, Alfano, and things that people were not aware of at the time. Even the orchestra was not aware of them. They had not played them. So, these recording sessions remain fixed in my memories as it was done in the summer when it was quite warm, but they went very well.

A very good friend, my best friend in Rome, Marco Verciani, was the chief contra-bass, the bass of the Rome Opera Orchestra and he was not playing, but he became my assistant in testing hearing how the recording was going and giving me suggestions. So, this recording took place in 1970 and was issued on the label that was familiar to all of us—Cetra. When I was growing up in America you always got recordings from Italy with singers on Cetra-Soria. Mr. Soria was an American in the recording business. He acquired all these Cetra rarities and added his name to Cetra—making it Cetra-Soria. Well, it turned out that in Rome when we did this it was issued by Cetra, but there was no Soria attached. It was simply called Cetra preceded by Fonit Cetra. Marcella acquired many and so did I to give to our friends and they were also famous because of the amount of photographs of Marcella in various costumes and the history of verismo.That was a superb account of that period in history which was written by our friend William Weaver, who had for years been a critic in Italy and a writer. He had written many books and appeared in America for ages at the Metropolitan Opera as one of the broadcast guests, one of the people who was on the quiz panel or as a lecturer in some phase of opera. Everyone in America is familiar with the Met broadcasts on the radio. At this time he was not yet that well-known, but he was known in Italy and he was engaged to write this superb history of verismo, which I cherish to this day. As a matter of fact, Marcella just asked for a reprint of it for another purpose for another record.

Well the record had a lot things going for it and loads of press reviews.

Also in that same year I returned to the Teatro San Carlo in Naples with a guitar soloist, Diego Blanco, who performed the guitar concerto by Italian *Castelnuovo Tedesco* and in addition, the American soprano, Irene Oliver, who had been in Rome for years studying, was announced as the soloist and she and I did two selections that were wonderful: from Barber's "Knoxville Summer of 1915"and also she did the "Cantilena" from the "Bachianas Brasileiras No. 5" of Villa-Lobos with the leading cellist of the orchestra as a soloist with her. It was excellent. I did a lot of small symphonic works by Copland, Mennin, Barber, Gershwin and others.

So, it was a program made up of many short works, but all very effective. It was well-received. I would say particularly the work with which I closed it and did in many concerts in Europe, the "Schuman: Variations On America," a work written by Charles Ives and orchestrated by William Schuman, and it always draws enormous reception. And it did for me there and elsewhere in Europe.

After that I returned to Rome and I had a normal year teaching, with certain absences, for various reasons—either conducting or for just visits to other places. I returned to Torino in addition to Naples and at one point had a concert at the other chamber orchestra in Milano at the Pomerigii Musicali which was attended then by my mentor Gavazzeni who then gave me push and also credit for having done a fine concert. Speaking of Gavazzeni also brings me to Gui and the others.

Over the years I kept up with some of them. I met Maestro Tullio Serafin, the best name of all, through all of the reviews at the Met, his discovery of Callas, his promotion of her and all his work and recordings. I met him in Rome after a performance, then saw him in Naples and heard him there and asked him later if I could visit him. So he accepted that and brought me to his apartment in Rome and talked to me about my career. Well he was aged by that time. He had no particular suggestions. He thought I was doing the right thing having learned so much under the conductors of the Rome Opera and also being in touch with Gavazzeni and Gui. He just wished me the best, but he wrote me a very nice letter and when I think of the time it took to write letters, I'm astounded at the letters I received from Gui and Gavazzini—I think some 23 to 30 in all. Whenever they were on a tour, let's say to Palermo or to Florence to do an opera, they would have time off between performances. Well normally if they go to Florence to do an opera, they would have time off between rehearsals, and they would just rest. But then (these two) would always take the time to sit down and write by hand or at home by the typewriter a letter to me, a personal letter replying to my requests and my comments with their questions, commenting on my career, what they had done, and they are very personal and cherished possessions and some of them will be included I will insert some letters. (Text continues on page (204).

Above—A photograph and remembrance to Mr. Feist from Maestro Gavazzeni signed: "As a cordial remembrance, 1985.
Right—A dramatic photograph of the great Maestro Gavazzeni conducting.

Introduction to the Letters From Maestro Gavazzeni

In an article from *Opera News* from 1977 is one of the few if only articles that appeared or that I read on this wonderful maestro in any newspaper or magazine in the USA, thought he was extremely prominent in Europe. I met him as a student in Rome when I was assisting him playing piano rehearsals and doing all the backstage work for his many productions there along with the others. So, I was able to access all the Italian conductors. Many were better known in the U.S. In periods of time, they were at the Metropolitan Opera, such as Vincenza Bellezza, di Fabritiis, and of course, Tullio Serafin, who was the best known. He was there for a long time, perhaps 20 years and at the same time La Scala and everywhere else in Rome. So, he got to be known all over in American more so than the others. The reason Gavazzeni was not known was because he was somewhat a reclusive person, meaning he was not out searching for publicity. He was extremely competent and a clear-cut musician and many people considered him didactic or even cold. It did not. I found him *somewhat* cold or somewhat unfriendly, but not open as other people are.

Yet he welcomed me whenever he saw me and when I got to play rehearsals with him he was very happy and was very congratulative. As a matter of fact, soon after I got to know him he began corresponding with me. I would write in the period when I was in Germany at the opera house there and he would reply which surprised me. But, I was grateful for this amazing return of interest in a student whom he watched mature over many years.

Then began this constant exchange. Sometimes his letters were typewritten, and sometimes they were not. But they covered an extensive period indeed, including when he was conducting at the Metropolitan Opera in 1976. At that time I had just returned to American and he invited me to his performance of *Trovatore* and afterwards to his apartment in New York after the performance and we had hors d' oeuvres and wine with his wife. The next day I accompanied him on a walk down Fifth Avenue to St. Patrick's Cathedral where his wife was attending a religious ceremony. We walked back with her, which was a pleasant thing. Now this is a culmination of many, many years because he kept up with my career through all his notes and remembered everything I had written and made comments as you will read about why the situation in Italy was bad and why the situation in Germany was not as good as it should have been and so forth. He apparently was not happy with the critics because he said the critics (especially in Milano) disliked him as in Rome too. He had rather hard terms for them, as you will read.

He was very clear in his approach to all the operas. He knew them backwards. He studied profusely as a young man, as a pianist and later as a conductor. And, not only his studies in that, but he watched everyone else and I think he grew in his appreciation through watching great conductors, such as Serafin and even some Germans he admired. So, he was very, very straightforward and stuck to the text and stuck to the notes as we would say. That is why I got to admire him and he always had a pleasant greeting for me.

When I was out of town and I would come to Rome, let's say I was in Germany, he would invite me after the performance to have dinner with him at a restaurant where he used to go as a student. On the other hand, when I went to see him conducting at La Scala, which was his home base, and where he was artistic director for several years, he always gave tickets to me through his assistant and afterwards I could visit him and we would go out again to have a dinner or bit to eat or something like that. He never minded. He liked to do this and he would share insights with me. That continued all the way up to until he came to leave La Scala to go to the Montreal Expo of 1976. But he came again a few years later in 1984 or so and brought La Scala with him to Vancouver, British Columbia which is just north of us. We had corresponded before that. In fact, he talked to Kurt H. Adler, the Artistic Director of the San Franciso Opera about me, However, when he was in Vancouver, he invited me up and of course I went there and I took a friend, a woman friend, that I had known for a long time who lives in Vancouver and gave us gratis tickets to this wonderful performance out-of-doors in a big arena, almost an arena, where they did Verdi's *Lombardi* and I had seen him do that in Rome with Pavarotti and Scotto many years before. It plainly was the first time they had done it in Canada. After the performance, as usual, I went backstage and saw him. I even saw him getting a doctor's examination. They always had the La Scala doctor some along on these kind of trips. He promised he would write to me or send me a photo when he got back to Italy, which he did. But I never saw him again because I never went back and he, of course, did not come back to Canada or America. Where we find a lot of amazing introspection in his letters, there was not just a lot of casual chitchat but always reflected what he was thinking about at the moment. This is why many of the letters are quite brief, even a few sentences or a few paragraphs, unless he became enthused about a subject. It was his faithful recognition of me as a student and a conductor that really made me feel so good.

So, the contact with Gavazzeni was very important. Why he is not world-wide known is a mystery. I think it is because he spent most of his time in Italy conducting all over, mainly at La Scala. Occasionally he would be with them in another country such as Spain or Germany or even Edinburgh where he conducted often. But, very seldom did anyone else know of him because he was not the "show-off" many conductors are—such as the ones who followed him. Even conductors such as Oliviero de Fabritiis, who was well-known all over Italy, but he was not nearly as good as Gavazzeni, but he conducted in San Francisco regularly and that is why he was known in America for nearly ten years.

Other conductors that were very, very well-known surpassed Gavazzeni in public recognition because of their constant moving around to other countries; not that they were better, but they were constantly on the move to make themselves better-known. I can really say that I can't think of any other conductor who would have taken the time in the middle of rehearsing and performances or at home to write me so many letters. I haven't counted them, but between he and Gui, maybe 30 letters over those 22 years. It is really amazing and I am eternally grateful for his contact and for all I learned from him; all of which I marked in my scores, and particularly one thinks of special things such as being asked suddenly to play a rehearsal with piano of the second act of Puccini's *Manon Lescaut* with my favorites at the time, Petrella and di Stefano, which was a real, real joy.

Baveno (Novara) Villa Franca
August 1967

Dear Feist,

I received your letter and I am very happy for your successes and your activities. That which you tell me of the fervor of musical Australians is very interesting. *(I had just come back from the first year of conducting there).* Just like in Italy where the music is always more tired and sleepy—I've had a very, very unpleasant year—an irritating year. I had had hopes of reposing my nerves and my mind even if I am not conducting. We are going to Montreal soon with La Scala in October then back to Milano. I am going to write to Dr. Paone to make him remember you.

Many greetings and most cordial salutes.

Porta Dipinta, 5
Bergamo Alta
September, 1966

Thanks for what you tell me about *Aida* at La Scala (which I heard). As far as opera is concerned what are we going to do with the critics and the public who speak English. It doesn't work. Well, have patience. By now they are speaking of the few years or months. The game is finished (or the dice is thrown whichever is suitable to you).

Anyway in Milano, the vote for me is always displeasing and unpleasant.

So, arrivederci when you are in Italy.

Much cordial greetings.

Comment from the Author: *This letter indicates that he has moments when he does not get along with the press or the press do not like him.*

```
Bergamo 8 aprile 1977
 Caro Feist,
ho ricevuto alcuni giorni fa la Sua
lettera del 22 marzo.
Ho inviato oggi a Lombardo, quanto
Lei mi ha richiesto.
Almeno fin dove ho potuto capire poic
la Sua lettera era alquanto confusa.
A d Adler mi riprometto di parlare dir
mente quando sarò a San Francisco.
( Dal 22 agosto al 27 novembre, nulla
accadendo in contrario; e se la situaz
italiana lo permetterà;siamo oramai in
clima di guerra civile .Non c'è più li
a nulla ...Quindi potrà darsi ,se le c
continuano a peggiorare che io non mi
di allontanarmi da tutta la gente di f
glia . Lei che ha conosciuto e amato il
nostro Paese,può ben capire quanto tutto
questo sia triste ....!)
Mi scriva se occorre altro. Ma con indi=
cazioni ben chiare .
Rallegramenti per i prossimi impegni .
In fretta. molti saluti e auguri , aLei
e ai Genitori
```

Gianandrea Gavazzeni

April, 1977

Dear Feist,
 ...From 22 August to 27 November if nothing happens to the contrary and if the situation in Italy will permit it because we are now in a state of civil war.
 There's nothing here. Therefore it may be that the situation will continue to get worse. So, I will not feel like leaving all my family and friends behind.
 You who have known and loved our country can well understand how all of this is very sad. Write to me if other things happen, but with clear indication. Good luck on your next project.
 In haste, many greetings and good wishes to you and your parents.
 Gianandrea Gavazzeni

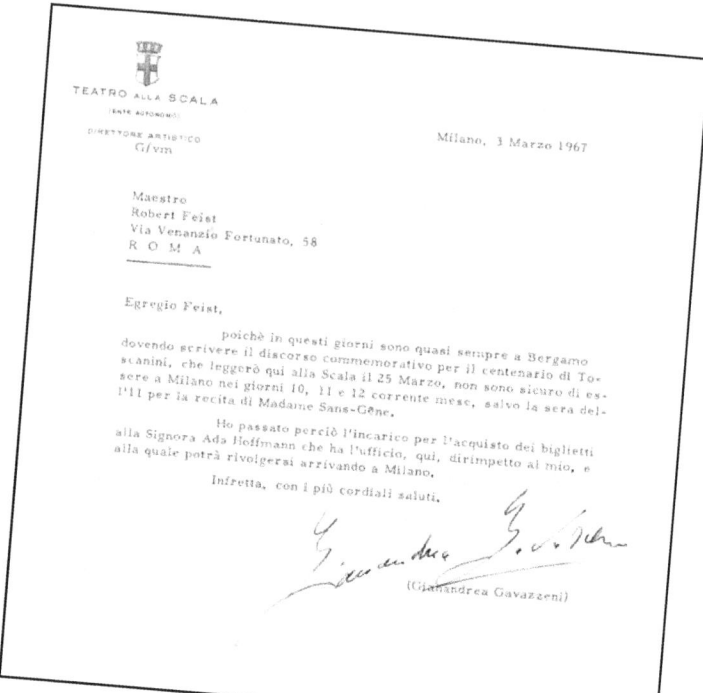

Teatro a la Scala
1967

Dear Feist,
These days I always at home in Bergamo because I have to write a big commemorative lecture for the Centenary of Toscanini which I will have to read at La Scala, the 25th of March. So, I am not sure that I will be there on the 10th, 11th or 12th when you may be coming to town, except for the evening of the 11th for the performance of *Madame Sans Gene*. I passed the burden of getting tickets for you to Signora Hoffman who has an office here, right next to mine and whom you can greet when you arrive in Milano. Now in haste, with cordial greetings,
Maestro Gavazzeni

Comment from the author: *This letter brings up an interesting point. He mentions an opera that he is going to conduct; this opera is called* Madame Sans Gene. *That is a very rare opera by Giordano and we all know his great opera* Andrea Chenier.

I was lucky because I had recorded an aria from a rare opera of his with Marcella Reale and she invited me to join her in a box at La Scala for this performance with the Giordano family and I was very, very overjoyed because I had already met, as iI told you, the daughter of Franco Alfano and I met the granddaughter of Puccini at some point, all the heirs of Verdi at his home and now Giordano. He lived quite a long time and this party at this performance where we were in a box was with his daughter (I forget her name) and so Marcella and I were with her and some other people to hear this performance and an opera that I had never heard ever in my life. It's not one of his best and it is very rarely done and I have never seen it before or after. But it gave me a chance to meet the daughter of the great composer Giordano and to hear a rare performance of the opera.

Baveno Lago Maggiore

7 agosto 1977

Caro Feist,

rispondo con ritardo alla Sua lettera del 15 luglio.

Sono stato in giugno a Roma per la Messa di Chimay di Cherubini (stupenda) alla Rai Foro Italico, e a chiusura del "Maggio Fiorentino" con tre esecuzioni del Requiem di Brahms.

Pochi giorni fa un concerto a Montecarlo.

Rispondo in fretta : parto il 20 agosto per San Francisco -senza fermarmi a New York - tre ore al Kennedy -.

Resto, nulla accadendo in contrario, fino al 28 novembre. Alloggio al Fox Plaza Residence, vicino al teatro.

Parlerò di Lei ad Adler, e se sarà utile Le telefonerò per venire a San Francisco.

Lombardo mi telefona stasera da Zurigo.

Ho visto la bella intervista su Opera News di Fremann.

Scusi la fretta. Ho tante cose da fare prima di partire.

Mucchi di posta e tante disposizioni da lasciare per il lavoro d'inverno e primavera in Italia.

E' veramente incredibile che con i direttori che Lei mi nomina -americani o mezzi americani o europei mediocri - che dirigono nel suo Paese non si siano ancora accorti di Lei !

Ma io penso che la situazione dovrà sbloccarsi.

Molti cari saluti

Babeno Lago Maggiore

7 August 1977

Dear Feist,

…Pardon my haste, I have so many things to do before I leave—tons of mail and things to arrange so the work will continue here until I come back.

(Mr. Feist was trying to get a job at a university at that time and Gavazzeni comments):

This is truly incredible that with the directors (conductors) that you mentioned ot me, Americans or half Americans or mediocre Europeans that conduct in your country, that they have not yet become aware of you! But I think this situation must become unblocked soon.

Many fond greetings.

PORTA DIPINTA, 5
BERGAMO ALTA

28 aprile 1970

Caro Feist,
rientrato da Ginevra trovo la

Sua lettera.
In data odierna ho scritto a

Paone per Lei, insistendo.
Mi ha fatto molto piacere quanto

mi ha detto per il Mozart di

Roma.
Non so cosa ne abbiano pensato

nella "cloaca massima" della
critica romana. Non ho letto

nulla, essendo ripartito subito

Riascolterò volentieri la signorina Reale. Le dica che mi

cerchi a Bergamo nell'ultima
settimana di maggio.

Sarò a Roma per incidere il Pirata

dal 17 al 30 luglio (Rai).

hotel Leonardo da Vinci. —
Molti cordialissimi saluti

Porta Dipinta, 5
Bergamo Alta

April, 1970

Dear Feist,
...I don't know what we should think about the "huge sewer" of the Roman critics. I have never yet read anything that you read having left town immediately after the concert. I will very, very gladly meet and listen to Signorina Reale when I can. Tell her to look for me in Bergamo in May and I will then be in rome to record the *Pirata* of Bellini. That is in July for the RAI.

Many most cordial greetings

November, 1973
Dear Maestro Feist,
   ...I am going to send all of your curriculum to Maestro Raffaello De Banfield, Directtore Artistico di Trieste. He is a man of a high level, personable with exceptional confidence and experience. He speaks in Italian, French, English and German and I will speak of you. He visited new York for some time and he has a residence also in Paris and he also knew the young Karajan and he was an assistant to him. I am leaving for Trieste Monday and I send many most cordial greetings.

February, 1973

(Mr. Feist conducted a conert in Milano of the Pomeriggi Musicali which was an orchestra where Maestro Gavazzeni knew the manager and he wrote to him on behalf of Mr. Feist. At that time Mr. Gavazzeni was conducting right across from the Galleria at La Scala and during a break Gavazzeni came to hear Mr. Feist's concert).

Dear Feist,
   Thanks for your letter. I had much pleasure to be present at your concert and also very much admired you and was able to examine and to appreciate your eminent qualities of being a concert maker and your directorial capacity. Bravo!
   In haste, many greetings and good wishes.

18 December 1962

…I don't have time to respond to a letter like yours full of arguments (rather bitter). I am very, very busy at La Scala and I'm tired.

…That which you tell me of the happenings in German theater is incredible and serious. And also on their additions and manipulations. I do not know what to advise you to do—or better—I would advise you to have patience.

Meanwhile you can make yourself a big, big experience that would not be possible somewhere else. In Italy the theater situation, except for La Scala, is every year more difficult and precarious. When you come here I will see you very gladly and we will chat. Many greetings and good works.

Gianandrea Gavazzeni

3 May 1962

…I am replying in haste because I am very tired. We passed a very brutal period in my family due to the long illness and death of my wife's only sister, still young.

I had to absolutely leave immediately to go to Rome and conduct with the RAI and with Benedetti Michelangeli in a concert at the Vatican in the presence of the Pope who is from Bergamo like me and was a close friend of my father in his youth.

Up to now I have conducted *Battaglia di Legnano*—nine performances: *La Favorita*—fifteen performances; *Trittico* di Puccini—five performances; *Faust*—nine performances.

At the end of June I'll be in Rome to open the Caracalla season with *Aida* and then up to Verona, August 15th to conduct *Nabucco* and *Ballo in Maschera*.

All this if nothing happens to the contrary and if I remain well.

Many greetings.

Gianandrea Gavazzeni

(A letter written by Mr. Gavazzeni as a recommendation for Mr. Feist. Gavazzeni went to the trouble of having it written in English)

Mr. William B. Christ, Associate Dean
Indiana University, School of Music
Bloomington, Indiana

6 November 1976

Dear Mr. Christ,

Mr. Robert Feist has been known to me for many years and I can personally vouch for his integrity and serious approach to music.

I first met him when he came to the Teatro dell'Opera, Roma in a Fulbright Scholarship in order to gain experience in Italian operas and since then I have followed his career with interest. After this period in Rome he spent a few years at the Opera house in Augsburg, West Germany widening his operatic experience, this time in the German repertoire. At the same time he had the opportunity of learning the Russian and Czech operas. Indeed, two years ago, interest was generated in the Italian musical world when he conducted a hitherto unknown Smetana opera for the Italian Radio in Milan. Recently in Italy his activities have been mainly symphonic. In 1976 he conducted with great success two concerts at the Academia di Santa Cecilia in Rome and two at the Teatro Comunale in Florence. Mr. Feist is also very gifted as a teacher with a comprehensive knowledge of the various operatic styles.

For these reason I consider Mr. Feist admirably qualified and suitable for the post at Indiana University mentioned in your letter.

With kindest regards, I remain,

    Yours sincerely

    Mr. Gianandrea Gavazzeni

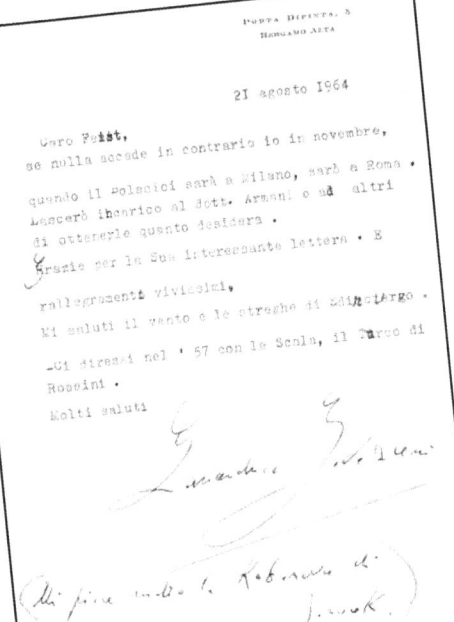

Porta Dipinta, 5
Bergama Alta
21 August 1964

Dear Feist,

Thank you for your interesting letter and many, many vivid greetings to you and while you are up there please greet the winds and all the witches of Edinburgh. *(This was the year of the Rockefeller Grant and I was in Edinburgh). (The Gavazzeni goes on).* I conducted in Edinburgh in 1957 with La Scala and I did the *Il Turco in Italia* by Rossini.

Many greetings.

P.S. I very much like the *Kabanova* by Janacek.
(That is one of Janacek's big operas).

Gianandrea Gavazzeni

Corriere della Sera — TERZA PAGINA

MAESTRI *È morto a ottantasette anni il grande direttore d'orchestra. Domani i funerali alla Scala con l'«Eroica» diretta da Muti a porte aperte. Come per Toscanini*

Addio a Gavazzeni. Un lungo inno alla vita

Vanitoso e testardo, ma ci lascia più poveri
di PAOLO ISOTTA

di FRANCESCO M. COLOMBO

Porta Dipinta, 5
Bergamo Alta

May, 1986

Dear Feist,

I have had much trouble with my health. Since early in January I have had thrombosis which has cut out the use of my right eye and I was absolutely infirm for two months giving up all the repeats of "Lombardi" at La Scala and other engagements in Vienna where I had been two times before with much satisfaction. However, in March I repeated *La Sonnambula* at La Scala and a concerto by Respighi at the RAI. I get along as much as I can. I will have to go to Vancouver with La Scala for "Lombardi." I hope so. I don't know yet the name of the hotel that La Scala has picked for us, but I will write to you. I will be there from the 17th of August with one of my sons. Excuse me if I am short, but I am old and I am tired. In three months I will be 77. So, it makes me very tired to write at length. But I am always grateful for the kind remembrances that you have of me.

Gianandrea Gavazzeni

24100 BERGAMO ALTA
Via Porta Dipinta, 5

16 maggio 1986

Caro Feist,
ho ricevuto con piacere e interesse la Sua lettera del 28 aprile. Mi rallegro per le Sue ottime notizie. Io ho avuto guai di salute: ai primi di gennaio una trombosi mi ha tolto l'uso dell'occhio destro. Sono stato fermo due mesi rinunciando alla ripresa dei "Lombardi" alla Scala e a due impegni a Vienna (Sinfoniker e Staatsoper, dove ero stato due volte, ai Sinfoniker [illegible] con molta soddisfazione). Ho ripreso in marzo con recite di Sonnambula alla Scala e con un concerto Respighi a Rai Torino. Mi arrangio come posso.
Dovrei appunto venire a Vancouver con la Scala per i Lombardi. Speriamo. Non so ancora il nome dell'albergo che la Scala ha fissato. Glielo scriverò: sarò lì dal 17 agosto all'8 settembre, con un mio figlio.
Scusi se sono breve: sono vecchio e stanco (tra due mesi 77 anni !!!). Mi affatica molto scrivere a lungo.
Molti cari saluti e auguri di buon lavoro, sempre grato del buon ricordo

Gianandrea Gavazzeni

Mi comunichi, a suo tempo, il nuovo suo indirizzo.

A newspaper story on the death of Maestro Gavazzeni. He is pictured above left with Luciano Pavarotti and he is with his second wife in the photograph on the right.

PRIDE OF BERGAMO: GIANANDREA GAVAZZENI
BY JOHN W. FREEMAN

Conductors always seem to have plenty to say, and Gianandrea Gavazzeni is no exception. An avid reader, he has written twenty or so books of his own, embracing not only music but literature and poetry. He loves art and considers the Frick Collection in New York "a masterpiece among museums." As for the U.S., which he never visited until he came to Lyric Opera of Chicago in 1957, he says, "Nothing surprised me here. You see, I've always read American novelists and historians." Now, after a busy life as biographer and musicologist and until 1967 (the year he led La Scala at Montreal's Expo) artistic director at La Scala, he has fulfilled a long-standing dream of conducting at the Met, opening the current season with *Il Trovatore*.

"The Bing management had discussed with me the possibility of coming, but our schedules couldn't be worked out. I felt at home here right away—very good, active collaborators. And now in New York I had a chance to visit old friends, Wanda [Toscanini] Horowitz and her husband. After dinner, Horowitz played a Clementi sonata, and then we listened to his recording of the Scriabin Fifth Sonata, in which the piano is treated like an orchestra. I love the piano, you know, though I haven't played solo in public since Beethoven's Third Concerto at the conservatory in Milan. I graduated in 1929. Wanda Horowitz reminded me they used to call me *il ragazzo Gavazzeni*, 'the Gavazzeni kid,' in her father's house on Via Durini.

"Yes, I composed too, with the avant-garde tendencies of the time, but when your head is so full of the music of others it's impossible to write, so for thirty-six years I haven't composed a note. I studied with Pizzetti, and we were friends until his death. An odd thing happened at a rehearsal some time ago: as I was leaving the podium, the first cellist played a theme and asked if I recognized it. 'How come you don't?' he said—'it's the opening theme of your own Cello Concerto!' But I heard it with complete indifference."

A source of pride to Maestro Gavazzeni is the musical heritage of Bergamo, where he was born in 1909 and still lives. Donizetti is Bergamo's most famous musical native son, and it was under Gavazzeni that his *Anna Bolena* made a triumphal return to La Scala in the spring of 1957. The maestro's light, penetrating eyes briefly seem to look into the distance as he recalls the event: "We took our bows, Callas and Simionato and I, and I told them, 'In our lifetime we'll never see anything like this again.' The audience was in an

uproar beyond belief. Yet people say operas like that are old-fashioned, dead today!" In the bel canto repertory, Gavazzeni is careful to distinguish between the classical and the romantic elements. *Norma* in particular he feels needs special care: "The opera comes from the tradition of Gluck and Spontini, and it's wrong to play it with too much freedom." His performance of *Norma* with Caballé at La Scala, the first international opera broadcast by satellite, reached the U.S. airwaves last winter. Not since the days of Ettore Panizza at the Met has *Norma* been heard here with such stylistic integrity and dramatic force.

Most of his conducting is on the opera podium, but he has always liked to give symphony concerts, and he remembers leading Adolf Busch's last performance in Milan—the Brahms Violin Concerto—as well as Alfred Cortot's last concert in Italy. "Specialization is wrong. With singers, where there's a biological basis for their mastery of their own language, there's some justification, but otherwise a musician shouldn't be limited. Yet in Italy they want a German conductor, even a bad one, every time a German opera is given. The great theater conductors of modern times, like Mitropoulos and Rodzinski, conducted everything. For myself, I love Russian music and Janáček's operas and introduced *From the House of the Dead* at La Scala. I'd love to conduct *Peter Grimes*, and I love Mozart, but since my young days I haven't been asked to conduct any.

"In the French repertory, *Le Jongleur de Notre Dame* is worth reviving. I had the good fortune to lead *Werther* with Tagliavini and Schipa, also *Manon*, and at La Scala *Samson et Dalila* with Barbieri and Vinay, as well as *Mignon* with Simionato, which we repeated in Chicago. In symphonic music I've been fond of Bruckner ever since the early 1920s, when my father, a lawyer who loved music—he was a deputy until fascism came—gave me a piano four-hand score of the Sixth Symphony. I played it with a Japanese professor from the Berlitz School in Rome. The adagio and scherzo especially impressed me. Besides that, I've conducted Bruckner's Third Mass and Te Deum. There's a good audience nowadays in Italy for this repertory."

At the Toscanini Congress in Florence in 1967, Gavazzeni remarked sadly that most of the vocal scores with Toscanini's markings had disappeared from La Scala. "After the bombing, people took things away. Anyhow, those scores belonged to the theater and were in constant use, so many of them just wore out. That's what happens to our great traditions if we don't treat them carefully." In his researches on Donizetti he found that "Tu che a Dio spiegasti l'ali" in the last scene of *Lucia di Lammermoor* was originally meant as a cabaletta. "But when the tenor tried it slowly, so as to learn it, Donizetti said, 'Keep it that way—I like it better!' It helps to understand the music, I think, if you know about its origins in performance. *Don Carlos*, for instance, sounds better in French than in Italian, because it was written that way, but *Jérusalem* doesn't sound as good as *I Lombardi*, because the French words are a translation and don't fit the music."

How does this conductor, who is no longer young but has the enthusiasm and vigor of a boy, find time to do everything? "There's plenty of time," he says simply, "but you have to organize it. There has to be time to read. Regardless of my schedule, I start every day at the piano with the *Well-Tempered Clavier*, perhaps followed by some Scarlatti, Mozart, Debussy, Ravel. Gide liked to do the same, according to his *Journals*, but he preferred Albéniz and Granados. I've loved music since I was born! When I was five or six, my father would play through operas at the piano and I'd stand on a chair and conduct with a pencil."

It's been a career of lifelong curiosity and conviction. Donizetti of Lombardy could hardly ask for a more responsible deputy. Neither could Verdi of neighboring Emilia-Romagna, or the many other composers Maestro Gavazzeni has loved and served so well. ☐

photo: © Erika Davidson 1977

(An interview of Gianandrea Gavazzeni in *Opera News*, 1977).

Introduction to Letters from Maestro Gui

Now as one can read from his letters Maestro Gui was the opposite. He was somewhat—let's call him a braggart. He was never quiet. He was always a big talker. When I visited him in his beautiful villa in Fiesole on the hills above Florence, he would serve me something to drink. He would always get to reminiscing about what it was like when he was in Glyndebourne conducting there for some 20 years and all the Germans he met and the French and the repertoire he did and how he revised the entire Rossini repertoire. He never really was quiet much, but interested in what I was doing. But that he took the time to do this amazed me, plus the letters.

The letters are not brief letters. Many conductors on their day or so off from the middle of a run of performances would stay in their hotel or go out and take walks or be entertained. He would actually take the time to sit down and type a letter to me or write in handwriting a letter to me telling me many, many aspects of his life as you will see. I think they are quite amazing because I met him I think the first year in Rome and assisted him in performances of the *Magic Flute* and then a wonderful performance of *Cenerentola* which he introduced me to the real type of singer that should do it—Giulietta Simionato. And those were the type of things he did chiefly with affection because he was the reviver, if that is the word, of Rossini. He mentions it in one of his letters and all of Italy knows it and he was tired of the tendencies and bad habits of all singers and conductors in Italy at the time he was growing up.

They were distorting, adding things, adding cadenzas, changing the vocal lines of Rossini until he brought about in 1925 this amazing production of *L'Italiana in Algeri* and he cast it as it should be with a mezzo of coloratura ability. Well, that really "knocked" everybody. They were stunned that this is the way Rossini should be done, sticking to the notes and to what Rossini meant. That led to a revival of all Rossini eventually. Well, we can't say all because he wrote over 35 operas, but in Glyndebourne where he was the chief, he would always do a rare Rossini plus all the Mozart and even to *Pelleas* and operas such as that. But, when he was doing Rossini, he stuck to the absolute basis of it and the correct interpretation and the right notes with no additions, no cadenzas and no things that were improper.

And what I am mentioning caught on in Italy and other countries. So, finally Rossini because known not only for *The Barber of Seville*, which up to until this time, was the only opera of Rossini's that anybody knew—America, Germany, Europe, the only one that anyone knew well. Suddenly we get all the other ones which are much more commonly performed—and not the rare ones such as *Otello* but we certainly now know so many more than we did, like in *Il Turco in Italia*. So, Gui had an international reputation that often when people talk about him, singers that I have talked to, who would not brush him off, but would say: "Oh, he is so didactic. He is so hard. He is so demanding," or words to that effect. Well, they knew very well that he made them "get to the bottom" of the score and do it exactly as Rossini had meant it to be. That is what I admired on many of his recordings and the many performances that I saw him conduct. I also saw him conduct other things like operas by Gluck in Rome or even Pizzetti—unusual enough. So, the memories of both these men are firmly ensconced not only through constant meetings and lunches and talks but through this parade, this collection of letters, which I think is very unusual for anyone to possess and to receive from prominent conductors and the two are the most prominent in Italy. I cannot imagine de Fabritiis or even Serafin writing such long letters. I had a short note from Serafin when I met him and he invited me to his apartment in Rome and we discussed my career, but it was just one meeting. He was very polite and very nice, but it didn't continue into a friendship as it did with these two).

The headline on this page from the Italian newspaper *Il Tempo,* 17 October, 1995 reads: "Great Sorrow for Art and Culture. Maestro Vittorio Gui has died. He was 90 years old. On October 4th last year he inaugurated the symphonic season in Florence where he had founded the "Maggio Musicale." Following this page are excerpts from over 25 letters that Maestro Gui wrote to Mr. Feist as his mentor and as the greatest Rossini conductor and historian in Italy.

MARATEA(Potenza) 9 ottobre 1961

Egregio Maestro,

La Sua lettera mi ha raggiunto qui dove da tre settimane mi trovo per un periodo di riposo del quale, dopo il lavoro di tutto l'anno, sentivo urgente bisogno. Abbiamo costruito, con mia moglie, una casetta qua nell'Italia del sud, al mare, in Lucania, in un posto bellissimo; la casa l'ho chiamata "La solitaria" perché veramente qui mi rifugio per non veder nessuno e star lontano dal mondo. Potrei considerarla la mia "Wahnfried" se il riferimento non fosse un po' troppo... presuntuoso! Quanto Lei mi dice del Barbiere udito e visto alla T.V. mi fa molto piacere. Ho dedicato molti anni di studio al grande Rossini, e al suo stile, spintovi anche da un sentimento di reazione contro le pessime esecuzioni che sempre sentivo in giro, e che si moltiplicavano sotto l'usbergo delle cosidette "tradizioni" quasi sempre pessime abitudini inveterate e nate da capricci di cantanti. Già nel lontano 1925 io rimettevo in circolazione la sua Italiana in Algeri che sembrava dimenticata da anni; nel 1942, centocinquantesimo anniversario della nascita di Rossini, a Firenze nel Maggio realizzammo un'esecuzione sull'originale della partitura autografa che sta a Bologna. Lo stesso sto facendo da alcuni anni in Glyndebourne. Non è necessario trovare dei cantanti "divi", ma è molto meglio addestrare delle giovani voci con un serio studio e molte prove, come a Glyndebourne abbiamo sempre. Uno dei buonissimi spettacoli del nostro repertorio è anche per l'opera italiana il Falstaff, che fu trasmesso per T.V. l'anno scorso. Un altro bello spettacolo è il Fidelio. Ogni opera viene eseguita nel testo originale sempre con grande cura. Il successo grosso è stabilito per sempre; 75 rappresentazioni ogni anno, e il teatro sempre esaurito. In Italia, in genere dirigo molto raramente l'opera, perché le condizioni dei nostri teatri diventano ogni anno più difficili. L'anno prossimo farò solo un'opera a Venezia (Macbeth di Verdi) e due a Firenze, e parecchi concerti in giro. Avrei dovuto andare in settembre a Monaco per la commemorazione di Strauss, ma un indisposto fisico me l'ha impedito; questione di denti, nella mia vecchia bocca!!! Ora va tutto bene. La salute regge in modo sorprendente se pensa al numero dei miei anni...76...

Mi ha molto interessato quanto Lei mi narra della Sua sopracittà. Conosco molto bene la città di Augsburg, dove diressi dei concerti anni or sono; era una interessantissima città allora, prima delle distruzioni di guerra. Chissà che cosa ne è rimasto... J'erano le più antiche vetrate di Chiesa del mondo nella Cattedrale di Sant'Ulrico, e il quartiere "Fuggerei" era assai caratteristico. Là ebbi la gioia di incontrare e conoscere il vecchio critico, suocero delle Münchener Nachrichten, che venne

apposta da München, Alexander Berrsche, e che dopo la mia 4ª di Brahms scrisse una pagina per me indimenticabile riprodotta poi insieme con altre critiche di lui nel volume postumo "Trösterin Musica" che Lei potrà forse trovare in Augsburg. (..)

Mi farebbe piacere rivederla, ma quando e dove? Faccio una corsa a Glyndebourne la prossima estate; la dirigerò, per il centenario di Debussy (della nascita 1862) un Pelleas che sarà riuscito bene, e una ripresa del Cosi fan tutte. Quest'anno abbiamo dato posto anche alla musica odierna con l'esecuzione dell'opera di Hans Werner dei giovani cantanti su libretto inglese del poeta Auden. Fu bene accolta.

La saluto di tondo di cuore, e la ringrazio di non aver dimenticato il vecchio Maestro Gui!

Saluti cordiali. Il mio indirizzo stabile Lei lo conosce, è sempre FIESOLE(Firenze) Villa San Michele. Io vado lì dopo il 15 corr. avrò forse notizie della morte del caro maestro Bertolli all'Opera, che Lei se ne ricorderà. Mi ha molto addolorato; era il migliore tra tutti in ogni senso!

[signature: Vittorio Gui]

(..) Io non conosco più di Augsburg. Ho il proprio Fugger in sub. Strauss ... di Vogel ... un certo Weber. Saranno ancora al mondo, o chissà... qualcuno dell'orchestra ...

Potenza, Italy
October 1961

Egregio Maestro,

Your letter reached me here where I am having three weeks of repose after the work for a whole year having this urgent need to repose. We have with (name) my wife, this beautiful little house which is in south Italy which is on the sea at Luciana, a delicious place and a house that we call La Solitaria meaning "the solitary place." For me it is a refuge to not see anybody and to escape far away from the world. You can consider this my "Wahnfried," that's the German word that Wagner used for his own house, if you don't think this reference that I am making a little too presumptious.

What you tell me about the *Barber* (meaning the *Barber of Seville*) which you saw and heard on TV gives me much pleasure. I dedicated many years of study to the great Rossini and his style, pushed into this also by a sentiment of reaction against the terrible executions that are always in circuit in Italy. These performances keep repeating themselves under the term "traditions," which are always the worst possible inveterate habits of singers and are borne by the caprices of singers. Even in 1925, a long time ago, I put in circulation in Italy the wonderful *L'Italiana in Algeri* and that had consequences in circulation to all of Italy and it had been forgotten for years and years and years.

The 50th anniversary of the birth of Rossini in Florence in the festival we put on a premiere performance of the original of the autographed score of the opera which is in Bologna in an archive, the same thing that I am doing for some years now performing in Glyndebourne in England. It is not necessary to find singers who are divas, as we say, instead better to just simply to find young voices who have had serious study, many rehearsals as at Glyndebourne we had all the time. Then these wonderful spectacles of our repertoire is also of the opera *Falstaff*, it was telecast by the TV last year. Another one that we did was *Fidelio*. Every opera becomes performed in the original text with great care in Glyndebourne. The success is absolutely stable for something like 75 performances every year and the theater is always sold out.

In Italy, in general, I rarely conduct opera because the conditions at many theaters becomes more difficult. Next year I will only do an opera in Venice, Macbeth, and two in Florence and several concerts. I would have liked to go to Munich in September for a concert commemorating Richard Strauss, but a physical impediment has kept me from this, that is my own mouth. Everything else is okay. My health seems to go on in a surprising way as I pass that number of my years—76. *(Author's comment: Gui went on conducting until he was 90—amazing).*

It interested me very much which you tell me about your operatic activities. I know very well the city of Augsburg *(where author was stationed)* where I conducted several concerts for years. It was a very, very interesting city then before the destruction of the war. Who knows what is left of it. *(Author: well, as a matter of fact, I know, as they rebuilt the entire city).*

There are the most wonderful windows of the churches of the cathedral and the church of St. Ulrich and the wonderful quarter of town called the Fuggerei *(which I knew very well)* which were very characteristic. That is the place where all the poor of the city were given living quarters during and after the war. There I had the chance to meet an old music critic from the Munich newspaper who came purposely to Munich to meet me and I was conducting the Brahms "Fourth Symphony" and he wrote a page for me in the paper which was an unforgettable reproduction with other critics and me in a posthumous volume that he wrote called: "Trösstserin Musica" which you may be able to find somewhere in Augsburg. *(Author: I did look for it, I couldn't find it).*

It would please me to see you, but when and how. I do a course this summer in Glyndebourne and conduct for the centenarian of Debussy, *Pelléas et Mélisance,* that I hope will go well and a repeat of *Cosi Fan Tutte*. This year we have been given room for music contemporary, the execution of the opera di Henze, *The Elegy of the Young Lovers* with an English libretto by the poet Auden. It was very well received.

I will send you many, many greetings and I think you for not having forgotten your old Maestro Gui.

All my cordial greetings. My address you know very well. It's always in Florence in Fiesole and I'll be there the 15th of this month and maybe I will have the chance to talk to you then.

(Author: He adds a list of names of all the people he knew when he was in Augsburg, but they are nobody that I knew when I was there).

Vittorio Gui

Fiesole 5 giugno 1966

aro Feist, Grazie della lettera e dell'accluso articolo che ho già tradotto io stesso;adesso cercheremo di sistemarlo in qualche rivista cosa non facile qui dove riviste musicali non esistono più....
Mi ha molto interessato,tanto che ieri,giornata di riposo per me, dopo esaurite le recite di Alceste,mi sono messo alla macchina da scrivere e ne ho fatto la traduzione italiana.Unica parola il cui senso mi è sfuggita è "indeed"; che significa? Me lo scriva.
L'Alceste di Gluck ha avuto qui un inaspettato esplosivo successo, al disopra dei meriti dell'esecuzione, in generale.Naturalmente sopravviene sempre il senso di "relatività" e si capisce che quando io dirigo e sopra tutto un'opera che ho nel sangue da più di 35 anni (la mia prima esumazione,dopo 70 anni di oblio in Italia risale al 1927 a Torino, poi venne quella memorabile en plein air a Boboli nel 1935,e in seguito per due o tre anni le molte e acclamatissime esecuzioni a Glyndebourne......)anche se la preparazione,come sempre orami qui e da per tutto,sia stata limitata a pochi giorni, il senso dell'opera,che è un autentico capolavoro,è uscito fuori abbastanza chiaro,tanto da portare la folla a un vero e sincero entusiasmo. Io mi consolo dei difetti pensando che essendo "immortale" avrò altra occasione di farla con più calma e meglio!!!!
Ho realizzato questa volta un terzo atto piuttosto differente da quello che si usa fare seguendo la versione gluckiana del 1776 di Parigi,su libretto rifatto dal Du Roullet;ho cioè preso il meglio della versione viennese e lasciato il meglio della francese,riducendo a Corazzo di ringraziamento un trio che c'è verso la fine e rinunciando a tutte le Danze, dato che un vero e proprio corpo di ballo oggi qui non l'abbiamo e così (anche ricordando che il poeta Calzabigi, autore del primo libretto di Alceste, si era mostrato contrario alle danze che Gluck a Parigi non potè rifiutare di fare e ce ne sono anche delle belle) è rimasta la pura e nuda tragedia greca da Euripide senza discordanze stilistiche,con l'immissione di musica leggera e frivola settecentesca in mezzo a una Stimmung continuamente e profondamente tragica....
Appena potrò Le farò vedere il lavoro fatto che La interesserà di certo. Conosce bene Lei Gluck? Tutta la moderna forma del dramma musicale nasce da lui,e sopra tutto da questa Alceste.
Oggi o domani telefonerò a Pinsauti per vedere se sarà possibile pubblicare il Suo articolo sopra un numero di Approdo,ma non sul prossimo che è già destinato a onorare Busoni per il centenario della nascita.
A giorni andiamo a riposarci finalmente a Maratea (indirizzo è: MARATEA-porto- Prov.di Potenza)Villa solitaria. È veramente solitaria lo è;una casetta entro una larga zona di bosco con carrubi e ulivi,degradante sugli scogli.E vista di mare mare mare da tutte le parti;veso il sorgere e il tramontare del sole.dietro le montagne sorge ,dietro il Capo degli Infreschi, cala;e ancora dietro c'è (ma non si vede) il famoso Capo Palinuro, dove passò la nave di Enea mentre veniva a scoprire l'Italia,e il suo pilota,che aveva forse bevuto troppo,cadde in mare, affogò e non ritrovarono più la salma;finchè, alcun tempo dopo, Enea sceso all'Erebo, lo ritrovò in spirito e conobbe il luogo dove era finito il corpo e potè fargli dare la sepoltura dovuta. Miti e ricordi di classici studiati in gioventù...
Io là mi sono da tempo rimesso a leggere Orazio e altri autori latini. Una delizia dell'intelletto....E la musica intanto tace e...aspetta.
Mi tenga al corrente dei suoi viaggi e del suo lavoro.
La seguo con interesse,con amicizia e con tanti buoni auguri.
Un abbraccio cordiale

Fiesole
1966

Maestro Feist,

Thank you for the letter with the enclosed article which I had translated for myself. I will try to get it placed in some kind of magazine which is not easy here where all the musical magazines don't exist any more. It interested me very much, so much so, that yesterday, after a little bit of rest for me, when I finish the performances of *Alceste* by Gluck, I sit down to the typewriter and I started making this translation into Italian and the only word that escaped me was the word "jaded." What does that mean. Please tell me.

L'Alceste de Gluck has had an unexpected, explosive success in general. Naturally there is always the question of relativity and you understand that this means that what I conduct, especially in opera that has not been heard for a long time, but I have known for 35 years, there is going to be some kind of confusion about whether it is correct or not. The first one that I did was in 1927 in Torino and then came a memorable one in the open-air Boboli Gardens in 1935 and it continued for two or three years in very accurate performances in Glyndebourne in England. But the preparation here and everywhere else was limited to two or three days. So, in the sense that the opera is an authentic masterpiece and it came out rather clearly so much to carry the audience to a true and sincere enthusiasm as in Glyndebourne and in here. I am concerning myself with any defects thinking that to be immortal you have to wait for another occasion when I'm more calm and in better shape. I realized this time and I concern myself with defects thinking that to become immortal needs more calm. I did a throwback quite different from that which had been done before from 1976 which was a Gluck version in Paris and by different libretto. To reveal these and later French versions which reduced the story to a trio that was then considered proper which was a ballet and in those days they thought it was normal, but not now.

(Author: He goes on and on about the use of ballet and the different traditions for Gluck that we don't repeat here. He even mentions Euripides *because it is based on* Euripedes *and so forth).*

I may be able to show you this work when it is finished and it will interest you certainly. Do you know Gluck very well? All the forms of a drama musical, the music of drama were born within and especially *Alceste*. Wagner knew this very well.

Tomorrow I will call Pinzauti *(a leading critic in Florence)* to see if it is possible to publish your article on the number of things that you mentioned, not in the coming issue which is already set to honor Busoni on the centenarian of his birth.

Near me you see the famous Capo Palinuro where the ship of Eneas came to discover Italy and his pilot had perhaps drunk too much, fell into the ocean and drowned and they never find this corpse anywhere until some time after Eneas descended to the earth and found his spirit and saw the exact place where his pilot had fallen into the water and he could make a very normal burial. These are all myths and remembrances of classical studies of their youth. In those days I was always placed to read Horace and all the other great Latin writers. It was a delicious thing for the intellect.

But, in the meantime, music just waited and waited. Well anyway, I follow with interest everything you say with great friendship and many, many good salutes.

A very cordial embrace.

Vittorio Gui

Comment by author:
It is remarkable that a man this famous who began the whole Rossini revival in Italy in 1925 would take all this time to write to me two or three typewritten pages at his age of 76 or so. I am amazed.

FIESOLE   Villa San Maurizio   10 XII 1962

Caro Feist,

La Sua cara e lunga lettera e i dischi che ho assai apprezzato e di cui La ringrazio vivamente, mi hanno recato un grandissimo piacere, e sopra tutto arrivano in un momento triste per me perchè esco da una malattia (non ero mai stato a letto malato dal 1904...!) una nevrite orribile al braccio destro, che mi ha fatto soffrire per più d'un mese, e mi ha lasciato ancora debole e pieno di acciacchi! ho dovuto sospendere tutto il lavoro per cui m'ero già impegnato qui a Firenze (Freyschütz) e Roma (concerti, di cui uno per il Papa! che s'è poi ammalato anche lui...) spero poter riprendere verso la fine di Gennaio...! Può immaginare il mio umore, costretto a cure noiose e a starmene fermo a casa, con un braccio (il destro!) e una mano infermi... Pazienza!

Quanto Lei mi descrive dell'ambiente di costà e della vita musicale della Germania, non mi arriva nuovo. Io ho fatto poche scappate in Germania nella mia carriera, avendo anche rischiato di essere assorbito dalla vita musicale di quel paese quando nel lontano 1911 mi fu offerto un posto a Berlino; poi ancora nel 1925 Riccardo Strauss mi fece di nuovo invitare al teatro di Berlino. Accettai invece qualche invito per concerti e visitai la Filarmonica per invito personale di Furtwängler, che io invitavo anche spesso a Firenze: e fin dal primo concerto - anzi fin dalla prima prova:- fu un trionfo con Brahms! Nel 1933 Bruno Walter mi fece invitare a Salzburg con Brahms, anche là fu un altro memorabile successo. Poi fui ad Augsburg (4° di Brahms) a Monaco, a Stuttgart, a Dresda, a Vienna e sempre ebbi grandi soddisfazioni, ma non avrei mai potuto fermarmi come "fisso" in quei paesi, nè so perchè! Adesso da circa 15 anni ho il mio posto a Glyndebourne che è un ambiente assolutamente internazionale, dove capitano anche a volte dei tedeschi; e andiamo tutti d'accordo, perchè il livello artistico è altissimo sempre, forse ogni anno superiore. (Pelléas, Fidelio, tutto Mozart, 4 opere di Rossini, Falstaff, sono esecuzioni eccezionali, perfezionate a tre sempre i rapporti sono perfetti!/// Perchè" Ricordo sempre il mio caro amico Adolfo Busch, il quale mi diceva "il paese dove si sa la musica, ma dove la si capisce meno, è la Germania!" Busch non pareva davvero un tedesco di razza pura! invece il fratello Fritz lo era, e io ho dovuto faticare abbastanza a Glyndebourne, per modificare le abitudini e il gusto da lui portato in quel teatro (da lui fondato) nelle opere di Mozart!... ma adesso ho vinto e non si discute più. Se io nei miei 50 anni di attività avessi seguito il sistema di farmi sentire in giro per il mondo (come fa la più parte dei direttori) avrei oggi una più larga fama mondiale e più quattrini... ma non rimpiango di aver servito lealmente la mia Arte con devozione e spirito di sacrificio, dei materiali interessi... La vita è un sogno che passa prestissimo, e alla fine il solo conforto è quello di non aver tradito sé stessi!

Fama danaro sono tutto fumo che non lascia traccia...Ha ragione
l'Ecclesiaste nell' antico testamento...tutto è vanità,si dimentica
tutto,ogni due generazioni.al massimo,e tutto è ingoiato dall'oblio.
Ne la pena agitarsi tanto? Ma l'amore dell'Arte è un "assoluto"
che non si discute:ed essendo un fenomeno d'amore,si riceve in
fondo quel che si è donato! La basta con le prediche! Vorrei
aver l'occasione di vederLa e fare la chiacchierata direttamente.
Peccato non sia venuto a Bregenz;non tanto l'opera,quanto la
Messa di Verdi con i solisti italiani e le masse di Vienna,
mi dette una immensa soddisfazione,fu forse la più bella esecuzione
che io abbia (della Messa) realizzato in tutta la mia vita!
Vorrei parlare un po' del caso Suo e dare qualche consiglio,ma
purtroppo anche lo scrivere a macchina mi stanca molto il braccio e la mano destra.Le scriverò ancora;Lei mi tenga a contatto.
Io per ora non mi muovo da qui.
Un abbraccio....paterno e affettuoso e tutti i miei migliori
auguri.

P.S.Ho collaudato ieri qui la mia ultima inci-
padrone ingl.) del Barbiere di Glyndebourne;ma
Lei conosce già Cenerentola e Conte Ory,credo.

Fiesole
1962

Dear Feist,

Your long and dear letter and the records you sent I have really appreciated and I thank you vividly because they have given me a most grand pleasure. Mainly because they arrived a moment that is sad for me because I am getting out of an illness (I have never been sick in bed since 1904) from nephritis to my right arm that has caused me to suffer for more than a month and left me weak and filled with annoyance. I had to suspend all my work that was set for me in Florence, the Freyschütz and in Rome—concerts; one of which was for the Pope himself. Now I hope to start again and all my efforts are work in January. You can imagine my humor about this. I am forced to take various cures and to stay home all the time with a bad arm that makes my right hand infirm.

What you tell me of the surroundings of the musical life of Germany does not strike me good. I have had many runs up into Germany in my career, having also absorbed the musical life in that country since 1911 when a post was offered to me in Berlin. And again by Richard Strauss in 1925 who invited me to a theater in Berlin. I accepted instead an invitation for concerts and visited the Berlin Philharmonic at the personal invitation of the Furtwängler whom I had invited several times to Florence. Ever since the first concert, in fact from the first rehearsal, it was a triumph with Brahms.

(continued)

In 1933 I knew Bruno Walter. He got me invited to Salzburg again with Brahms and that was another memorable success. Then I was in Augsburg as I mentioned, in Munich, Stuttgart, Dresden, Vienna and I always had great satisfaction, but I was never able to stay fixed, as we say, in those countries. I don't know why. Maybe the 15 years that I had in my post in Glyndebourne is a place that is so absolutely international where we get at times Germans and we all get along well because the level of artistic excellence is so high. maybe every year it is even higher; *Pelleas, Fidelio* all of the Mozart, Rossini, *Falstaff*—they are all exceptional, perfections and they cover the study of years on my part.

But also there with Tedeschi (with the Germans) the rapport between us are perfect. Why? Because I am a member of my dear friend Adolf Busch. "The country that knows music, but the country that doesn't understand, it is Germany." Busch did not seem to be a German of pure race instead he is brother Fritz, who is well-known, was of a pure race and I had to work very hard at Glyndebourne to modify all the habits and his tastes that he brought to that theater in the operas of Mozart which were wrong. Now I won and we don't argue any more.

If I, in 50 years of activity, had followed the system of making myself heard in trips around the whole world as most conductors do, I would have had to go to much bigger fame world-wide and more money. But I don't regret at all to have so very legally and faithfully that my art is devotion and sacrifice and not with material interests.

Life is a dream that passes very quickly and at the end the only comfort is that of not having betrayed yourself. Fame and fortune are all smoke and it doesn't leave a trace. And it is certainly clear in Ecclesiates and in the Old Testament where they say: "Everything is vanity." Forget everything. Every two generations at the most, everything becomes swallowed up by oblivion. So, is it worth the effort to get so excited. Love of art is an absolute that does not have any argument about it. Being a phenomenon of love, you receive it in depth that is given to you. So enough of these lectures.

I would like to have the occasion to see you and to talk to you perfectly—face to face. It is a shame you can't come to Breganz when I will be there to conduct the Verdi Requiem.

I would like to speak of more of your affairs and give you some advice but unfortunately the typewriter tires me out and especially my arm, so I will write to you another time. Keep me in contact and you know that I am here.

I bid you adieu, paternal and affectionate with all my best greetings.

Vittorio Gui

(Text continued from page 178).

These occasions, these casual visits, went on for two hours or more, and are etched in my memory and I think they are rare in America to have this experience with such luminaries in the Italian operatic world.

At the same time Antonietta Stella and I had maintained contact whenever she was learning a new opera. She invited me to her house and I would teach it to her—rarities such as Spontini This was his *Fernando Cortez*, one of his rare operas and also Verdi's *Attila*, which she had never done. She did that for the RAI in Rome in public performances conducted by Muti, which I heard. He was very good and I have it on tape. And also, strangely enough, she had to learn Euridice in the Gluck opera *Orfeo and Euridice* for the RAI in Torino It was a very unusual choice. I did not know why the RAI wanted to put her, a spinto soprano, in the role of Euridice, which is usually sung by a very light lyric, but they did and she recorded and the broadcast was very fine. I would not have cast her in that role, but that is neither here nor there. We often talked together with her husband after rehearsing, and we'd go to dinner at a restaurant with mutual friends of their and very, very pleasant times together. That went on for years, as long as I was in Rome.

To my great pleasure, quite a few years ago when I returned on one of the several trips to Europe, I made a point to contact her. This was around 1999 and I called and she was delighted that I called. Her husband had been extremely ill with cancer and she was taking care of him. She had retired from singing way before that. I do not recall what year, but it seemed rather young for her to quit singing at the age, of say, 48-49.

But, when we met at their house, she welcomed me and served me some tea and brandy and we covered everything that had happened between the time we had last seen each other. And, of course, the subject did get around to singers. Well, she and many other singers that I talked to agree with my current thesis; that singers are not singing well and the reason.

She said "Bob, there are not any voice teachers who are any good anymore in Italy or in any other country." She was very much down on voice teachers and what they allow you to sing. She said: "You hear them, they are all screaming and pushing singers to other repertoire and agents push them into roles that they should not be singing at their age and with their vocal equipment." Well, this discussion took quite some time. But she was very fixed on her position and I tended to agree with her and we shared opinions about the current singers that we knew that we had heard singing today.

My visit with Stella was incredibly pungent and beautiful and her husband was pleasant through the whole thing. He didn't say much, he was there and I remember always with great affection, especially because she gave me two new photos of herself. I had had one since her Rome Opera days, but there were two more of her as Tosca and Elisabetta in *Don Carlo*, which I cherish and they are on the wall with all of my other famous singers.

During the Rome years teaching, there was an experience in 1973 when the U.S. State Department, through the embassy there, where I had known the cultural attaché for years, invited me and at the time, Marcella Reale, to do a tour performing in several cities in the Mid East or North Africa. We went directly from Rome to Tunis (or Tunisia). We did a very nice recital there and it was welcomed enthusiastically. And then the American Ambassador there invited us to his home which was very near the ancient city of Carthage. Carthage, which I looked out on with amazement for what was left of it from the old, old days of the Trojan Wars. We had a very nice reception at this home and Reale sang again and we had a very fine dinner and a lot of interesting conversationwith his friends.

Then we went back to Tunis, looked around and took a plane again. We went over to Egypt. The plane first touched down in the country of Libya and we visited nothing but the airport in Tripoli and looked at a little gift shop right there and saw nothing of interest. We got on the plane and flew to Cairo. The Cairo stay was also interesting because we got to see all of the city in little bus tours plus two expansive tours given by the American Embassy. We saw quite a bit of Cairo, including the pyramids and the sphinx and it was fascinating. And then we saw there the conservatory of music in Cairo for students and we covered many aspects of singing including opera. Marcella explained many aspects of her repertoire to the students who were very interested. She sang in French, Italian and German.

From there, the next stop on this little Egyptian tour took us on just a really pleasant excursion. We flew down to Luxor. She didn't sing there, we didn't perform. We looked at the ruins of the temple which was magnificent and the remains of the tombs of the pharaohs. That remains fixed in my memory as well as a stop in the middle of the desert at the Giza Pyramids somewhere near Cairo, where we had a view of the sphinx and where we got out and looked

Above—Shahyad Ayra, the name of the mosque in Teheran.

Left—The Municipal Theater in Teheran in 1975, during the Shah's regime.

Above—Soprano Marcella Reale and Mr. Feist on their U.S. sponsored tour to North Africa. In Egypt they visited the famous pyramids of Giza in 1973.

Right—During a concert engagement in Teheran, Iran, Mr. Feist, on a side trip, visited the famed ruins of the historic city of Persepolis, the original capitol of the Persian Empire.

Robert Feist at the Manila Cultural Center and in front of a restaurant in Manila.

OPERA NEWS

NAMES, DATES

(From an *Opera News* clipping). Mr. Feist standing in front of the new cultural center of the Philippines in Manila where he conducted the first opera excerpts to be staged there. He also led the season's first symphony concert and was a guest with many foreign ambassadors at the Presidential Palace, Malacañing, hosted by Imelda Marcos, the first lady.

Mr. Feist, while a guest conductor in Seoul, Korea, visited the DMZ (zone) overlooking North Korea. He was required to wear the uniform of the U.S. troops.

Quote from *Opera News*

Robert Feist in late September conducted the first opera excerpts to be staged in Manila's Cultural Centera four-year-old structure of 2,000 seats suitable for concerts, ballet and opera. Under the aegis of the Manila Symphony Society, the American maestro led native singers in full staged scenes from *Madama Butterfly*, *Faust* and *Rigoletto*. The theater has been a pet project of Imelda Marcos, first lady of the Philippines, who attended the season's first symphony program, also conducted by Feist, and sponsored a reception for the participating artists at Malacañing, the presidential palace. According to Feist, the theater has excellent acoustics and audience support is enthusiastic. So successful, in fact, was the operatic evening that it was videotaped in color for a telecast.

at the sphinx. We also got on a camel back, separately, on several camels and I have photos of that. It was my first time on a camel and we laughed quite a bit, but it was a very interesting experience to be on a camel in Egypt.

Then we went back to Cairo and then went on a plane trip that took us to Alexandria which was, of course, the famous home of Cleopatra and that empire. In that city of Alexandria, we did another recital. It was in a recital hall and not really a big concert hall, but a small theater and it went very well. Again, she sang the same repertoire we had done in Cairo and it was very interesting to see the reaction of the students there and the public in general . Also we saw everything around Alexandria including the port and ruins still in existence. This trip has remained in my mind as one of the most fascinating I've ever had.

Another fascinating experience however occured later in 1975; I was invited probably through the United States Embassy to conduct in Teheran, Iran which I did not expect. I visited it once enroute back from the Phillipines for one day because I was tired, but I did not meet anyone there. This time when the invitation occurred I flew directly to Teheran, was welcomed there and lodged in a very nice modern apartment building. The whole city was as I had seen it before, very modern, very Americanized with taxi service and shops and everything and people dressed as they would in Europe.

There were three orchestras in the city, amazingly; the Teheran Symphony, whose conductor I met at lunch one day, and the Teheran Opera where major singers like Gobbi had sung in the previous years and I conducted the National Iranian Radio/Television Orchestra, a chamber orchestra made up mainly of Eastern Europeans. Well, this was a wonderful experience. The orchestra played well. We talked to them in rehearsal in English and in German, whatever worked and we did what I think was a remarkable program for Teheran at the time; a "Suite For Strings" by Janacèk from 1877, never heard there, David Diamond's "Rounds for String Orchestra," which I conducted in Naples.

Then after intermission, the "Adagio For Strings" by Samuel Barber and finally, the very difficult, "Piano Concerto, No 1" by Shostakovich This was really a tricky work for both the orchestra, for the solo trumpet and the piano soloist and it was a very, very successful concert. It was highly reviewed in the papers in Teheran, also in a French paper in Teheran as well as in America. And I made a lot of friends there. I've never seen them since, but I was invited to various parties and remained active seeing all of the city that I had not seen the first time when I was only there for a day or two.

So, that is another great experience. However, they wanted me back, but it never happened because as we all know the Cold War occurred. This wasn't part of the Cold War from Russia or anywhere else. This was simply the overtaking of the city by the Ayatolah Khomeni which caused the ejection of the Shah of Iran into exile which he spent in various countries for years with his wife.

Now when that occurred which is probably in 1979 or so, I'm not quite sure, that ended, of course, with the overtaking of the American Embassy and with our Americans in it being hostages and they were released on the day President Reagan was inaugurated. As a matter of fact I had even called the Iranian Embassy in Washington, D.C. to ask about returning. That was not after the Ayahtolah had come in but before that and they said: "We find it impossible to arrange for you to return because the country is absolutely in chaos and no western music is allowed or anything western in nature." And that, we know, persisted for years and years and years. So, my only trip to Teheran that was important was that in 1975 in May.

And then we went back to Rome and I resumed my teaching. Among the students I had had in Rome a couple of years before was a woman by the name of Alia Toukan and she was of Jordanian ancestry in the middle east in general. Her father was very prominent in Rome as the Ambassador of the Arab League in Rome and she was a student of the university where I was teaching, Loyola, as well as her brothers. She was not in my class, but she often visited with me at my apartment and brought her two brothers and I played tennis with them. There was a big tennis court there, right on the university grounds and we played tennis a few times and we became friends. To my amazement, not only that, soon after, her father was transferred to New York in some ambassadorial position and she went with him and she actually got a job, a position working for American Express or some such company, and corresponded with me from New York.

Well, she was of Arab origin from Jordan and it turned out that the king had just lost his wife or divorced his wife and she being of the right ethnic origins, asked for her hand in marriage. She was very surprised, but her father emphatically agreed with this, so Alia became Queen Alia al Hussein of Jordan after she moved back to Jordan and to the royal palace at

Above—This wedding photograph of King Hussein of Jordan and his wife, Alia, was sent to Mr. Feist with the inscription: "To Robert with my best wishes, Sincerely, Alia Hussein." Alia and her brothers and family were students and friends of Mr. Feist at the Loyola University Cultural Center in Rome (approximately 1973).

Opposite—This letter from the Royal Palace was one of several from Queen Alia (to Bob) and they are fondly retained.

THE ROYAL PALACE
Amman, Jordan
February 26, 1976

Dear Bob:

It was so nice to receive your card and letter. Thank you for your best wishes on the birth of Ali. He is a fine baby and we are very proud of him.

From the sound of your letter, you have been quite busy. Not only do your concerts, classes and articles keep you busy, but I am sure your decision to leave Europe took much time and consideration. You have my best wishes on your decision and I hope things work out as you would wish.

Tammy tells me you plan to be in the Middle East in May. We would be most happy to see you if you should be able to arrange your trip through Jordan. We have no symphony orchestra for you to conduct, of course, but it would be nice to talk over old times!

Looking forward to seeing you in Spring, I remain

Oman She actually kept up a correspondence with me writing very, very nice letters occasionally from the royal palace, signed by her as Queen Alia of Jordan, and sent me a wonderful photo of her and Hussein, which I have on my wall. She said: "I'm sorry but we have no orchestra here, so I cannot invite you to conduct here, but if you want to visit, you are welcome to come here." But that never turned out. I had no opportunity to go to Jordan and visit her and her husband.

Years later in 1977, (I'm jumping ahead now) came the shock. I was then living in America, but I had to fly to Europe to do a concert. The concert was with the Italian Radio, the RAI, in Milano and another interesting concert with the same orchestra. But I remember, at breakfast, at my hotel, I picked up the local newspaper, the *Corriere della sera*, and to my astonishment I read an article on one of the front pages that Queen Alia of Jordan had just died. She was on a mission with some of her friends to visit the poor and the impoverished on the outskirts of her country. She was in a small plane, I don't think it was a helicopter, but it crashed. But in this crash, she died. This took up quite a bit of space in the paper because of her position and the fact that her husband was very prominent in the Arab League and the Arab world. It really bothered me because that very morning, following reading this article, I had to rehearse with the orchestra and there was nothing I could do. I sent a card of some kind later to the Palace in Oman, expressing my sorrow at her passing. There was no reply and I had no more connection with Alia Toukan or her husband or her family.

Meanwhile I had maintained contact with my friends who directed the American College called Fleming College in Lugano, Switzerland, and they invited us, Marcella and me there to sing a concert. This was soon after my first return from Australia and we did a concert in the main theater in town with the Lugano Symphony which is called the Orchestra della Radio Svizzera Italiana, the Swiss-Italian Radio Orchestra.. All the students of the college were there and the citizens of the city and she sang the Barber: "Knoxville, Summer of 1915" and a few other things and it went very, very well. I was pleased that we got to do another concert together and especially in a city where my friends were in charge of the musical activity in the college itself.

Prior to that, I don't know exactly what year, I had been invited by the radio orchestra, the Radio Svizzera Italiana, to conduct a concert which would commemorate the 20th anniversary of the founding of UNESCO. And so, that occurred in Lugano and not only that, it was a concert that had music from many countries; America, Russia, Germany, and it was broadcast live, and I have a tape of it. And not only that but the concert was repeated in two or three neighboring small towns. The names escape me, but they are near Lugano around the lake. So, we did the concert three times in a row, more or less every night, or every other night—the same program and this was purely symphonic. There was no singing by Marcella. She was not involved, but it did involve the duo of pianists, Gorini and Lorenzi who were friends with me in Italy and we had played before and we did the same piece called *Homage to Paul Klee*, composed by Sandor Veress who was very well-known in Switzerland because he was actually living there and had been teaching in Zurich and Basel. So, we did the concert always inviting these two pianists and it was very, very effective.

Later on I returned to that school and I did a concert that celebrated the anniversary, let's say of the "Year of Czech Music" because I had already been to Czechloslovakia and somehow Europe was celebrating a Czechoslovakian week. So, the entire program had music by main Czech composers, not only Dvorak and Smetana, but also Janàcek and Klusak It was an interesting concert because of the concept and the fact that we were performing something familiar, but much unfamiliar music by all of the leading Czech composers in Switzerland. It was very well attended, recorded and broadcast by the Swiss-Italian Radio. This is another one of my prime memories of connections with Czechoslovakia and with Switzerland.

About this time I had begun to think very seriously of returning to America I saw still no particular hope in starting in a new theater in Germany with a leading position. It was still not really available to Americans. And I could see no change occurring in that direction. So, I decided I would return to America and trust my luck there. I made many inquiries by mail and by phone and with friends and an agent in New York, and I finally made the decision to return and I closed my tenure with the American University in Rome in 1974. That means that actually still taught there in the fall of 1975 and I firstwas in New York checking things there with agents and so forth and then I spent, luckily some time, a couple of years, in Cincinnati as my mother's health was declining and I knew it was very good to be there to help my father and also to be near her.

So, my departure from Rome had taken place only after a very nice event had occurred which was around 1972 when Marcella came down from Milano, where she lived, and our record had been issued, of course, and we did a special benefit recital in the University itself for all of the students and for anyone else to celebrate the 50th Anniversary of Giacomo Puccini, and this was interesting because on the program were many Puccini arias and we had the help of this wonderful tenor, Umberto Borsò who was a friend of mine and lived in Rome. So, the concert involved arias and duets from many operas of Puccini and it was very successful, not only for the faculty and the students, but for all others who were there. This included a friend of mine, the assistant conductor at the Rome Opera, Maestro Franco Cavaniglia.

This was, more or less, a farewell although I had not yet left the university. More important that that, in that same period which was roughly 1972-1973, I had managed to convince the Italian Radio, the RAI in Rome to let me perform an opera in concert which would then be recorded.. They knew very little of Czech repertoire except the well-known *The Bartered Bride* and perhaps Dvorak and Janácek and one or two or his. So, I proposed a very rare Smetana opera called *The Two Widows*, which I had loved in Prague when I saw it there. It was almost like a comic Italian opera, an Italian light opera, an opera buffa, which resembled an Italian opera which could have come from the time of sometime after Rossini or Verdi or Donizetti. Luckily we didn't have to do it in Czech because the RAI hired a man who was adept in languages to translate the entire opera into Italian. All of the score was in perfect Italian text and also my conductor's score. This is one of my highlights because the singers chosen by the RAI and by me were not Italy's leading singers, but they were all extremely good and they remain active, so the radio audience would know of them. We all went to Milano. I started the first rehearsal and then came another blow—the orchestra went on strike, not because of me, but because of the union problems—the usual questions, wanting more rehearsal time or wanting more money or something. It had happened in Rome also, not that year, but around that time. Thomas Schippers was then conducting *Manon Lescaut* and something else and a rare opera by Tchaikovsky, and the same thing happened. The Rome Opera struck and they had to postpone one opera completely and the other one was just missing from the schedule completely.

Robert Feist conductor and Gino Gorini, piano soloist at the Aug. 5, 1976 concert in the Roman Forum for the Bicentennial of the U.S Independence with the orchestra Nationale di Santa Cecilia.

So, Schippers was aggravated and though the orchestra was not striking against him, but they were simply striking for better wages and such things. He accepted this and just wasted time staying around Rome while the first opera disappeared into the air. But he did stay around to conduct the *Manon Lescaut* which involved Virginia Zeani who had moved from the coloratura repertoire of *Lucia* and *Sonnambula*, etc. into heavier lyric roles which eventually included *Alzira* by Verdi which I saw her do in Rome and *Aida* and similar heavier spinto roles. I personally didn't think she should make the move, but she did and the *Manon Lescaut* was exciting. The tenor should have been Richard Tucker, who was assigned to it, but because of the strike, he could not stay and so he departed. Another tenor, whom I don't recall, sang the role of des Grieux and he was very fine. The orchestra played very well for Schippers and I was very glad to be there.

Meanwhile my *Two Widows* by Smetana had resumed rehearsals after the strike. I played the piano for the singers alone and finally we got back to the orchestra and continued it. The only difficulty was, that time was running out. And we ended up with me recording the accompaniment to one soprano's aria and she came in and sang over it later with the recorded orchestral part and also the overture which was the kind of thing that had to be done with no rehearsal because we had no time. But it was all recorded and broadcast all over Italy, not live, but a few weeks later, with a lot of publicity in the papers for this Czech opera, *The Two Widows* and it remains one of my favorite rarities in the Czech repertoire and I'm glad to have a recording of it.

Getting back to where I had been, back to the question of leaving, by the time I returned in 1974-1975, I realized I that I would move back to the States and I finished the fall quarter of 1975 and returned to the States around Christmas expecting to stay. I had said my farewell to the university in Rome and I thought I would stay in Cincinnati and plan letters and calls for different positions and it happened that I was also called back to Italy because I had many more engagements that were pending and I had to return to do them.

These were not all casual concerts. They all were instigated by the Italian government and by the various opera houses and concert halls such as the RAI to honor, to acknowledge, the American Bicentennial of our independence which was in 1976. I was sure to be asked to do it because I had done so many concerts. And the first was to be in Naples, which occurred early before the Bicentennial, in the fall of 1975 when I did an honorary concert in Naples at the San Carlo with a guest Italian pianist who played the Gershwin "Rhapsody in Blue" and also with an American soprano, who had married an Italian. Her name was Lynne Strow Piccolo and she sang the Italian premiere of a suite of songs called *Songs of the Rose of Sharon* by the composer John La Montaine, which I did not know and learned. They were very, very effective, in a lyrical, conservative vein. That same concert or parts of it would be repeated the next year in Milano. Then I realized that my stay in Cincinnati was not to be that long.

So, I went and played for various master classes in various places including the University of Kansas, where a friend of mine was voice professor and, she brought in people like the accompanist to Leontyne Price for master classes which I also did. I was also invited to Chicago, not by the symphony, but by the Chicago Civic Orchestra, whose conductor was attached to the Chicago Symphony, and there I did a rehearsal in a long reading session to acquaint myself to the orchestra and to a new style. We did many works of different composers, not just American, and that was a very high point.

So, a few weeks and months passed rather quickly and by May I had returned to Europe. So I turned again to American works, because the next concert coming up was the official concert in Milano observing the American Bicentennial, sponsored by the American consulate or embassy and again we had the soprano, Lynne Strow Piccolo, who sang *The Songs of the Rose of Sharon* and I did other American works by famous composers including Copland and Barber. This was done as a very special concert for the entire public, but some by invitation and it was done in the concert hall of the RAI, a very wonderful theater. It was attached to a part of the Giuseppe Verdi Conservatory of Music Orchestra. Having done that I realized I was going to conduct again in Rome in about a month or so, so there was no reason to return to America. So, I arranged my lodging at the university where I had been teaching and I stayed there for the rest of the summer, visiting and studying and this was another summer of the Olympics which were held in Montreal, Canada. We saw all those events on TV in the lounge at the university.

The most important concert occurred in Rome and it happened that year in the summer of 1976 of the Bicentennial. It took place not in the hall where the orchestra dell' Accademia di Santa Cecilia performed, but in the Roman Forum. The summer season of the Santa Cecilia

Orchestra, which is the main orchestra of Italy, was performing out-of-doors in a specially constructed theater inside the Roman Forum right in the Basilica of Massenzio. It is a huge gaping opening which used to be inside a famous pagan temple in the days when the Roman Forum was built. But at this time in the summer, it is a big, built-up stage for the orchestra and a big auditorium installing chairs all over the place for the thousands of people. And the summer season included eight or ten guest conductors and with various repertoire. When I came on, it was the first time I had conducted the leading orchestra of the country, meaning the Academy of Santa Cecilia, based in Rome, and it was a great pleasure and a great thrill. Rehearsals went well.

The concert involved all American music; Copland, Bernstein, Barber and the Gershwin "Rhapsody in Blue," which was played by one of that famed duo of pianists, Gino.Gorini, as the soloist. And they were done in two sessions, meaning they were performed on a Saturday night and a Sunday afternoon, out-of-doors in the open air with thousands of people in the audience and the reception was absolutely wonderful. The press was terrific. The American Consulate and the Cultural Attaché, Rich Arndt, came and they took me and others to a special dinner afterwards to celebrate the American Bicentennial of Independence and it was one of the most memorable experiences of my career. I might mention here that the role of a cultural attaché (in this case Mr. Arndt), cannot be ignored, as I learned throughout my career in Europe and Asia, etc. In Rome, I was invited directly by the Accademia di Santa Cecilia to conduct, but the U.S. Embassy was already aware of the importance and hence Mr. Arndt's presence and preliminary support and post concert reception. Before this, the RAI Milano concert was under the "auspices" of the U.S. Embassy in Italy. The list goes on in other countries; as earlier in this book, the support of Leo Wiener, the U.S. Cultural Attaché in Moscow is evident and similar support was offered to me by the attaché in Prague at the time of the "cold war," and the Communist refusal to let me conduct there. Similar support and kind help was offered in Paris, Japan, Teheran (very important there), Germany, in many cities, in Australia and more. I also must thank Mr. Arndt's predecessor as our U.S. Rome Attaché, Mr. Russell Harris and his wife, who invited me to their home several times, followed the cultural scene carefully and eventually moved to Paris in a similar position. Then we lost touch, but my thanks go out to all of them for supportive action when needed on my behalf.

PROGRAMMA

LEONARD BERNSTEIN — Candide, ouverture
(prima esecuzione nei concerti dell'Accademia)

SAMUEL BARBER — Musica per una scena di Shelley
(prima esecuzione nei concerti dell'Accademia)

AARON COPLAND — Billy the Kid, suite dal balletto

GEORGE GERSHWIN — Porgy and Bess, quadro sinfonico
(trascr. di Robert Russell Bennett)

— Rhapsody in blue, per jazz-band e pianoforte

Above—A program cover of the most important of the four concerts conducted by Mr. Feist to commemorate the Bicentennial of the United States Independence.

Right—Maestro Feist at the podium for this concert by the National Orchestra of Saint Cecilia in the historic Basilica of Massenzio in the Roman Forum, 1976.

ROBERT FEIST, nato a Cincinnati, (Ohio, USA), ha studiato pianoforte, direzione d'orchestra e composizione presso il Conservatorio di quella città e successivamente all'Università dell'Indiana. Nel 1954, con una borsa di studio Fulbright, ha iniziato un corso di perfezionamento al Teatro dell'Opera di Roma che, in breve, gli ha consentito di diventare sostituto direttore accanto ai maestri Gui, Gavazzeni e Santini. In seguito è stato assistente di Wolfgang Wagner a Bayreuth. In Italia ha debuttato al Teatro Nuovo di Spoleto, nel settembre 1955, dirigendo l'orchestra del Teatro dell'Opera di Roma. Primo americano « Kapellmeister » in un teatro tedesco, ha diretto opere di Mozart e di Wagner, specializzandosi però nel repertorio lirico italiano, al Teatro Municipale di Augsburg. Ha diretto inoltre concerti e spettacoli di balletti, proponendo all'attenzione del pubblico parecchie prime esecuzioni assolute. Ha effettuato lunghe tournées in Estremo Oriente, in Nuova Zelanda, in Australia, dirigendo centinaia di recite di Verdi, Puccini, Mozart, Wagner, Strauss, fra cui le « prime » di « Don Carlos » e « Fanciulla del West » in Australia; concerti alla RAI di Torino, al San Carlo di Napoli, con l'Orchestra Sinfonica Siciliana di Palermo, la Filarmonica di San Remo, l'Angelicum e i Pomeriggi Musicali di Milano, la Filarmonica di Monaco di Baviera, la Radio Svizzera Italiana di Lugano, la Chicago Civic Orchestra, la New Orleans Philharmonic e la National Iranian Radio Television Orchestra a Teheran. Ha inciso per la Cetra con l'Orchestra dell'Opera di Roma. A Milano ha diretto la prima esecuzione in Italia delle « Due Vedove » di Smetana, alla RAI, in occasione del centocinquantesimo anniversario della nascita di Smetana e del centenario della prima esecuzione dell'opera a Praga.

ACCADEMIA NAZIONALE DI SANTA CECILIA
GESTIONE AUTONOMA DEI CONCERTI

BASILICA DI MASSENZIO
STAGIONE ESTIVA 1976

Giovedì 5 agosto 1976 · ore 21.30
tagliando n. 16

Venerdì 6 agosto 1976 · ore 21.30
tagliando n. 17

5950-5951 dalla fondazione dei concerti

CONCERTO NEL BICENTENARIO DELL'INDIPENDENZA DEGLI STATI UNITI

DIRETTORE

ROBERT FEIST

PIANISTA

GINO GORINI

ORCHESTRA STABILE DELL'ACCADEMIA

Mr. Feist acknowledging applause at the end of his concert in the Roman Forum for the Bicentennial of the U.S. Independence.

Rai
radiotelevisione italiana

In occasione del
BICENTENARIO
degli Stati Uniti

CONCERTO SINFONICO

PROGRAMMA

Sala Grande del Conservatorio G. Verdi di Milano
venerdì 11 giugno 1976 ore 21.00

WILLIAM SCHUMAN
CIRCUS OUVERTURE (1944)
per orchestra

PETER MENNIN
CANTO
per orchestra

JOHN LA MONTAINE
SONGS OF THE ROSE OF SHARON OP. 6
per soprano e orchestra
— I am the rose of Sharon and the lily of the valleys (Lentamente, ma scorrevole)
— I sat down under my head, and his right and doth embrace me (Molto adagio)
— O my dove, that art in the clefts of the rock (Moderato)
— My beloved is mine and I am his (Sereno e scorrevole)
— The voice of my beloved! Shold, he cometh (Molto lentamente)
— Rise up, my love, my fair one, and come away (Moderatamente veloce e con grande fervore)
Soprano: Lynne Strow Piccolo

SAMUEL BARBER
MUSIC FOR A SCENE FROM SHELLEY OP. 7
per orchestra

NORMAN DELLO JOIO
VARIAZIONI, CIACCONA E FINALE
per orchestra
— Semplice (Tema) - Semplice e grazioso - Andante religioso - Semplice e grazioso - Vivacissimo - Allegro pesante - Amabile Funebre
— Adagio serioso
— Allegro vivo, giocoso e ritmico

La Radiotelevisione Italiana ha il piacere di invitarLa al Concerto Sinfonico diretto da

ROBERT FEIST

Orchestra Sinfonica di Milano
della Radiotelevisione Italiana

Program from the observance of the United States Bicentennial in Milan with the orchestra of the RAI (Radio Television Orchestra) with soloist; the American soprano, Lynne Strow Piccolo.

A program observing the U.S. Bicentennial in Florence, Italy at the Teatro Comunale, the city's major opera house with an all Gershwin program at the request of the opera manager.

So, I was glad that I had stayed. But I had to stay on because after that came another concert in Florence. Florence decided to acknowledge the Bicentennial as well. They added after their season, two special concerts in September of that year in their main theater, the Teatro Comunale in Florence with all American music. It was planned to be all Gershwin and a rarity, in the city as was the case early in Rome, and I had the privilege and this was again involving the pianist, Mr. Gorini who played with me the "Rhapsody in Blue."

This concert was repeated and it had a wonderful reception. My best friend in Florence that I had known for years, Hilda Kanzler, an American, came to it and also her daughter Barbara. (Her daughter visited me here in America later and I visited them there).. They were present along with others and we had a reception afterwards at a nearby palace at which the artistic and the general director of the Florence Opera came and his staff. Everybody that I invited came to this big reception in honoring us and in honor of the Bicentennial.

It was my first opportunity to conduct the Florence Orchestra after all those years and it was a marvelous orchestra. They are well-known for their Maggio Musicale, which happens in the spring and summer, but this was not part of it. It was a special concert in late summer, early fall.

Having done that I realized that there was not reason to stay longer and I had to get back to America. So I flew back from Florence or from Rome to New York. I checked various possibilities there including a possible tenure as a professor at a university in Maine or Massachusetts and that didn't pan out, but it is just as well because I had had enough of that, actually, in Rome. It would have been with musical students. I spent the next period of time basically in Cincinnati, but doing a lot of visiting as a lecturer. One of the lectures involved an invitation from the society called "Opera America," which is a combination of all the opera houses in America and this was to take place in Oklahoma. The reason for it was to discuss verismo and on the panel with me was the editor of *Opera News*, Patrick Smith, at the time, and also singers such as Martial Singher and Blanche Thebom, and we then became well acquainted. So, we all addressed the audience and the panel itself and exchanged comments about verismo and our experiences with it and what we thought of it. This was not open to the public, it was simply a conference with members of the Opera America Society and they came from all over the country. This happened in one day and was very eventful and I got to not only see the other singers and the other panelists, but also much of Tulsa.

Soon afterwards this came an invitation to return to Milano again to the RAI and I went there and did a concert involving American works including *The Gershwin Concerto* for the piano, but also some novelties by Ives and Honneger. They wanted Honneger for some reason, and I did two works by him which are fairly well-known. One was *Pacific 231* quite well-known, and the other was *Rugby* which had never been done in Italy and it was very successful, with the exception of the Communist press. *L'Unità*, was the name of the newspaper. For some reason they didn't like it; didn't like the program; didn't like my conducting and yet the orchestra played wonderfully and the reviews in the other papers were excellent. But the director of the RAI there, Giorgio Vidusso, whom I had known well, replied when I asked him why this was so. "Well, look at the newspaper—it is a Communist newspaper; they are not necessarily in favor of programs featuring American music." This explanation is, I guess, the truth.

Soon after that, the following year, came an invitation to return to Switzerland and this was first time for me in the main orchestra city, let us say, Geneva, and it was l' Orchestre de la Suisse Romande, very well-known, and I was there to do a special concert, meaning a public concert and had works by Europeans as well as the world premiere by Jean Perrin whom I did not know. He was a Swiss-Frenchman and the piano concerto was the "Fifth" by Beethoven, "The Emperor" played by the wonderful American pianist Barbara Nissman and she played excellently and I was very, very glad to work with her. And I saw her again a year later in Chicago playing out-of-doors at Grant Park. This was a short visit. I was only there for the concert and there was a dinner afterwards with her and various friends of hers including the well-known composer, Ginastera, whose piano concerto she had premiered in Geneva that year. Then I returned again to America expecting and indeed awaiting agents to call from Europe.

Meanwhile I kept running around in America doing master classes and occasionally back to Europe for concerts in Switzerland, Italy and Germany, where I had first done a concert around 1978 in Munich with the Munich Philharmonic and this was for the German Radio station, the Bavarian Radio Network. They recorded and broadcast it, but the orchestra was not their orchestra but the Munich Philharmonic.

This was a concert involving not only American works but some European works as well and they had unfortunately scheduled a very difficult piano concerto by Rochberg. The concerto was so difficult that it took so much rehearsal time that we even had to drop a piece, which was the Ives: Schuman, "Variations on America" which was a shame because several of the Americans in the orchestra playing tuba or trombone really wanted play it, were ready to play it, but we couldn't get around to it. There was no audience. It was simply recorded for future broadcasts, which, thank goodness, I do have and it went well. The soloist was excellent; Veronica, the daughter of the famous conductor, Eugen Jochum. I later met with her in a Munich hospital to visit her father who was ill.

Back in America again from Germany I followed various leads and this agent advised that I might take over the Omaha Opera and I said I would meet them, but they were not interested. I was not and they were not. I was just as glad because I did not want return to American and sit in Omaha for the next few years. So, I looked for university positions. And as it turned out, several offers came, but not to my liking until I had suddenly the offer from the University of Washington here in Seattle, which wished me to come as the professor of orchestral studies, meaning graduate studies in conducting for masters and doctoral students and to conduct all of the symphony concerts and operas. This was absolutely to my liking because I had spent two years in the army in Washington at the old Hanford Works in the area of Richland and I had known Seattle briefly and liked it. Well, I was that summer so busy with my European schedule, I actually didn't even have time to audition. I simply went directly from Cincinnati to Seattle in the fall of 1981 and assumed my position, which went on then for the next seven years. It was a very interesting period.

I would dwell on it, in that I had a very good class of doctoral and masters students in conducting whom I taught using my staff for opera. I would sing the role or either another pianist on the faculty played the symphonic scores in piano arrangements, symphonies of everybody; Beethoven, Mozart, Tchaikovsky and Brahms, and they learned that way. If they made a mistake, the pianist would stop and we would do it again. They were not doing it with recordings which would not have made more sense. It had occurred to me when I was at Indiana University, that's all we did in conducting class was to conduct with recordings.

Well my tenure there at the U.W. (as we called the University of Washington) involved conducting maybe five or six symphony concerts a year, scattered throughout the year and also in the spring and in the fall—a major opera. In all, I conducted 18 operas at the university, always highly praised and with the best singers, many of whom had gone on from there to positions elsewhere including in Europe.

Among these students were several that stand out; several of my conducting students now have posts either at this city or in community orchestras or with major universities. As my principal student, Joseph White, who is now in a similar position to mine at a university in Virginia. Another is Kirk Gustafson, Conductor for Grand Junction Symphony. Many of them went on to careers, some in America, some in Europe. Among those should certainly be mentioned Jeffrey Francis who moved to New York and began working with a professor who worked him into the high Rossini repertoire in which he flourished. He sang these very difficult roles in New York and the New York City Opera and elsewhere in America. He became, as well, a member of the Berlin State Opera where he sang extremely difficult roles such as Rossini, Donizetti and even more modern composers which he did all over Europe including, to my amazement, his debut at the Rome Opera itself where I had worked, singing the tenor lead in Donizetti's *Roberto Devereaux*. This was an astonishing achievement and then he showed up here in Seattle a year ago singing the tenor lead in Donizetti's *Don Pasquale* and his improvement over the course of those ten or more years was amazing and thrilling.

In addition to him there were others such as the soprano Juliana Rambaldi who sang very much on the West Coast in regional companies and now is on the faculty of the University of Washington. There were more than that, but it would be too much to list them all. But Francis and Rambaldi really stand out. Others were the tenor, Barton Green (*Bohème* etc. at NYCO); bass, Mel Ulrich, now reviewed in *Opera News* in countless U.S. regional theaters; even San Francisco Opera,; the stage and set designer Erhard Rom; baritone Keith Harris, my most recent student here; and Marcia Bellamy, who went to Germany and sang for years at Deutsche Oper in Berlin, later marrying and moving to London.

Among the singers who auditioned and won the regional auditions for the Met in New York were several of my own best students. One was the aforementioned Jeffrey Francis who went on to New York to the finals and the other was another excellent tenor, the Korean, Pil Sung Kim who also went to the Met finals. Neither got to the Met Opera but they did work with the Met Opera Training Program at that time. Later Jeffrey Francis made his Met debut in *Idomeneo* in the fall of 2006. And then came the surprise that one year Menotti himself arrived in Seattle around 1988 for the premiere of a new work of his for chorus for the Seattle Men's Chorus and I met him and he, of course, remembered me from 1958 in Spoleto.

Well, he was looking for a tenor because he had written a new opera on commission for the Olympic Games in Seoul, Korea for that summer. And this opera needed a tenor and he had no Korean tenor, but I did. My tenor, Pil Sung Kim auditioned for him and Menotti was thrilled and he engaged him on the spot and Pil flew to Korea, his home country that summer and sang the world premiere of Menotti's new opera, *A Wedding Party* or a similar name. And I later engaged Kim himself to come to San Francisco to sing with me when we opened our opera company called Opera Peninsula, which I will get to later. At any rate he was an excellent tenor and since that time he has disappeared and we don't know where he is. I think he went back to Korea. (He *did* and just returned here to visit me in September of 2006.)

I will pause and then indicate that when my invitation to take the position there came when I was then in Europe. The whole spring and summer of 1981, I was conducting in Italy and Germany. I went over for a performance that was somewhat a repeat of the Bicentennial concert which took place with the orchestra of the arena in Verona, a superb group and in the winter they played in a theater, a wonderful theater in the city called Teatro Filarmonico. Again there was the same Gershwin program with Gino Gorini playing Gershwin and at that same summer, before or after that, I did another concert in San Remo on the Riviera and with Marcella Reale This was based on her verismo activity and it was a verismo concert with arias by Puccini, Mascagni, Leoncavallo and Giordano, the same people we had recorded.. That was done twice, once inside the opera house, which was attached to a casino in the city of San Remo and the other a few day later, out-of-doors, at an outdoor auditorium which was called the Franco Alfano Auditorium. It was a wonderful public and with wonderful acoustics and there again, it was the same concert. But, very interestingly enough we had just recorded one of Alfano's arias in our recording of verismo, an aria from *Cyrano de Bergerac* and his daughter knew of this and wanted to meet me, so I met Signora Alfano at her home in San Remo. We had a wonderful discussion with her about her father and his life and it got me very, very impressed with his activities then unknown to most of the world. It turned out, however that she and I continued a correspondence that went on for several years. At the university in Seattle, she wrote to me and I replied always to her in Italian until she passed away.

So, the Alfano connection was very fine but in that same period in Italy, besides the events in San Remo and at the RAI, I returned to Munich to the Philharmonic and did another concert with them which was basically American works though there were other works involved. That was my second time with the Munich Philharmonic and I cherished the memory very much..

Then I returned and had the job in Seattle which began in the fall of 1981 and continued. Although as I was a tenured professor and knew that I could stay there as long as I wished. The work was extremely taxing because after a concert I would be involved in an opera and the rehearsals went on and on and on. So, to get away, to absent myself, caused a problem as there was no one to take my place. So, I would find that when I first went over to judge a competition in eastern Washington, the Dean of Fine Arts complained that I was gone for two days and that, of course, irritated me.

Later that year or the next, I was invited to conduct the orchestra of the Netherlands Radio in Amsterdam through a connection that I had acquired earlier and this involved a departure for some time for, I think, ten days or so. But, they let me do it because they thought it was important. That concert was a very, very eventful one. I flew to Amsterdam and immediately went outside of town to a suburb where the recordings took place—where the Radio was established, in Hilversum. I stayed at a hotel there, rehearsed the orchestra and it was all American music—some that I had done before and others that were new to me and to them and the recording went very well. I also have it on tape, as it was sent to me. Other than that, my departures consisted mainly of events occurring here and at neighboring places as a judge.

First of all is the connection with the radio. Well, the radio connection is a very big one in my career and it started in Cincinnati. On my return from Europe I became acquainted with the director of the National Public Radio station there, Mr. Albert Hulsen, and we became friends. He knew of my career in Europe and he had been there often. He suggested: "Why not do a series of programs dedicated to opera and symphony?" All of my choice. Well, we formulated the first group of 13 programs dedicated to many aspects of opera and symphony and famous composers and so forth. We recorded in the studios in Cincinnati, WGUC, and then it was sent all over the country and he had letters coming from all corners praising these broadcasts which I wrote and narrated.

I would spend time writing the script, choosing the records, and then go into the studio recording my voice and they would insert the recordings that I had brought, Well, this first one, which was in 1977 or 1978 led to others. In short, I continued to make them. So, by the time I left Cincinnati with all my other absences and came to Seattle, I was still involved in this recording process which could continue here as well and I did that. When recording, Mr. Hulsen came here and I had the script and records ready and we recorded in the NPR studios here at the University of Washington which was KUOW. He was succeeded in Cincinnati by Ann Santen, a well-known and marvelous woman who did an excellent job.

A program cover for "Exploring Opera with Robert Feist." This was a series of radio programs written and hosted by Mr. Feist from the WGUC in Cincinnati which aired on National Public Radio.

And that was the last series that I did here. I had already done four or five series of 13 programs and they were broadcast nationally and some were picked up internationally by English- speaking countries such as Australia or New Zealand. Knowing this, the local district and regional auditions for the Metropolitan Opera, asked me to help because when we had the regional auditions, Seattle would head the Northwest Region including five states, and the finals took place in the auditorium of the university, a very beautiful theater where all of my operas and concerts took place. They asked me to be the host mainly because of the pronunciation of all the composers and works that were done. So, that started that year and continued all the periods I was in Seattle. I would be backstage with the singers, the judges would hear someone, I would announce what they had chosen into the mike and the singer would go out and sing another aria.

And so it happened with all of the singers. There would be 15 or 20 singers in one, long Regional audition period. This happened only once a year and it came at different times. It could have been January or February and now it even happens earlier in December (Following what we call the district auditions, because districts included other states and cities like Portland, Vancouver, Montana and Idaho and elsewhere). But, when it got to the final one, that occurred in Seattle and it was called the Regional Audition. So, all of my time was spent not only conducting and teaching, even advanced vocal studies, giving singers all sorts of unusual repertoire to learn, and accompanying them, occasionally in recital, I was doing all this regular work, which took considerable time and I enjoyed it very much.

But, there was little opportunity to return to Europe even though invitations occurred from time to time, but they didn't want me to leave the university for such prolonged periods of time, to my regret. Therefore, at a certain point, I realized that I really was tiring of the university activities which kept me from doing any major conducting elsewhere and therefore I decided that I would retire or resign from the university and go on to other things which began with an invitation from Mr. Hulsen, of National Public Radio, who was then based in Hawaii. He wanted me to do a long, fifty-week series on all the music of the Pacific Rim countries. That involved, of course, China, Korea, Japan, Australia, New Zealand, etc.

This was fascinating. But it was too much to do while I was at the University. I could never have handled that. But, just before that invitation occurred, I was invited by a friend of mine whom I had known from Spoleto, William Lewis, to California, where he had created a new festival in Lake Tahoe, called The Festival of American Opera. This occurred in the summer of 1988 and it was to be a festival including only American operas and I was the director, the singers were all American. It turned out that at that time I knew that Mr. Hulsen had invited me to continue with recording, a project of the music of the Pacific Rim, so it was too much to do while I was at the university, so I resigned. I simply left and I moved to California for a stay of approximately two years and it started out with this festival at Lake Tahoe where we did operas. I did the famous opera, *The Ballad of Baby Doe* and there were others on the roster that I did not conduct, including Gordon Getty's opera *Plump Jack* which has since been repeated in New York and elsewhere in the USA—he was based in California.

After that summer I knew, that through Bill Lewis, I was invited to take over the Oakland Opera and the Oakland Symphony which at that time had no permanent conductor. Oakland was then struggling to regain its position, so I moved, initially, to Oakland. I conducted first an opera in the fall, which was *Carmen* with the mezzo soprano, Wendy Hillhouse, who was already at the Met and later San Francisco. We did the *Carmen* and Bill Lewis sang the tenor role and there was a bass brought in from elsewhere and a soprano who had been a student of mine at the time, Sheila Burkh, who later married Bill Lewis. The *Carmen* was an introduction to a new opera season in Oakland and it went very well. It was followed by several other operas, one of which I didn't conduct, *Traviata,* and then came *Madame Butterfly* and *Tosca*. The *Butterfly* included my prime student and protégé, who was the baritone Ralph Wells, who had won the San Francisco auditions and was a member of the Merola Program and Apprentice Program of the San Francisco Opera which took him all over the country. Here he was the Sharpless, but the soprano and mezzo were really unknown to me. But the *Butterfly* went very, very well. The *Tosca* was even more important because it had the soprano everyone knew from the movie *DIVA*, Wilhelminia Fernandez who did the *Tosca* and her husband, Andrew Smith, was the baritone, Baron Scarpia. Both had sung with me leading roles in the Houston Grand Opera production of *Porgy and Bess* which I had led for two weeks in Miami, Florida in 1978. They were both excellent and I was very, very glad to run into them again in Oakland, California and we remembered many things about the *Porgy and Bess* production.

The tenor was a discovery for me. He was a local tenor, Keith Ikaia-Purdy, a double name, and he was a marvelous, sensational artist as I found out later as his career suddenly blossomed. He was heard in the East and then he was engaged in Europe and before I knew it, he was in Vienna as a star tenor in the Vienna State Opera, where I heard him years later. But he began really in Oakland and that was a great joy to conduct these people in that opera.

At that time, the Oakland Symphony, which played for the opera, was searching for a new conductor. I was invited to do their introductory concert, which was done for a small audience and it went very well. They didn't appoint me permanent conductor because they were shuffling around and they had several possibilities. But, it turned out that during the course of that fall or spring, they did three official concerts in the big theater in Oakland, the Paramount Theater. One of them was conducted by Jorge Mester; one was conducted by the ballet conductor of the San Francisco Opera and I conducted another concert. They all went well and I did not expect to be asked to take it over. It turned that, of course, they were basically looking for a black conductor because Oakland, as we all know, is a very much a black-oriented, African-American city in general. So, at the time I decided that I would prefer to live not there where I had rented a room, but to live in San Francisco to continue my recording projects. I had met a friend from the summer opera festival at Tahoe and they had a room in their house and I moved in there which was in South San Francisco, right next to San Francisco and I stayed there for the next year approximately.

From there I continued on this radio series of 50 programs hearing all the recordings that were sent to me by Mr. Hulsen in Hawaii and wrote the scripts according to the works which involved Japanese, Australia, New Zealand, Chinese and Korean music and it was very interesting to do all of these things while living in San Francisco and going in every day by the Bart, the subway, to the recording studios which were in the big radio station, KKHI in the main hotel of Union Square. It was not NPR, but they were the ones that recorded all of my programs. I was very glad to meet the staff which was exceptionally favorable and helpful in all ways. So, that series of 50 programs was finally finished with my recording sessions.

And in between came another excursion, this is to backtrack a bit, because this was a return in 1970 to the Far East. And it occurred while I was still living in Rome and I was invited to conduct the Seoul Philharmonic Orchestra in Korea because its conductor was then on leave and I looked forward to it because at the same time the Manila Symphony had engaged me again. So, I flew from Rome to the Far East to Korea and was there for a long time and I did several concerts with them. The orchestra was fine, not as professional as one of the RAI orchestras in Italy, but I did several excellent concerts which I think brought them into prominence and they liked what I did. In between two of them I flew from Korea to Manila and did another concert which was symbolic because it was the introduction to everyone of the new "Manila Theater of the Performing Arts," a brand new building constructed under the auspices of Imelda Marcos, the wife of the President, and it was right on the shores of the ocean.

It was a beautiful place and an excellent facility. This concert was memorable because of the fact that Mrs. Marcos came with her entourage and after the concert invited me to the presidential palace for a reception in which all of the heads of state were there. All the ambassadors etc. from various countries nearby or far away were present in the palace for this presidential reception. I was tired because of the rehearsals and the performance and yet when we got to the reception in her own limousine, sitting with her and the violin soloist, they told me that at a certain point Mrs. Marcos was going to want to sing because she always liked to sing for her guests. Well, this was some time before their expulsion into exile. So, I waited, we had dinner and then at some point they announced Mrs. Marcos would sing. She sang popular and folk songs. I told the French ambassador that I was worn out and really had to get home. He said: "I will take care of it." So, he very cautiously, in an intermission, approached her and the staff and said: "Mr. Feist is really worn out and has to go home to rest," and they agreed. So, he and his wife, who were also glad to leave this event, drove me home and at that time it was the home of the Mannings, the wonderful woman who really ran the Manila Symphony and at other times I stayed in a hotel or a private residence in downtown Manila.

That particular trip in 1970 brought me from Manila back to Korea for another concert. From there I flew to San Francisco and from San Francisco up to Seattle to meet the then, general director of the Seattle Opera, Glynn Ross, who just recently passed away. He had learned of me and Marcella Reale and he had invited her to sing there before this, but I thought that I would have an invitation, but it did not turn out because he had his permanent conductor, Henry Holt, so all we did was to have lunch and talk and that was that. I ran into him once later in Cincinnati at a performance of the "Opera America" crowd and Beverly Sills sang

Traviata. Then he approached me and asked if I would I like to come to Seattle next year and conduct her in her *Traviata* in Seattle. It didn't fit in with my schedule and I declined because I knew that this way of making a debut in the city was not to my advantage. It would only be to the advantage of Beverly Sills, whom I admired in many things like Lucia, but I did not care for her Violetta in *Traviata* and now we have also recently lost this great artist, famous in countless roles.

So, I returned to Rome. After that, at various intervals I was invited back to Manila both from Rome and also from Seattle. It occurred later that year and occurred several times, as a matter of fact while I was living in Seattle and with returns to the Philippines. In that time my work continued in San Francisco. I finished the recording project completely. I did the first concert that I had planned to do with the Oakland Symphony and I did a concert in Marin County, north of San Francisco in a very affluent area. I also conducted a concert of modern works including choral works with soloists in the theater next to the San Francisco Opera. It was a concert with invited guests and we did all this contemporary American music which went very well and I was very glad. It turned out that I met excellent friends who I often stayed with or visited in San Francisco. They were very supportive of me.. These were Mr. and Mrs. Tede. Margery was a singer, a mezzo, and I worked with her often at her home in San Francisco and through her met a lot of people there.

As it turned out, around that time, or a little later, I became a judge for the Metropolitan auditions, which I had done once in Louisville, Kentucky. I judged the Met District and Regional Auditions in San Francisco and in Portland, Oregon as well as Seattle. I was the co-judge in San Francisco with Sam Ramey, which was fine. We got to know each other and he was very easy to deal with and to work with and we all agreed on the winner at that time.

So the judging continued even up to the time I had returned to Seattle—judging various competitions. But when I saw that I would not conduct the Oakland Symphony as the permanent conductor, I had finished the recording project and the trips to Manila etc., I realized that I didn't think I would want to live in San Francisco. I was not invited to conduct the San Francisco Opera though the general manager knew me from Europe. This was Lotfi Mansouri. He heard me do the *Tosca*. But they preferred to have the usual Italian or foreign conductors which has gone on to this day.

THE OREGONIAN, WEDNESDAY, JUNE 5, 1991

ARTS & ENTERTAINMENT / TELEVISION

Italian opera specialist to lead class

By DAVID STABLER
of The Oregonian staff

Italian opera, so laden with tradition, means smooth, beautiful singing, known as bel canto. It means executing florid ornaments and high-flying cadenzas with perfect breath control. It also means a blood-and-guts delivery in the realistic operas of Giacomo Puccini and other turn-of-the-century composers.

Italian operatic traditions have historically been handed down from teacher to student, conductor to orchestra player. The specialists learned their craft from the composers themselves. Now, the experts are getting old and dying, taking their precious knowledge with them.

Today, opera singers who want to succeed in the Italian repertoire must either have the good fortune of being born in Italy, or pick the brain of someone who knew someone who knew someone who worked with Puccini or Pietro Mascagni.

Every year, scores of serious young singers travel to Milan or Rome or Florence to learn from these experts twice or thrice removed. They spend years working closely with vocal coaches, conductors and accompanists.

One person who did just that has moved to Portland. Robert Feist is a conductor and vocal coach, now teaching at Portland State University. Feist hopes to teach Portland singers some of what he learned from working in Italy for 13 years.

Feist will lead a master class for singers at Portland State University on Wednesday. The class will take place at 7 p.m. in Room 75, downstairs in Lincoln Hall.

Singers and auditors are welcome. Admission for auditors is $5.

During three years as a Fulbright scholar and conductor at the Rome Opera, Feist learned from some of the best in the business: Tullio Serafin, who taught Maria Callas most everything she knew; Gabriele Santini; and Vittorio Gui.

While conducting orchestras in Milan, Turin, Naples and Verona, Feist brushed up against the best interpreters of Italian opera of the day: Callas, Renata Tebaldi, Tito Gobbi and Giuseppe Di Stefano.

Feist is one of the few specialists in Italian opera in Oregon. "The tradition hasn't been carried on in this country," Feist says. "Singers must learn this, but most voice teachers don't know the traditions. We're trying to open the door to anybody who

---

Friday, May 17, 1991 The Seattle Times E 5

A&E BRIEFING

Feist heads troupe

Conductor Robert Feist, formerly of the University of Washington School of Music, now heads a new company called Opera Peninsula in San Mateo, Calif. Following a January gala and last month's "Cosi fan tutte," the company will produce Verdi's "Jerusalem" in its first staged production in the United States since 1850, this July 3-13 with Feist conducting. "Jerusalem" is Verdi's French-language reworking of his "I Lombardi alla Prima Crociata" for ticket and other information, call Opera Peninsula at 415-508-2178.

Articles from the Portland, Oregon *Oregonian* regarding Feist's work at Portland State University and from the *Seattle Times* about his work with Opera Peninsula in San Mateo, California.

Willamette Week OCTOBER 8—OCTOBER 14, 1992

Feist Puts on a Show

By David Maclaine

**The Portland Rossini Festival
First United Methodist Church
Sunday, Oct. 4**

FOR A LONG TIME we've had it wrong about Mickey and Judy. Those musicals in which Master Rooney and Miss Garland played a couple of teen-agers who had a barn and said, "Let's put on a show!" always felt absurd because the gifted

CLASSICAL MUSIC

young stars and the Hollywood chorus lines seemed way too classy for small-town USA. But the second concert of the Portland Rossini Festival—the first was last spring; the last comes Oct. 16—was a forceful reminder that in our city it's really not unusual to stumble on talent that overshadows its humble settings. What's more often missing here is the happy ending in which the crowded audience roars its appreciation and the big-city producers realize they've just discovered a new star.

Although he's been in town for a couple of years now, this was the first chance the widely traveled conductor Robert Feist has had to show the locals what he can do with an orchestra. The program was devoted to music written by Rossini when the composer was still a precocious teenager, and the narrow range of the young Italian's style leaves little room for error. Before his craft had been perfected and full sophistication attained, Gioacchino simply relied on the lilt of his melodies and the forward push of his rhythms.

Feist knows his Rossini. In the three instrumental works that filled the first half of the program, he proved he can make orchestral players treat their lines as real tunes rather than the mechanical patterns on a page they remain when our city's more perfunctory conductors wiggle their batons. An occasional astringency from the violins could not dampen the easygoing pleasure of the Overture to *La Scala di Seta* and the String Sonata No. 3. A few breathy patches in Stan Stanford's solo work during the Introduction, Theme and Variations for clarinet and chamber orchestra were a trivial price to pay for his rich tone and expressive virtuosity.

The limitations of a low-budget show cramped the concert's second half. Rossini's first opera, *La Cambiale di Matrimonio*, relies on stock *opéra bouffe* situations—young lovers thwarting silly old men to attain a happy union—and half the fun of the genre is the broad physical comedy with which the plots play out. This *Cambiale*—a Portland première—managed to entertain despite a concert-style presentation that jammed the uncostumed singers behind music stands at a side of the stage. The performers who made us yearn for full staging still offered

> **F**eist knows his Rossini—he proved he can make orchestral players treat their lines as real tunes rather than mechanical patterns on a page.

enough energetic, *bouffe*-in-a-closet to hold the show together. As the two elders whose respective efforts to buy and sell a wife fling them into farcical strife, David Jimerson and Ralph Wells merged gesture and vocal acting to make their characters' every bluster and quaver understandable and hilarious, despite the absence of a Supertext to translate their Italian.

The modest audience did its best to fill the barnlike space of the First United Methodist Church with applause, but they lacked the sheer numbers of Hollywood extras who, in the movies, could always overpower the echoes with their cheers as they propelled the dark-eyed girl with the incredible voice and the sawed-off dynamo with the freckles on to Broadway stardom. But as show after underattended show by gifted locals can attest, this is not a city that can recognize a star out of costume or a conductor who's not perched in front of the Oregon Symphony. Start them at the bottom in Portland and Mickey and Judy might never have escaped the purgatory of half-empty high school auditoriums and the earnest, ineffectual praises of family and friends. •

A part of the program for Giuseppe Verdi's *Jerusalem* produced and presented by co-founders Robert Feist and Michael Morris of Opera Peninsula.

ROBERT FEIST

A native of Cincinnati, Ohio, Mr. Feist completed his undergraduate work at the Cincinnati College of Music and his Master's at Indiana University. A Fulbright Fellowship brought him to for his conducting apprenticeship at the Rome Opera House with the major conductors and singers of the era; his chief mentors were Gui, Gavazzeni, Santini, Serafin, and others at Bayreuth where he studied on the invitation of Wolfgang Wagner. Since his conducting debut in 1955 with the Rome Opera House Orchestra, Mr. Feist has led many of the world's major orchestras in concert and in opera on four continents, chiefly in Europe during more than two decades residence in Italy and Germany, with long sojourns in France, Russia and Czechoslovakia, and some 10 tours to the Far East, Middle East, Australia and New Zealand. Prominent among these have been the Teatro San Carlos in Naples, L'Accademia di Santa Cecilia in Rome, The Teatro Comunale/Maggio Musicale in Florence, the RAI orchestras of Milan and Turin, L'Arena di Verona, as well as others in Milan, Palermo, Trieste, Spoleto (Festival of Two Worlds), San Remo, The Munich Philharmonic and Augsburg Philharmonic, L'Orchestre de la Suisse Romande in Geneva, the Swiss-Italian Radio Orchestra in Lugano, the Netherlands Radio Orchestra, the Seoul Philharmonic, Manila Symphony and the Australian and New Zealand Operas. Since his American debut in New Orleans with *Tosca*, he has conducted in his native Cincinnati, Miami, Chicago, St. Petersburg, the Seattle Symphony and the University of Washington Symphony where he served as Director of Opera and Symphony for seven years; and in California at the Festival at Lake Tahoe, the Oakland Opera, the New Oakland East Bay Symphony and the Marin Civic Light Opera.

In addition to the standard repertoire, Mr. Feist has pioneered contemporary works in concert with a list of over one hundred regional premieres conducted throughout the world, and over fifty operas of all eras from Handel and Mozart to the twentieth century, chiefly the Italian repertoire from Rossini to Puccini, and including some seven West Coast or Northwest premieres in Seattle and the USA premiere there of Martinů's *Julietta* in 1988. For CETRA in Italy he has recorded rare verismo excerpts with the Rome Opera Orchestra.

Mr. Feist is also known as a radio host and commentator. He has written and hosted five nationally (and one internationally) broadcast series for NPR and APR ("Exploring Opera" and "Orchestras of the Pacific"). His most extensive endeavor in this area, "Winds of the East", a 52-week series on all major orchestras, as well as opera, chamber and indigenous music of all countries of the Pacific Rim, is due for national and international broadcast in 1991-92, and is currently being aired by KKHI in San Francisco (where it was recorded), and other stations in Portland, Honolulu, Eugene, etc. Mr. Feist has served as judge or host of the Metropolitan and San Francisco Opera regional auditions, has been panelist for national conferences of the Metropolitan Central Opera Service and the American Symphony Orchestra League, and given Master Classes throughout the United States.

A Rare Verdi Gem on the Peninsula

By Joshua Kosman
Chronicle Staff Critic

Opera Peninsula did a cagey thing by concluding its maiden season with an attention-getting operatic rarity, Verdi's "Jerusalem." The fledgling company did an even cagier thing by giving the piece a thoroughly creditable and often excellent account.

Under conductor Robert Feist, Saturday night's performance — the second of two in the San Mateo Performing Arts Center — offered impeccable musical values, including first-rate orchestral playing and vibrant, skillful singing from two of the principals. If the evening was a bit short on dramatic power, that seemed an acceptable price to pay for a presentation so much richer than what regional opera usually has to offer.

Inspiring

Musically, however, the performance was of an inspiringly high quality. Feist paced the flow with consummate sensitivity throughout; charging ahead in the more dramatic passages and relaxing for the score's lyrical interludes. The orchestra proved to be an unusually fine ensemble, playing with sureness and tonal beauty.

A review from the *San Francisco Chronicle* for the attention-getting operatic rarity, *Jerusalem* by Opera Peninsula, and another from the San Jose *Mercury News*.

San Jose Mercury News ■ Saturday, July 6, 1991 5C

Opera Review

A Verdi jewel shines after years of darkness

By Paul Hertelendy
Mercury News Music Writer

A PRICELESS jewel of an early Verdi opera was unveiled this week by one of the smallest, newest and least-publicized troupes on the West Coast.

Opera Peninsula is presenting Verdi's French opera, "Jérusalem" (1847), a revised and improved version of his Italian opera "I Lombardi" (1843), in a rare production that has caught the elite troupes sleeping.

Choice pit work

Opera Peninsula's conductor, the veteran Robert Feist, achieves greater success here than many a podium star at the Opera House in San Francisco. While the back-up cast and chorus are rather amateurish, the 48-member orchestra of free-lancers proves itself one of the Bay Area's best pit ensembles.

Opera Peninsula
"Jérusalem," by Guiseppe Verdi
Performed in French, conducted by Robert Feist
When: 8 tonight
Where: Foothill College Theater, 1235 El Monte Rd., Los Altos Hills
Tickets: $20, $18 students/seniors, $15 children under 12
Call: (415) 948-4444
Also: July 11 and 13 at San Mateo Performing Arts Center; (415) 329-2623.

This Belmont-based company has made a quantum leap in quality and production standards, this time under producer Michael Morris, since its low-budget inaugural production of "Cosí fan tutte" in mid-April.

So, I decided it was time to move again and I did not want to immediately return to Seattle and I said: "In between is Portland." So, I checked with all of my friends in Portland, and I liked that area and I moved there. I became the Adjunct Associate Professor of Voice and Opera at the Portland State University. This was a pleasure because I coached most of the fine singers in Portland and in addition to that got to know everyone in that area and judged the Met auditions there. It also gave me an opportunity to produce things on my own, such as, most importantly, the Rossini Festival. I created the *only* observance of the Rossini Bicentennial that I can remember in the West, meaning even San Francisco. This was a bicentennial occasion for a composer that I loved and through him, my mentor, Maestro Gui, was very memorable to me.

So, I arranged a series of four concerts, one as a recital with the leading singers of Portland, including those from the university and that covered a whole array of Rossini arias from his operas. That was done in a theater in Portland. After that, some time later, we arranged for the orchestral concerts. One was done in the very big Episcopal Church in Portland where all the symphony concerts were held by other orchestras. For this concert I hired the Dean of the Portland State University Music Department, Professor Stanford, who played Rossini's *Variations for Clarinet and Orchestra*. I did an overture and a string symphony and then did the local premiere of Rossini's early opera, *La Cambiale di Matrimonio*. It is a wonderful work in one act and I used the best singers that I knew in that area including my baritone friend Ralph Wells, and the leading baritone professor at the university who was David Jimerson and the soprano, Ruth Dobson, from there as well and it went very well. We did that two times. To conclude the Rossini Bicentennial there were two concerts of choral music which meant his famous last work, "Petite Messe Solennelle," a small solemn mass, which was done in that same theater or church with four soloists, two pianos and organ. I played one of the piano parts and the soloists were excellent and that created a lot of applause. We repeated that down the road, meaning some distance away, in Eugene, Oregon, where we performed the same work in another church there.

And these Rossini events created quite an impression for me and the city observing the Bicentennial. In fact, it was sponsored by Italian Consulate General in San Francisco who had been a lot of help in this case and who came up for these concerts. Prior to this, the same Italian Consulate helped me out in another major adventure or venture, which took place in California and that was, at the time when I lived in Portland, but still commuted to San Francisco for various events that involved my presence.

This involved the creation of a new opera company that a friend of mine and I conceived called the "Opera Peninsula" on the peninsula which neighbors the San Francisco Bay and it was to include several operas. It turned out to be a public success but not financial, because we didn't have a strong enough board who would support another opera company in the vicinity of San Francisco Opera. But we did achieve something very big: an American premiere of a rare work that no one knew.

In this case it was an opera that I had on tape from a performance in Italy and it was Verdi's *Jerusalem*, his first opera commissioned by the Paris Opera, way before *Don Carlo* and he had later revised it into an Italian version which he called *I Lombardi*. *I Lombardi* is familiar to everybody. I had seen it in Rome under Gavazzeni with Scotto and Pavarotti. Later I got the tape with Gavazzeni conducting the first version, the *Jerusalem*. With the help of the San Francisco Italian Consul General, they obtained the music which was not recorded. It was owned by the Italian RAI, the Radio Corporation. They paid for the rental and the shipment and all the materials came to us in San Francisco.

We engaged a cast. I auditioned many people, especially the soprano, who had come from Montreal, and we knew of her and so she came down to audition for me in Seattle, of all places, for the leading role. And we engaged her. Her name is Maureen Brown, who later went on to become a leading singer at the opera in Graz, Austria. The rehearsals went very well. We decided that we would first, prior to that, do another opera, more familiar, and it was *Cosi Fan Tutte* with all the local singers that we knew from their history and their performances including Wendy Hillhouse, who had already sung with me in the *Carmen* in Oakland and who lived there. This *Cosi Fan Tutte* was first done in a smaller theater below San Mateo and San Mateo was going to be our home base basically because they had a big theater.

So, we did the *Cosi Fan Tutte* in the original Italian version and it went very, very well. It was our introduction to the city and that area, except for a prior concert, which was an orchestral symphony concert with vocal solos. That had taken place earlier and involved local singers in addition to whom we had the famous Carol Neblett, from the Met, who lived in the San Diego. area and she very gladly agreed to do this. Others were Michael Morris, co founder of the company, a fine baritone, and my former university tenor student, Pil Sung Kim, whom I mentioned earlier. The concert involved arias and duets from *Il Trovatore, Norma* with Wendy Hillhouse and *Lucia* and *Trovatore* and other operas. That was our real start for this opera company, the concert, and it went very well.

Following that came the *Cosi Fan Tutte* in that small town and the *Cosi Fan Tutte* was done twice. Then it came time for the *Jerusalem*. We rehearsed it very, very much and we did it four times. We did it twice in the smaller theater near San Jose, and we did it twice more in the San Mateo Performing Arts Center. This was with Maureen Brown, local basses and a wonderful tenor from the New York City Opera, Jianyi Zhang, a Chinese tenor, who had a career extending from the New York City Opera to the Paris Opèra Comique and the Opèra. .He was very good in French and was very happy to do this.

So, the premiere went exceeding well and when we got up to San Mateo Performing Arts Center, it received absolutely rave reviews from the entire San Mateo and San Francisco press. All of them came and welcomed us as the new opera company in the area who they said left all the others in their tracks or in their wake. Well, this was very encouraging except for the fact the cost of this production of *Jerusalem* was excessive. We had planned to have in the next year two operas, one a double bill and another major opera, but by the time we got around to it, we realized it was going to be difficult. I was then in Portland. I was even in Portland for the performances of *Jerusalem* and I flew down for the performances and when we planned the new season we had an introductory recital for the public, which went alright, but did not generate that much enthusiasm.

So, we thought about it for some length and realized to put on two more major productions in San Mateo would be a total waste of time and bankruptcy, which it did. It drove this small, new company into bankruptcy so we could not continue with the company we had envisioned as being a new one to rival Oakland but not San Francisco, of course, or to even rival San Jose, which was still functioning with minor singers and in a very small theater. I had seen one or two of them. So, we realized there was no point in continuing our Opera Peninsula and I simply stayed in Portland then for approximately three years and finally finished the Rossini Bicentennial and was about to continue and then I began to think about returning to Seattle.

I had had many friends visit me in Portland, of course, but then came an invitation from the woman who had been helping us with Opera Peninsula in housing one or two of the singers and she was a very big help to us, this was Nell Arnold, who was by then not only a voice teacher, but a very good business woman who had the post which was offered to her as Director of the Business School of the Queensland State University in Australia. She took that very gladly and went to Australia with her husband, who was a singer and a voice teacher and that lasted for several years.

In her second year there she was guiding and hosting a tour of business people, all the business men in Queensland and elsewhere, to China to further business ties with China and said it would be a good experience for me as well to do more for them musically and to introduce me to China which the Chinese Embassy in San Francisco also wished. So, this was a welcome departure and I did this from Portland. I flew directly from Portland alone to Japan and stayed one night in Japan and then flew by Chinese airline to Beijing. In Beijing I was welcomed by Mrs. Arnold and her colleagues in business and was housed in a very excellent hotel. Then I engaged in teaching which they had arranged.

I became visiting professor of conducting at the Conservatory of Music in Beijing. This was not a permanent thing, just one or two sessions, in which I worked with all the conducting students on their ability to conduct, using recordings or using a pianist to play for these sessions which they conducted and I criticized and worked with them and helped them. They liked that very much and so did I and, of course, along the way, I got to know all of Beijing. I saw it all, the entire city. I saw the Tiananmen Square, I saw the palace, the Forbidden City from which Americans had been excluded and I even went up north on a tour to the Great Wall. I climbed the Great Wall of China and walked along it for some time. That ended, and this group of business people moved from there to Shanghai and I went with them. The same thing occurred; I got to know Shanghai and I was a professor for a visiting session of the Conservatory of Music in Shanghai with all the conducting students who were there, teaching them, observing them while they conducted with either a piano or a recording. This went on for several hours in one or two days and it was very, very much appreciated as I appreciated the chance.

Those two sessions and seeing all of Shanghai and all of Beijing was very impressive. After that they wanted me to return with them to Australia. Now I had not been there since I left in 1968. So, this was 1973 and we flew from Shanghai to Guangzhou that was the big neighboring city to Hong Kong and I was there for a night or two and was enveloped in the most tremendous traffic I could imagine anywhere in the world. And then went on the next day to Hong Kong, where I stayed only one night and changed planes and flew right to Australia. The plane went first to Sydney, but we didn't stay there; we went back to Queensland where Mrs. Arnold was the professor.

When we got there I was lodged in a very nice hotel and was scheduled for master classes. It turned out that the famous Peruvian tenor who had been at La Scala for some twenty years, Luigi Alva, whom I very much admired in things of Rossini and Donizetti, was there as "artist in residence" giving master classes and vocal lessons and I got to know him very well.I also did master classes after him at the Queensland Conservatory. When I was there I still had time before I had to return to America. So, I took advantage of this by flying to Sydney to simply visit old friends. While I was in Sydney I saw many, many old friends and also had the great chance of seeing the new opera house which had been completed finally in 1973. I had been there in 1966, 1967 and 1968, so this was years later and I had never been in it and the people that I knew who ran it were old friends and they invited me, of course, and I had a tour of the whole opera house. I went to performances. I heard an entire *Meistersinger* there with a friend of mine, the famous baritone, Robert Allman, singing in the cast, and an excellent tenor was there from Germany, a leading permanent artist. I also saw *Salome* there which was very, very well done. This was a time when Richard Bonynge was there. He was not there at the time, but he was very much involved with the Australian Opera.

The reunion with my baritone friend Allman was an excellent occasion to catch up on news because he had sung with me years before and actually, I first encountered Allman when he was still in England. He was a famous baritone even then, and he was with the Royal Opera of Covent Garden. On my first visit to England in 1957 enroute back from Dublin, Ireland to Germany, I stopped in London and went to the opera and it was *Carmen*, and he sang Escamillo which was quite marvelous. I reminded him of that later because some years later when I was conducting in Augsburg, he was engaged from his German house-he was then a principal baritone in Cologne—to sing in my *La Forza del Destino*. So, I was so thrilled to run into him in Augsburg singing in German, this Italian opera, the baritone lead.

He was, of course, better than any of the baritones in our company and I will comment on them now. I will mention the sopranos; Norma Williams, who went on to a career elsewhere in Germany and in America and she finally retired from singing and was engaged by several Universities in Chicago, DePaul and Virginia, where she finally retired and we were always in touch. Another soprano was the Swedish, lovely girl, Gunnel Ohlsson, who sang in other houses in Germany after she left Augsburg in my second year and she stayed in touch with me to the present. She has even visited me here with her husband. She became a professor of voice in Salzburg at the famous Mozarteum then at the Munich Conservatory and finally the Frankfurt Conservatory, which in that country are called Hochschule Für Music. She had a very good teaching career, married a wonderful man and they had a wonderful son.

Now about the baritones; we had in Augsburg several. One of them was Grathwol who stayed there until he retired and then he passed away. And the other big one was Robert Anderson, a very good friend to this day. He was well-known all over Germany as a "helden" baritone or bass baritone, singing the major baritone roles in Wagner and the Ring Cycle in many cities in Germany. And in addition to that, through my suggestion to Schippers he was engaged for the Spoleto Festival in around 1962 to sing in *Salome* in Spoleto. After that he was engaged at the Teatro San Carlo, the major house in the South to sing the same role, but in Italian. So, with me, he relearned the roles in Italian.

Soon after that, maybe a year later, he was engaged in Sicily, Catania or Palermo, to sing the role of Kurvenal in *Tristan and Isolde*. So, that was quite a career, not to mention his year or season in San Francisco where he sang many roles with the San Francisco Opera and with great success. He finally left Germany and retired to a wonderful teaching position in Kansas. Then when he was really ready to retire, he moved to Portland when I was living there and we resumed our great friendship. They followed me to Seattle. They live near me in Seattle and we are in touch all the time. So, that was a big career for him. Another baritone was George Fortune who sang light baritone roles in Augsburg but, as I later learned—he "moved up the ladder" to Berlin where he was singing major Verdi roles and even Wagner as I noted when I stayed in Berlin on a visit in 1998.

The only other one to mention is the other tenor, Gerd Brenneis, who had gone on from Augsburg singing lyric roles such as Rossini and *Bohème* and he went on to Berlin where to my amazement he was put into dramatic roles and he was singing Wagner of all things which got him to the Met. He even sang *Meistersinger* at the Metropolitan Opera and I congratulated him, but I don't know how he did it with what was basically a very lyric voice. But voices change over a period of ten or twelve years. So, I am very happy that these people did have the success they did—very happy. Also the soprano, Elizabeth Wrancher, who took the place of Lippert when she moved to Stuttgart. Wrancher was a superb lyric spinto singing Verdi and Strauss. She sang *Turandot* in my farewell to Augsburg at the Red Gate. Later she had a great teaching career at the University in Orlando, Florida.

Not only did I do that, but I saw more performances—not opera. I saw drama in one of the other theaters in the Sydney Opera House, which by the way, has three theaters and other rooms and I heard a symphony concert with the famous Britten "Mass." At any rate their concert hall of the Sydney Opera House is used only for symphony concerts. It is huge. It is much bigger than the opera theater which is much smaller, acoustically excellent, but I think a little bit too small. But, I got to talk to all of the artists including many of whom I had worked with in 1968 and they were all wonderful to talk to and I visited with the artistic staff and saw much of the city that I had known well and which had changed enormously. It had expanded and had become much more international and the area called Kings Cross where I had stayed became even more of a bawdy, raucous Times Square which was somewhat disappointing, but that is what happens to many places.

From there I flew back to America, from Sydney and I stopped at Hawaii as I had often done on the way before to see the Fiji Islands, then to L.A. and from L.A. back to Portland. After I was in Portland for approximately another year, with many visitors coming and I continued my coaching and doing coaching recitals, I realized that my home base really was Seattle. I had tried San Francisco, Oakland, L.A. to an extent, and that I really wanted to get back to where I had roots and of all places in America besides Cincinnati, it was Seattle. So, I moved. I moved back to Seattle in 1995 and was very glad to do so. I moved into an excellent house, immediately got in touch with all of my old friends, who all welcomed me back, very overjoyed that I had returned and started off with coaching.

I didn't intend to have anything to do with the university and I was not searching for another conducting position. I had done enough of it on four continents, in every possible city and environment and I really did not want to do that. I had even been invited twice to conduct the Seattle Symphony while I was in Seattle as a professor, the former conductor, Rainier Miedel and Gerard Schwarz, both invited me and I conducted the Seattle Symphony in two excellent concerts which thrilled me.

But, by this time, I realized time was going and I had no desire to face that series of events again and I didn't want to apply elsewhere and I was very, very happy to settle in a semi-retired position which left me time to do a lot of coaching and piano work. So, most of the singers came to me on their own or through the persuasion or the advice of professors at the University of Washington, such as Mary Curtis Verna, Frank Guarrera, Julian Patrick, who had joined the faculty about five years before and was a very good friend from my youth in Cincinnati and others such as soprano, Carmen Pelton, who coached with me herself and then later moved on to the University of Michigan. It was a thrill for me when I arrived at the University in 1981 to take over my teaching job to find Mary Curtis Verna and Frank Guarrera, both famous Metropolitan Opera stars for years on the faculty with me. We became very close friends and we remain so to this day. Frank is retired and lives in Philadelphia and Mary lives here.

In addition to them, there were two other excellent teachers, the tenor, Augusto Paglialunga, who had a career first in Europe and then he returned from Germany and took on his job here and later sang throughout America with regional companies with success until he left the University. He went on to teach in the East. The other one on our faculty and a close friend was the mezzo soprano, Montserat Alavedra and she sang with me in concert with the orchestra and unfortunately in my last year she became very ill with cancer and returned to her home town in Spain and passed away to our great regret.

So, actually the period in Seattle has turned out to be a wonderful retirement area. I had achieved a lot, was grateful for it and had a lot of friends and many, many students and this went on until the present. Here, I have many friends in the musical world, either in the orchestra or the conductor of the symphony, Gerard Schwarz, who is a very good friend, whom I admire immensely and whose concerts I hear often and I also hear other guest conductors as well. I go to the opera frequently. The new general director took over in 1983 from Glynn Ross who is Speight Jenkins from Texas, well-known to everyone in music and also for his appearances on the Met intermission features. I still go to performances. Of course that leads to a discussion of what the singers are like today compared to the past.

Now, on to the poorer state of things vocally in America. I'm returning now to the period in the 1970s when I returned from Europe and I knew what was going on there and I could sense already a decline in Italy and in Germany. All of the greats I've occasionally mentioned. They ranged not only from people like Corelli and del Monaco and di Stefano, Tebaldi, Callas, Cerquetti, but many more who did leading roles that were already suitable to them, but they have since passed on and the sopranos or mezzos who have taken their place are not up to that level, or the level I knew when I was in college, which involved people like Bruna Castagna and Stella Roman and Zinka Milanov.

Those days are not around. What we have to admit is the difference in roles and requirements. I don't want to be long about this, but we all know that we are in the era of the revival of not only bel canto, but the entire baroque era which has now come upon us. When I was in Europe and before that we had many mezzos doing *Cenerentola*. We had great mezzos doing Amneris, and Azucena and other great dramatic roles, singers like Barbieri, Simionato and a few others. Then this change gradually occurred and with it the emergence of some lyric mezzos and now we have so many who are great; Lorraine Hunt Lieberson (now deceased), Susan Graham, and many like that—too many to mention, who can sing both Rossini and Gluck and Handel and all the baroque composers.

Then we have the countertenors who never existed before and they sing all this repertoire as well. We also have a supply of very lyric leggiero tenors, such as Juan Diego Florez, at the Met and elsewhere. He can sing wonderful Rossini and Donizetti. There are others like that too. But, if you search for the lyric spinto or even the lyric tenor who sings *Bohème* and *Tosca* and *Butterfly*, there are a few, but they are not great like the variety we had when I grew up, such as Charles Kullman and Eugene Conley and people of that calibre.

In Italy, of course, we had the burgeoning of the careers of Pavarotti and Domingo and Carreras But they are not the only ones; many sang that repertoire, and I chiefly remember Bergonzi and Alfredo Kraus, who do not have an equal today. Kraus could go into the lyric repertoire beyond singing Donizetti and was superb. Today we have Alagna, we have Ramon Vargas and people of that stature. They are fine when they are in lyric repertoire, but even Alagna tries to do *Tosca, Il Trovatore* and the others, and we know that compared to the past, and to the era of Corelli, Monaco and di Stefano, he should not be doing those roles. It is a harm to the voice, but he does it and it is accepted until the recent scandal at La Scala, where he was booed and left the stage at the end of his aria. (Di Stefano also pushed himself too far in his repertoire).

Today everything is accepted on a lower level, meaning that lyrics do dramatic things they should not be doing as it is harmful to the voice, even baritones. It is very hard to find people like Tibbett, Merrill, Warren, and Guarrera. I could only find a few, but really to fill my goals in listening such as I just now heard on TV, only Dimitri Hvorostovsky whom I first heard way back in 1989 in the Welsh Opera competition, "Singer of the World," sits on top of the list. Other Russian baritones do not equal that, nor do the Americans. Thomas Hampson has his fulfillment in roles of more lyric baritones so that even Germont, even Posa in *Don Carlo* for me are a bit beyond him. I have heard him in the French version; it was not really the Verdi sound that I want in a baritone, such as Warren or Robert Weede, who was my favorite, actually, for years and years, as well as Silveri, Colzani, though he was not as prominent at the Met With basses, the era of Ramey is fading, Raimondi is, more or less, frayed and we have a few Russians.

But, to have a great bass, who equals all those of the past, like Ezio Pinza, we are not in that category anymore except for René Pape. So, with these performances that involve a role like the Grand Inquisitor in *Don Carlo*, you take what you get, but it is not what it should be. Mezzos can get by, such as Borodina who can sing Rossini. She can also sing Eboli or Amneris. But the Eboli or Amneris are not up to the Rossini because for her, they are both too heavy. They do not equal anyone like Simionato, or even Cossotto who was marvelous in that repertoire. So, what I'm getting at is the fact that everything has become more lyric. The people do not have the depth of voice to fulfill the Verdi requirements, or for that matter, the Wagnerian, because they are in equal trouble. I grew up in the era of Melchior, Traubel, Varnay and Flagstaff.

Below—At a reception after a University of Washington production of Mozart's *The Marriage of Figaro* with a special guest from the Metropolitan Opera, the well-known "Quiz Master" Edward Downes. Left to right: Frank Guarrera, Mary Curtis Verna, Edward Downes and Robert Feist.

Above—Edward Downes and Robert Feist chatting.

Above—Three very famous Metropolitan Opera baritones at a reunion at a New York musician event. Left to right: Frank Guarrera, Robert Merrill and Sherill Milnes.

Well, to find their equals is difficult. Voigt is very good, but she does not sound like a great Wagnerian, such as Traubel or Varnay and though Mattila is very good, for me she is not up to that level nor is Jean Eaglen. So, what persists is that we are in agreement—everyone is singing above their limits and it is hard to determine what can be done to change it. I attribute it, as I said earlier, to voice teachers, who get the young singers who can be only lyric and they haven't sung spinto repertoire. It is beyond them, like *Tosca* or *Trovatore,* which they shouldn't sing, but agents push this. They get the singers to sing repertoire beyond them because they know opera houses need them. So, they are getting lyric sopranos to sing too heavy roles (or a tenor) and then in a few years they are frayed or worn out. This has been commented on and mentioned in many newspapers and articles in the news and a *New York Times* article.

This is nothing new, but we have become accustomed to hearing very lyric voices singing spinto or dramatic roles in the Italian repertoire, which is, of course, not right and will ruin the voice and it doesn't give a dramatic impetus to the opera that is required. Naturally, one could sit and write a list of one hundred voices, but I think the few that I have indicated give an indication of the position that we are in right now with the world of opera and where it stands. It's a shame, because we are now in the world in which anything that is done in the baroque era or the early classical era is very fine, is very acceptable—*if* you like that repertoire. If you limit it to *Faust* and even *Bohème*, you may find sopranos singing them who should not be at that level and tenors too. We have become accustomed to Domingo and Pavarotti, who were very fine..

Certainly, they are excellent, but that era is going, and is almost gone. Their substitutes are the people who take their places and are not really at that level. It is very hard to name a couple in the spinto or dramatic repertoire either in Wagner or in Italian opera. So, the question remains, where are we going and who is at fault and who can guide the singers the right direction. Conductors, perhaps, accept all this. They are glad to conduct and if they are given a coloratura to sing *Tosca*, they will accept this, even though the soprano is certainly not right for the role. I can think of 20 examples of people who have followed this pursuit and have been wrong.

Robert F. Feist.

CHAPTER FOURTEEN
The Glory Years of the Past Are Gone

In reviewing my past experiences, including those when I returned to America in 1976, I'd been aware for a long time of this change in the operatic situation all over the world. For one thing, I returned to Europe in 1998 and 1999 to see all my old close friends, all involved in operas as former singers or intendants in Germany, in Vienna, Slovenia, Naples, Rome and Florence and their performances. The results for me were very disappointing. First of all, the state of the countries, which was so different than when I had left them. They were more disordered; they were more Americanized, if you can use this expression. They were less medieval or ancient or traditional as I knew them in the 1950s and early 60s. So, the operas I heard produced different results for me. Thinking of this today briefly, in Berlin I saw the Deutsche Oper Berlin performance of *Ring* excerpts and it had prominent singers, of which I knew only one, a bass or a bass baritone, Joll, who had sung in Seattle. It was a sort of overview of Wagner and it was not good. It did not enthuse me or my friends.

Then came Essen, which is basically a second-level theater and I knew the former intendant. He was Manfred Schnabel. He and his wife were very good friends of mine during my Augsburg years where he was a dramaturg. He moved from there to many other theaters, Heidelburg, Zurich. In both places I visited and stayed with them and caught up on news. We have been friends and correspondents ever since. As time went by he moved north and became an Intendant in Hagen and then in Essen which are noteworthy cities and noteworthy theaters. So, always keeping up with them during my last visit in 1998 I stayed with him and his wife which was a great joy in Essen when I went to the performance of *Aida*. Unfortunately since that time, in fact a year later, his wife was very ill and is still very ill. We do not know what the cause of it is and it has given him a lot of grief which is unfortunate, Alzheimers, I think.

And there I was a guest and I heard a performance of *Aida*. This was one of my first chances to see modern staging. I knew it happened here in Seattle and everywhere else, but this was a very avant garde staging of *Aida* that I did not anticipate nor did I like. The singers were fair. The only one who was impressive was the mezzo soprano and it passed without much comment. Before I go on I will say the Berlin Staatsoper, which is the one headed now by Barenboim, I heard a concert by the orchestra which was very good. They played Schönberg and a few other things, but at the opera they did the *Barber of Seville,* again in a modern staging that would not look like anything of the 1950s. The leading baritone was well-known and still is and he, Terkel, certainly was good. But he was in no way the equal of Taddei, Czaplicki, Guarrera, Gobbi and the other Figaros. His was a very lyric sound. He should have been doing the Count in *Nozze di Figaro*. But, it was well done and acceptable.

Then came Leipzig and Dresden, two cities I did not know even when I lived there because I did not want to go to the East Zone. So I heard in Leipzig the Gewandhaus Orchestra under a guest conductor and they did a very nice program of Bach and Brahms and a wild dissonant modern opera in Dresden. After this production, which was very modern and yet pleased us, we moved on to Prague and Prague was a totally different city then. It was no longer Communist, it was lively, everybody was friendly and everything that I had loved before 1964 or 1965 was unchanged, the squares, the wonderful clock; everything. I went to the old Estates Theater which used to be called something else and there we heard *Don Giovanni* which had had its world premiere there, which was an occasion. All the singers were unknown to me.

It was a small theater and yet, we sat up in the first balcony and it was really excellently done—traditionally fine singing and fine acting. In addition to that we went to the state opera house, the Narodni Divadlo, as it was known and still is, the national theater. We saw a performance of *La Forza del Destino* with all local singers. There were no singers from elsewhere and this was not good. It was a mediocre performance with singers who were not really in their Verdi element in this opera. The soprano was fair, the others less so and it was a disappointment to me because I had heard so many Czech works there. But the experience in the city was very, very good. On to Vienna.

In Vienna I had dinner one night with one of my best friends, a very great English baritone called Hugh Beresford who had sung all over Germany. I think he was based in Cologne, but I encountered him first in Augsburg and he was married to a wonderful woman, Hilda, and as time went on they moved to Vienna where he sang and then retired. (Unfortunately, about a year ago I heard of the death of his wife which made me quite sad). I visited with them, had dinner and that happened to be the 60th anniversary of the German invasion, the "Anschluss" or the "annexation" of Austria to Germany. It was quite an occasion. Nothing was happening in the streets. People tried to ignore the fact, but they had been taken over by the Germans so many years before in 1938 and there was no opera that night.

So, I waited for two days and in those two days I went down to Slovenia which used to be part of Yugoslavia and visited my former very good friend, the leading tenor of our Augsburg Opera, Jerney Plahuta, who had retired to live in his home in Maribor where he died in the past year or two. We had a fine time together. I visited him in his apartment We went out for dinner and had a wonderful time visiting and recounting all the events of the previous years. He was more or less happy, but retired and the radio saluted him by playing all of his recordings up until his death when he was 80.

Then I returned to Vienna for a business reason, the best, because the Vienna State Opera, the Staatsoper, had revived Verdi's *Jerusalem*. *Jerusalem* was the opera which I had done in its second premiere in America in San Mateo, California in 1991. (It was the second performance in America; the first had been done in 1850 in New Orleans and in French).

Well, here the Vienna Opera did it and of all things, they had the tenor who had sung with me in Oakland in *Tosca*, Keith Ikaia Purdy. It was an excellent performance. The bass baritone was Raimondi, in very good shape, but no longer the great bass that he had been, and at the end of the performance, the tenor and his agent took me to dinner and we hashed over many experiences. He had been leading tenor all over Germany and he had been recently in Vienna doing leading roles and sounded wonderful. Raimondi remembered me and my friendship with Gavazzeni whom he adored as a great conductor and I agreed with him. So *Jerusalem* in Vienna was a memorable occasion.

From there I went on to Augsburg through Salzburg and I was back in my "so called" hometown, where I stayed with another very best friend, Dr. Gerd and Helga Thürer and saw others, but heard no opera there. However, I took a train into Munich for one night to see what operas they were doing. I went to the secondary theater, the Gärtnerplatz Theater. There they did a Gluck opera. It was *Iphegenie in Aulide*. Again it was modern staging which Germany had apparently initiated years before and it was, more or less, intolerable. It looked like New York or any where, but it did not look like where it should have been. It was sung in a mediocre fashion, but I enjoyed it, yet left after the first act and that was my Munich opera experience after years of going there and hearing all of the great Strauss and Wagner with

Borkh and Varnay and Nilsson and all the great singers. That was gone. After Augsburg and my friends, I flew back to New York and from New York to Cincinnati and then back to Seattle.

The following year I made another trip to Europe to see the French and Italian friends. I started in Paris, stayed with a good friend of mine Claude Villanova and his wife, since deceased. After dinner, visits to Chartres, new to me, and all that, I went to the Paris Opera, the new one at the Bastille. I had never been there. I had only been to the Paris Grand Opera at the Place de l'Opéra, the Opera Square, but this time it was in the Bastille and I saw *Lucia* which I anticipated. Ha! Unfortunately we were back in the 1990s. It was sung by Sumi Jo, the coloratura from the Met, who was fine, but she was in no way the equal of any of the great coloraturas in Rome, including Sutherland whom I had heard at La Scala or Antoine or Sills, and others earlier. The others were also fairly mediocre including the conductor who was Campanella, who was well-known at the Met. His tempi did not interest me and the whole performance left me limp and I left again at the intermission.

Well, for the rest of the time, once I had moved back from Portland to Seattle, we had our usual assembly of operas, five a year, all based on the judgment and preferences of our general director, Speight Jenkins, who had his favorites as they all do. And, I heard many of them. If an opera had a cast I did not like, I did not go. If it was interesting by the appearance of a certain singer, I would go. I heard several that I liked over the years and many that I did not like.

One of the tenors that was highly prized by Mr. Jenkins was Vinson Cole, an extreme lyric tenor who was fine when he did his version of *Orfeo* and even *The Pearl Fishers*. But, then they had him do *Boheme, Traviata, Tosca, Butterfly*. They were beyond his limits. He was a lyric, lyric tenor and from my viewpoint, he tended to croon on the top. But, people accepted it as they accepted almost everything here and elsewhere.. The famous soprano from New York, Lauren Flanigan sung several roles. Her *Traviata* was fair, but she had none of the agility or the warmth of any of those I had seen such as Albanese and Sayao, even Tebaldi and people like that. But that went fairly well. The rest of the cast was not that important. (The baritone, as in most of the Verdi operas here, was Gordon Hawkins, who was okay). That is about all I can say. She also sang in a wonderful production by the Seattle Symphony which was a concert performance of *Peter Ibettson* by Deems Taylor, under Gerard Schwarz. In this, she and the cast were excellent and I think it was recorded by the Seattle Symphony and maybe issued commercially.

SEATTLE SYMPHONY

September 23, 2004

Robert F. Feist
14318 – 26th Ave NE
Seattle, WA 98125

Dear Bob,

Thanks so much for your card; I can't tell you how much it means to me to have you in the audience! To have someone of your integrity and knowledge there to hear and understand what we are trying to do. You are a remarkable man and I'm so thrilled to call you a friend! I send my warmest wishes always,

Sincerely,

Jerry Schwarz

GS/tmd

200 UNIVERSITY STREET
P.O. BOX 21906
SEATTLE, WA 98111-3906
206.215.4700
206.215.4701 FAX

GERARD SCHWARZ
MUSIC DIRECTOR

PAUL MEECHAM
EXECUTIVE DIRECTOR

A treasured letter from Seattle Symphony conductor Gerard Schwarz.

Left—Musical Director of the Seattle Symphony, Gerard Schwarz.

Photo by Yuen Lui Studio in Seattle.

Maestros Gerard Schwarz of the Seattle Symphony and Robert Feist on the balcony of Mr. Schwarz's home in Seattle, Washington circa 1984–1986.

In addition to this we had the usual singers returning all the time, Vinson Cole, the same sopranos and mezzos all of whom fall into the category of normal, conventional singers. We always had Gordon Hawkins doing Italian baritones. We also had the debut here of Jane Eaglen who then moved here. We had heard her in many Wagner operas here, *Isolde,* the Ring Cycle several times and we were used to that. I was impressed by her vocal ability, not by her staging abilities, which has been mentioned in other articles too. The *Ring* continued for many, many times, every few years and many of the same singers returned. Striking besides Eaglen was Stephanie Blythe and various tenors including an Englishman, who replaced another tenor on short notice. I stopped seeing Ring Cycles after three or four because I had seen enough of them and I heard them broadcast.

The normal repertoire continued with occasionally a modern American opera and occasionally the singers we did not know, but none of them were in the category of the great Met singers of the present era. Fredericka Von Stade came and sang Handel's *Semele,* which was excellent. And then the others that I can recall with enthusiasm was the reappearance of Andrea Gruber whom I had liked very much prior to this and then she had a fall or a period of absence. She returned, last summer and did a stunning *Fanciulla del West*, probably the best or one of the best I have ever seen. I had seen so many including the one who ruined herself with it in Italy called Frazzoni, who sang it all over Italy and I saw her in Bologna. But Gruber was excellent in a cast that did not live up to her calibre. But there was a brand new Italian tenor who arrived and sang the role of Dick Johnson, now at the Met, Antonello Palombi, excellent!

Aprile Millo appeared, recovered from an absence of some time, due to health or whatever, and she again was a star. I'll cite these two, Millo and Gruber among the two sopranos whom today I would call very much in the old style of great lyric spintos who handle the Verdi repertoire very exceptionally. Others that have done this that are fair, among them at the Met, was Maria Guleghina, the Russian soprano who does many Nabuccos there and even a lot of Verdi besides that, and she is very good in the top range but it is not an Italianate sound such as Leyla Gencer could achieve. Certainly Gencer was the best of all in that prior era. So, we had the usual category that flitted around America in all the other companies that were not the Met and sometimes they were in San Francisco or Chicago and we had them here occasionally.

But to name all the others that I call mediocre would include many, many, mezzos and sopranos whom I could not categorize as one or the other because, as I said, now we are in the era of the lyric coloratura mezzo, and you could not imagine them singing Verdi, (Amneris or Azucena). But they sang Handel, they sang Mozart and they sometimes sang Verdi, but it was not with the right sound, the one I had grown up to, or grown up used to in the 1940s, 1950s, and 1960s.

That era was gone, I think, also in Italy, except for Delora Zajick, the big American mezzo who really can do all of the Verdi repertoire very well, but she, of course, does not attempt any of the Rossini or those repertoire items. Among the mezzos we're stuck with, if you use the term, what I call the great era of Castagna, Thorborg, Simionato, Barbieri and Horne, Cossotto I heard often when she was still a very light mezzo in *Carmen* in Venice and it was such a lyric mezzo I didn't think she was a mezzo. But, she has had a huge reputation even in big Verdi roles which she has conquered quite well, but, for me does not equal Simionato or Barbieri. And that is another situation.

The tenor situation is worse because after the era of Corelli, Lauri-Volpi and del Monaco, di Stefano, we had a few others such as Limarilli whom I heard doing *Stiffelio* for the first time in Italy, in Bologna, a very good tenor, but the Italians at that time said: "Well, its not Corelli, but he's good." But today in the world we're in, he would be at the top of the list compared to the other tenors who attempt to sing *Trovatore, Aida* and all the other dramatic roles. He was up to that. Now, we have very, very few that can, and that is a big shame in the dramatic repertoire of the Italian tenors and the Italian dramatic sopranos. Certainly we have great lyric and coloraturas not only with the Handel and the baroque era, but into *Lucia* and those operas and their chief is Reneé Fleming, about whom I have no quibbles. Not only have I heard her often, I've met her and talked to her at intermissions here at the Seattle Symphony. She's a wonderful woman, a wonderful soprano, who knows exactly what she is doing and handles her voice with great care. Fleming stands at the top of the list.

And then there are all the mezzos such as Susan Graham, who do all the baroque repertoire extremely well, but should not sing the big Verdi operas and Lorraine unfortunately just died recently at the age of 52. And among the basses, I don't know where we are. Ramey is almost worn out, so is James Morris. We have René Pape, German bass who is exceptional. Every time I hear René Pape, I think we are in the era of Christoff and Ezio Pinza and people like lesser known baritones or basses of that era. But the point is that René Pape seems to reign among the basses. And the baritones, we talked about enough.

The world we are in is a totally different world and all young singers who go and are introduced to opera are hearing a whole new category. They are not used to the sounds of Simionato, Castagna, Barbieri, Tebaldi, Callas. They are hearing lesser voices, more lyric, often people who are not trained to do the repertoire but, they sing it anyway. And people are trying to get young people interested. And some do get interested and hooked on it. They may like the tunes and lullabies, but what they are missing is an entire era of great voices that you heard all the time in the 1940s, 1950s and 1960s into the 1970s when even Leyla Gencer sang *Lucia* and then moved from that into *Gioconda*—not to forget the great Ghena Dimitrova, the greatest dramatic soprano of the last 20 to 30 years who could sing *Nabucco, Turandot*, etc. like no one else. She also died recently.

That is the era that is gone. And I don't discourage the fact that young singers try the repertoire, and that young people like it, but I feel there is a lapse. The only way they can understand opera the way it should be and is done is through recordings of the great artists of the past. And by past, I don't mean 1915 or 1925, but the late 1940s or 1950s when we had Sayao, Albanese, Peerce, del Monaco, Tebaldi, and Callas. That is the way to learn how opera should be sung and was sung. I hope this era will return. I hope singers today and their teachers use the proper methods to have the students learn the right repertoire and not force their voices so we create more people who sing like Andrea Gruber or sing like Dolora Zajick.

And I, of course, cannot name a great dramatic tenor, I can name lyric tenors—yes, Vargas, Alagna, people like that. But, I mean the dramatic repertoire which is the one that is the hardest of all. I don't mean to be negative, but just that we are in a different era. It is not the era of the great periods of the 1940s, 1950s and 1960s. And I hope a new era will come with time and proper training and we will hear singers who are ready for the roles they are supposed to be singing. I'm sure the singers I know and have known, like Stella and Simionato and di Stefano would agree with me very much. They would very openly discuss this in their conversations or in their articles, as Stella did with me in her Rome apartment when I visited her there in 1999, I hope to come into a new era of great, great singing, especially of the Italian repertoire and I think that covers it pretty well. And, I hope those who read this will understand this and understand that I hope for the best because the world of opera deserves it.

Read the following excellent reviews:

A quote from *The New York Times*, March 13, 2007: (This is a review of Juan Diego Flórez singing at Carnegie Hall by Holland.)

> ... With the great Luciano Pavarotti faded into inoperability, and his equally great rival Placido Domingo now an aging though still formidable lion, opera houses and music managers are looking in high places and under rocks for new superstars. They are finding them in bits and pieces—good musicians without charisma, top ranges without bottoms and bottoms without tops, or beautiful sounds embedded in unacceptable coarseness.

Well, what you just read was an excerpt from a wonderful review by Bernard Holland in *The New York Times* very recently, March 13th of this year, 2007. And it was a rave review for Juan Diego Flórez and I agree with all of it including his comments for music managers of opera houses who are looking high and low for new superstars, despite the fact that they may not be adequate. And, of course, he gave a great review to Flórez. But it isn't only Holland who mentions this. Many of the excellent critics in *The New York Times* mainly Anthony Tommasini who reviews opera very, very often and very well and with whom I agree, but also the well-known female critic, Anne Midgette. At the time of both these farewell galas, I do not have the program here, it was sometime last summer, the article appeared in probably June or July in *The New York Times,* once by Tommasini who reviewed it in more or less casual terms, not generally enthusiastic. And it was preceded by the article from Midgette which was titled; "A Lost Generation Is Absent From Met Gala." The title hit me and as I read the article it really captivated me as she was writing about the subject of my book and that is why I am going to quote much of it. Because I have never read an article by a critic that so "nailed the matter on the head" as we might put it.

A quote from *The New York Times* article by Anne Midgette is on the following page.

Yes, indeed, in 20 years time, what will be the state of future Met farewells? I can add future Met performances or future Met broadcasts, or future Met performances in other cities such as Chicago, San Francisco, Cincinnati, Dallas or anywhere in America. It is an open question. Because of what Ms. Midgette has outlined every clearly and as other people have mentioned but very seldom put into print in such clear, unmistakable form, we are indeed in an era that has lost a generation of stars. In my particular view, the generation as I said, goes back into the 1970s.

Prior to that we had a gala year from the 1940s on. But in the 1970s, which was mentioned even by a former general director of San Francisco opera as he was departing. He is the one who said: "Well, you know, we are in a bad era now, because the 1970s had indicated that all the great singers are gone. You don't have any more. They've moved on elsewhere and what we are left with is nothing like the great eras before that."

And, of course, I agree with him and I agree with Ms. Midgette's final statement—in 20 years time we may have a rebirth of the great singers of the heavy Verdi repertoire. We may have a simple continuation of all the great coloratura mezzos, counter tenors and sopranos who are lyric, leggiero and can sing Handel, Monteverdi and anything up through Mozart and Donizetti, But when we get into the era of the heavier works—even the *Traviatas*, the *Trovatores*, *Aidas* and the heavier ones such as *Nabucco* and *Macbeth* and *Turandot*, we have a big question mark

What will we be facing in 20 years time? Maybe we will be hearing many more performances of Handel operas, more *Julius Caesars*, more *Monteverdis* and Gluck, *etc*. Then again we may also be stuck with hearing *Aida, Tosca, Trovatore* sung by lyric sopranos such as we have today who are almost spinto but nothing like the generations that I knew. And they attempt to at their management's urging or the opera company's directors. They sing repertoire that is too heavy for them. A lyric soprano who should be singing *Boheme, Butterfly, Pagliacci* is suddenly singing *Trovatore, Don Carlo* and roles like that. We hear them now.

CRITIC'S NOTEBOOK

Opera's Lost Generation Of Stars

By ANNE MIDGETTE

Galas are a big part of operatic tradition. You need to have one every few years. At the Met they have become practically part of the standard opera landscape. This Saturday's season-ending gala, a tribute to the departing general manager, Joseph Volpe, is being billed as a particular blockbuster. Yet, inevitably, people are already comparing it to another blockbuster gala in recent memory, the 1996 celebration of James Levine's 25th year at the house, which went on for more than seven hours.

Length is one measure of a gala, but the event rises and falls on the question of who is going to sing. Or who is not going to sing. At Mr. Volpe's gala, a whole generation of singers seems to be missing in action.

The point of a gala is to present a cross section of an era: generally, all the big current stars will perform, as well as a range of beloved elder statesmen and -women returning for a last farewell. The Levine gala represented the final Metropolitan appearances of James King, Bernd Weikl, Carlo Bergonzi, Ileana Cotrubas, Alfredo Kraus, Gwyneth Jones and Grace Bumbry. An august company indeed.

So it's interesting that Mr. Volpe's gala, celebrating a nearly 16-year reign that is being bruited (an inevitable accompaniment to the passing of the baton) as one of the Met's most illustrious, is focused so firmly on the present. Plenty of contemporary stars will raise their voices to Joe: Renée Fleming, Deborah Voigt, Susan Graham, René Pape, Dmitri Hvorostovsky. And there will be a few grand figures from earlier eras, including the redoubtable Plácido Domingo (still very much a part of the Met scene), Kiri Te Kanawa, Frederica von Stade and Mirella

CRITIC'S NOTEBOOK

A Lost Generation of Stars Is Absent From Met Gala

Continued From First Arts Page

Freni. Luciano Pavarotti is tentatively scheduled, but health problems may prevent him from performing. There will be relatively few touching farewells. Most singers appearing on Saturday are still active; most are still fairly young. A perusal of the schedule reveals what could be called a generation gap. Ms. Fleming and Ms. Voigt are in their 40's. Mr. Pavarotti is 70.

Where are the singers in between: the stars of the 1990's, of the early years of Mr. Volpe's tenure? Where are the stars now in their 50's? There are precious few of them.

Where, for example, is Jerry Hadley, the tenor whose star burned so brightly in the 1980's? He appeared in the news last week, for his arrest on a drunken-driving charge. (He didn't actually start the car.) News reports said he was 54, awfully young to be a has-been, but a recent recording of Bernstein's "Mass" documents a voice that is not in great shape.

I don't mean to pick on Mr. Hadley. He is far from the only 50-something whose prime is past. It's true that you can point to a few prominent singers of this age: the ever-reliable Dolora Zajick, for example, will offer a gala contribution, as will Thomas Hampson, still a star baritone, and James Morris, growl and all. But when you look at the soprano and tenor voices, there is a yawning void.

Richard Leech. Sharon Sweet. Susan Dunn. Francisco Araiza. June Anderson. Cheryl Studer. Carol Vaness. An entire catalog of singers is absent from Mr. Volpe's gala, and from the Met in general. (Neil Shicoff sings there from time to time, but he won't be singing at the gala.)

The blight extends to some singers in their 40's, like Aprile Millo, once a Met fixture, or Dawn Upshaw, another former Met regular who has since moved away from opera to colonize her own, predominantly contemporary terrain. So what has happened? The fault is not Mr. Volpe's, although the problem is symptomatic of a kind of approach to opera that has dominated the Met and other houses during his tenure. Career development is not a high priority in today's opera world. What is a priority is finding the latest stars and getting them up in front of the public, in as many places as possible, and in as many attractive roles as possible, regardless of how well suited they hap-

Sara Krulwich/The New York Times

Jerry Hadley is among an era o singers absent from a Met gala.

pen to be to a particular role. Mr Araiza is a perfect example of a fine young singer who sang himself ragged by trying to force his way into heavier roles.

And despite the Met's careful work grooming and encouraging the artists in the Lindemann Young Artist Development Program, its track record for helping its rising stars has been spotty. There are many examples of singers who were used a lot then cast aside when they ran into trouble. It is easy to blame the rise of jet travel, which enables singers to take on too much work, for short-lived careers. But a more significant cause is a lack of proper education not only about how to sing, but about which roles are appropriate for which voices and, equally important, how to say no.

Mr. Volpe's gala will be as long and as uneven, as occasionally exciting and frequently tedious, as such galas generally are. But what it will leave us with is not a picture of Mr. Volpe's tenure as much as a snapshot of the state of opera today: the state of a company that is not always as supportive of singers as it could be, and the state of a field that is looking anxiously to guardians of a tradition who seem, on Saturday's program, to be few and far between.

Ms. von Stade, Ms. Freni and Ms. Te Kanawa, whatever their vocal estates, can still deliver some serious wattage in the performance department. One wonders what, in 20 years' time, will be the state of future Met farewells.

So we are facing a great question mark. I can only hope and pray that indeed a change occurs in the country and even in Europe. The same situation applies there to a generation of singers and teachers that follow an old fashioned procedure of learning slowly and well and carefully the repertoire that suits their voice or their voices and does not force them to push into a harder repertoire for which they are not suited. This can be our hope for the future. It is indeed my hope that we are going to enter into a different era, another great era, because the world of opera as we have known since 1900 should continue as it did in the 1940s, 50s and 60s and not return to the era of Handel or the era of the baroque opera only. We have too much of a legacy of great works by Verdi, Puccini and on and on and on that must be attempted and must be proven to be sung with the right conductors and the right singers. Let us hope this comes to pass in the next 20 years or, if we are lucky, in the next 10 years. That we can hope for and cross our fingers that it will come to pass or the world of opera will not be the one that we and our parents knew and grew up with. I hope the audience and the reading public agrees with this to some extent and will agree with me that we are in a state now that, hopefully, will be altered within the next five to 20 years. That is my ideal, my farewell for this book, covering that great era that many of us of a certain age also lived through, although the young people of today who are getting into opera would not be hearing these things unless they heard records as I mentioned earlier of the great singers of the past. Let's hope that that era returns. I certainly do!

From Left to right: Mary Curtis Verna, Geraldina Sorrentino Hoefer, Robert Feist and Dwyla Donahue in the lobby of the Meany Theater at the University of Washington in Seattle after one of Mr. Feist's operas, 1987 or 1988.

Acknowledgments

I want to thank my very best friends here who have always been associated with me since I came here in 1981 as part of the music faculty at the University of Washington or simply friends in the city. Chief among there would be Professor Ralph Rosinbum and his wife Colleen. Ralph was the Stage Director at the University. Prior to my coming he staged all the operas for some 20 years and with me he staged two or three before he retired about two years after I arrived. Being a fanatic on opera and drama, he constantly goes to opera, drama and symphony and we rehash all these events. I visit his house very frequently just to talk about musical events and I know his entire family, which is a remarkable family and their children I know quite well.

Another of this group is, of course, is the soprano Mary Curtis Verna. I have known Mary since 1957 and she is one of those, as I have said, who came to Augsburg from Italy for our guest performances out-of-doors at the Roten Tor. There she sang in *Aida* and *Otello*. I met her then, coached her on a few things and we continued our friendship. I saw her in New York, which I mentioned earlier and at which time she invited me to several Met performances. She also was on the faculty of the University of Washington here and we spent much time together. I had engaged many of her vocal students in my operas and she was always present at all the performances, so our connections really go back to those performances at the University of Washington.

And at the same time that would have been true for Frank Guarrara, my dear friend Frank because he also was on the our faculty and his students also sang in my operas, depending on which opera and which role. So those two remain at the top of the list along with Ralph and the University faculty that I kept in touch with up to the present, though Frank died in 2007 in Philadelphia.

On the photo (page 266) that you will find of Mary Curtis Verna and myself there are two other women, one of whom is Geraldina Sorrentino. Her married name is Mrs. Roland Hoefer and Geri, as we call her, has always been a figure in my experiences here in Seattle because of her interest and her long passion for opera which she studied in Europe. She sang in several operas at the University and then she was engaged to sing in two operas at the Seattle Opera while I was here, *Jenufa* and *The Ballad of Baby Doe*. She and I share many, many views of opera all the time, exchanging ideas and so forth and then, of course, she became the Director of the Northwest Regional Metropolitan Opera Auditions The Northwest region includes five states including Alaska and this follows the various district auditions which are hold all over the country in smaller cities, not necessarily very small. For instance, Portland, Oregon is one of the districts for the auditions. Geri would assemble the singers who had been sent to us from these various districts and assimilate them into the program that was done here as the final performance or recital by these northwest singers to see who would go on from here to the Met finals in New York city which would occur several months later. That is the main reason for our contact, but it extended into countless times along with her and her husband in their home for dinners, for chats and for her two main big parties involving all the musical people in the city in the fall and also at Christmas and in the summer. They have a wonderful estate, even with peacocks and it was always fun to be there and have conversation with all the musical talent. So Geri remains one that I have to acknowledge along with the others.

Along with her is the third woman in that photograph, Miss Dwyla Donahue. Dwyla I met in my first year or so here and she came here after a long stint first in Vienna where was married and studying there, mainly in Austria and then later moved back to New York where

Professor Ralph Rosinbum and
his wife Colleen
at their home in Seattle.

Dr. Paul Mack and
family in their garden.

through her luck or her talent she became the personal assistant of Edward Downes, the famous host of the opera quiz of the broadcast intermissions of the Metropolitan Opera. You didn't hear her name mentioned, of course, but she had to tend to many of his editorial works in preparing the quizzes. So Dwyla knew everything about opera. While in New York for fifteen years she helped Edward Downes and heard everything at the Met and was very familiar with all of the singers I have mentioned. And then she came here and with me often went to the opera in Seattle and we had much to say about those and comparing them to the Met and to Europe. I am very grateful for all of her work in charge of the district auditions which she headed here for several years, the Metropolitan District Auditions for the city of Seattle. And then people would move from that after they were chosen by judges and it would move to the Regionals also in Seattle which were under the direction recently of Geri Sorrentino Hoefer. And, as I said earlier, it was due to her that we had Edward Downes as a guest at a performance of mine at the University, The Marriage of Figaro. Edward Downes flew here, stayed with Dwyla and came to our performance after which we had an informal lecture and quiz backstage with the cast of the opera which was very much of an experience for all of us. While here I took him on trips all around Seattle, up to the mountains, Snoqualmie Pass with a great view of Mount Rainier, which he enjoyed very much and I enjoyed that contact tremendously which happened really through Dwyla Donahue with whom I am always in touch. Her advice and help has always been a great boost to me. This is not to exclude all of my other friends, here and in Cincinnati and everywhere else who have followed my career with letters and phone calls and have been very supportive throughout my entire professional career.

Among those in Seattle that I must acknowledge as being close friends and helpful and very, very encouraging are the people who work for the big companies here. Tracy Stafford, who works for The Boeing Company, Mr. Mike Dodaro and his wife who wanted to have a career as a singer, but he turned to business instead and he is now in a very good position with Microsoft, but still goes to the opera and we hash those things over. And lastly, Mr. Alan Boyle, who is an executive at MSNBC which takes him all over the world for science. He is a big science expert and does all of that for his work for MSNBC but still goes to opera and symphony and we discuss those things either privately or at his home with his wife and children or if we go to an opera together.

So these people stand out along with an entire array of other friends that I have on the list which would be entirely too long which would probably take up ten more pages, so we can't go into all of those. But I want to mention those few.

In conclusion I must mention briefly the support given by many of the cultural attachés of the foreign embassies in cities where I conducted; that means Teheran, Prague, Moscow and a few others. Perhaps most important was the help that was given to me by the man who was the cultural attaché in Moscow at the embassy who kept in touch for a long time trying to arrange my conducting appearance with the symphony there, Leo Wiener. Also, the man already mentioned, Dick Arndt, the Cultural Attaché of the U.S. Rome Embassy at the occasion of the U.S. Bicentennial Concert in Italy.

To my best non-musical friends; Dr. Paul Mack and wife Ruth, his boys Gregory, Andrew and Aaron, with whom I share all my loving throughts and wishes.

My thanks to Roz Pape, who has been very helpful in the preparation of this manuscript, typing the transcription from my dictated tapes and the arrangement of illustrations. She is familiar with preparations needed for publication and has designed many books. Also she is a music fan, goes to the opera and symphony and belongs to the small group I have of extremely close friends with whom we play bridge with and ski together. She has made this book writing much more interesting and easier than I thought it would be.

www.ingramcontent.com/pod-product-compliance
Lightning Source LLC
Chambersburg PA
CBHW081454040426
42446CB00016B/3236